Having tried his hand at gravedigging, radio producing, running a pub and professional bed testing, George East now devotes his time to writing about his adventures as an innocent abroad. George and his wife Donella travel around the regions, restaurants and bars of France under the guise of carrying out 'research' for his work. George East is the author of *Home and Dry in Normandy*, also published by Orion.

French Kisses

LOVE, LIFE AND DISASTER
IN NORMANDY

George East

An Orion paperback

First published in Great Britain in 2006
by Orion
This paperback edition published in 2007
by Orion Books Ltd,
Orion House, 5 Upper St Martin's Lane,
London WC2H 9EA

1 3 5 7 9 10 8 6 4 2

Copyright © George East 2006

Illustrations drawn by Delia Delderfield
Maps drawn by Hemesh Alles

The right of George East to be identified as the
author of this work has been asserted by him in accordance
with the Copyright, Designs and Patents Act 1988.

1 3 5 7 9 10 8 6 4 2

A CIP catalogue record for this book
is available from the British Library.

ISBN 978-0-7528-6925-4

Typeset by Deltatype Ltd, Birkenhead, Merseyside
Printed in Great Britain by Clays Ltd, St Ives plc

The Orion Publishing Group's policy is to use papers
that are natural, renewable and recyclable and made
from wood grown in sustainable forests. The logging and
manufacturing processes are expected to conform to the
environmental regulations of the country of origin.

Contents

Glossary

Author's Note

All the following stories are true except for the ones that aren't, and were either experienced first-hand or passed on by others with a similar appreciation of the bizarre. Where necessary, names and locations have been changed to avoid possible embarrassment, aggressive legal action or a punch on the nose for me. As for the traditional acknowledgements and thanks to all the people who made this book possible, they are too many to mention and will anyway know who they are. However, particular thanks for knocking my meandering account of this chapter of our lives in France into shape are due to Lorraine Baxter, my editor at Orion. Anyone who can deal with my worst excesses of grammar, spelling, syntax and other liberties with the English and French languages and still retain her good humour and even sanity must warrant a mention in despatches.

French Kisses is dedicated to all those who, like us, have learned that while it may sometimes be better to travel in hope than to actually arrive, the journey can often be worthwhile. Always providing you are able to laugh about the horrendous cock-ups you make en route.

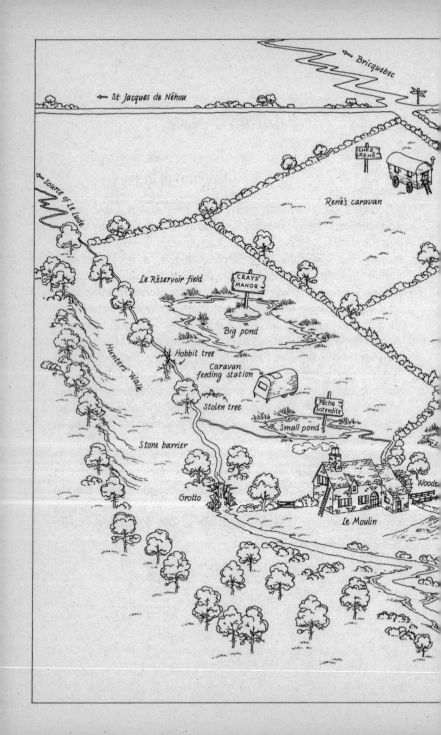

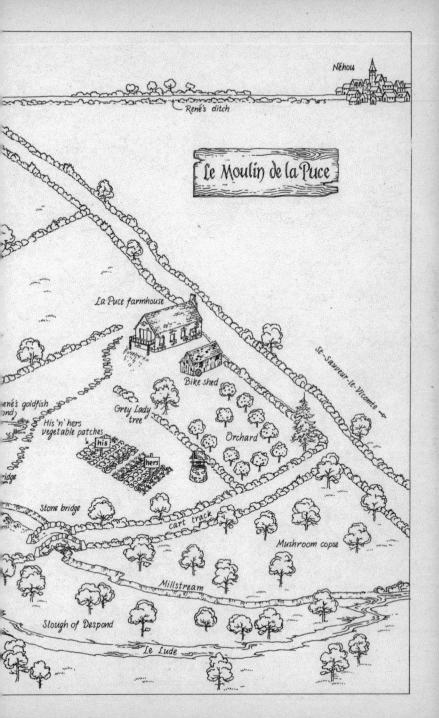

Néhou

René's ditch

Le Moulin de la Puce

La Puce farmhouse

St-Sauveur-le-Vicomte →

Bike shed

René's goldfish pond

His 'n' hers vegetable patches

Grey Lady tree

his

hers

Orchard

Stone bridge

Cart track

Mushroom copse

Millstream

Slough of Despond

Le Lude

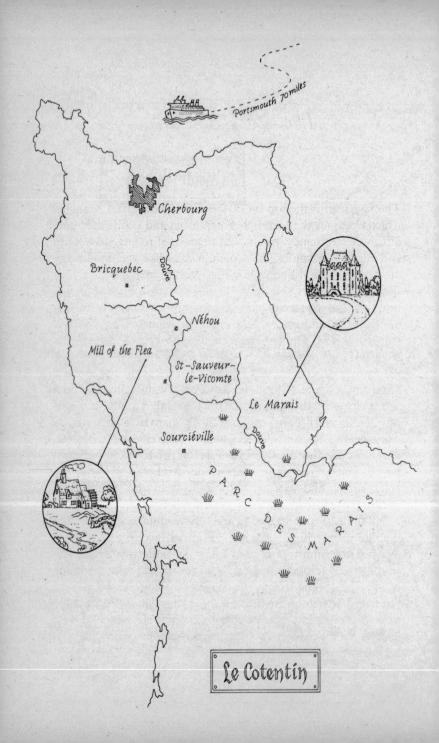

The Story So Far ...

The Cotentin is the top bit of the *département* of La Manche, which occupies the Cherbourg peninsula and is officially part of Lower Normandy. An ancient fiefdom of rolling landscapes and rugged coastlines, the Cotentin is as like and unlike any other area of rural France you may wish to imagine.

Our home, Le Moulin de la Puce, is to be found in the heart of the Cotentin, surrounded by ten acres of rivers, ponds, woodland and – during the notoriously long and wet winters – mud. The tiny eighteenth-century mill cottage sits alongside the small but lively River Lude, which flows through the 'grotto' – in truth an overgrown and tree-ringed water basin and cascade. Behind the cottage is a water meadow and a series of ponds; these are home to constantly warring tribes of murderous crayfish, psychotic goldfish, giant muskrats, mostly one-legged frogs, and other aquatic creatures that are savage, nimble or cunning enough to avoid their predators. Other non-paying guests who haunt the meadowlands include badgers, voles, shrews and an army of moles with an obsessive interest in creative landscaping.

At the far end of the meadow is a vintage caravan that doubles as a writing study for me and a favourite (and free) five-star restaurant, hotel and takeaway outlet for discerning wildlife from across the region. The caravan was once the home of my friend René Ribet, who moved on to our land and in to our lives to teach us the ways of the countryside and generally how to survive in a foreign and sometimes strange land. The lessons have occasionally been expensive, but we would not have it any other way.

The Mill of the Flea is on the outskirts of the village of

Néhou, which has one shop, a garage, a church and a population of around three hundred. The bar attached to the shop is run by the formidable but golden-hearted Madame Ghislaine, and is the committee room and debating centre for the Jolly Boys Club. The rules of this elite organisation require bona fide members to have been born before World War II and within the sound of the church clock; the regulations also stipulate that members be male and possessed of an insatiable thirst for philosophical discussion, gossip and strong drink. Exceptions are made for eminent and influential outsiders such as the area's champion moustache-grower and superchef, our double-agent postman who lives in the rival village on the other side of the crossroads ... and the sole overseas member and designated round-buyer who resides at the Mill of the Flea.

Most of the characters in this book live in the nearby towns of Bricquebec and St-Sauveur-le-Vicomte, while the others can be found in our local pub, the Flaming Curtains.

The British may not know much about music,
but they certainly love the noise it makes.
Thomas Beecham, orchestral conductor (1879–1961)

Singing for England

It is the week before Christmas and raining steadily as we drive to the first ever Franco-British carol service. Rain is more than common in the Cotentin, but this is serious stuff. Even the deep roadside ditches are struggling to cope, and the local soothsayers are making grim forecasts of the worst floods in living memory.

As we turn off the main road to cross the old stone bridge spanning the River Douve, a flash of lightning illuminates the turbulent scene below and the probing fingers of muddy water reaching out to a riverside farm. It won't be long before the Douve has the single-storey building in its clutch, explaining the local expression about farmers wearing their rubber boots to bed in the rainy season.

Victor the Volvo struggles manfully up the winding road to the hilltop village of Fierville-les-Mines, and the church where the carol service is to be held is dramatically silhouetted against the brooding night sky by another flash of lightning. As if by a miracle, it stops raining as we reach the square, and we are touched to see that an obliging sycamore tree has been draped with fairy lights to mark the occasion. There are already many cars parked in the square, and I note from the registration plates that the English and French are keeping their distance at either end of it.

Leaving Victor parked pointedly midway between the two camps, we squelch along the path leading to the church. My wife has made a concession to the occasion by wearing her best Wellington boots, and I have been persuaded to leave my Father Christmas hat at home. Threading our way between the gravestones towards the welcoming light of the church portals, we say hello to several English friends and see other obvious expatriates whom we have not as yet met.

Inside, we realise that it is going to be a full house, and a divided one. Although the French and English ushers at the door invite us to sit where we will as they hand out the dual-language song sheets, we find ourselves on the side of the aisle that has obviously been colonised by the British contingent. Settling down while the last stragglers are ushered in, I look around and reflect on the typically French approach to the maintenance and décor of this sturdy Norman church. Solidly constructed of stone from the quarry for which the village is named, the interior of the church is as ornate as the exterior is plain. Ancient frescoes forming a frieze around the walls depict the Stations of the Cross, and a giant brass crucifix dominates the altar. Above us, the candlelight reflects dully from the sleek bodies of a pair of brazen eagles perched high on either side of the pulpit. In stark contrast, a series of ugly gas-fed panels bodged on to the fluted stone columns provide the only source of heating, and I cannot help noticing that only half the heaters on the English side of the church have been lit.

Two figures appear at the altar. One is in full ecclesiastical fig and obviously on home ground, while the other is wearing a sensible and very British waxed jacket and an immaculate tweed suit. The effect is somewhat marred by a pair of Eskimo-style bootees; like all English settlers in the Cotentin, he has obviously learned the value of compromising between style and comfort during a long and cold winter.

After waiting for silence, which takes much longer on the French side of the aisle, our hosts welcome us to the church and the annual carol service, with the waxed jacket speaking in English, and his remarks being translated by the *curé* immediately afterwards. It is a nice touch, but I am somehow reminded of the Eurovision Song Contest.

Following the opening remarks, it is time for the first carol, and the curate of Fierville explains that we are going to alternate the service, with an English carol followed by a French one. We will find the translation printed alongside in each case, and he hopes we will all sing along in the appropriate language. We all nod earnestly and there is much throat-clearing as the massed bands of the local fire brigade and school strike up the familiar – at least to us – opening chords of 'Once in Royal David's City'. As I concentrate on finding approximately the note and my wife, Donella, shuffles away from my side in deep embarrassment, it becomes clear that we are not getting much support from those on the French side of the church. Most seem to be at least trying to mime the English words, but few are actually attempting to sing them. There was also an awkward moment at the start, as the entire English congregation rose to their feet when the music began, while the French stayed firmly rooted to their seats. This resulted in some confusion as a number of our hosts quickly stood up, while about half of us sat down. Eventually, an awkward compromise was reached, with the English half-crouching and the French sitting up straight.

Now it is time to air the first French carol, which according to my song sheet is called 'Il Est Né, Le Divin Enfant'. On comforting home territory, the band strikes up with gusto, and their enthusiasm is matched by the French congregation. Regrettably, the response from the English side is not so fulsome, and we receive some sour looks from across the aisle.

This seems to have set the pattern for the evening,

with each side ripping into their own familiar carols, then mumbling half-heartedly through the foreign variety.

While not wishing to take sides, I have to say that our carols seem somehow much more Christmassy, with 'The Holly and the Ivy' and 'God Rest Ye Merry Gentlemen' streets ahead of 'Dans Cette Etable' and 'Venez, Divin Messie' in terms of overall melody and jollity. Like the church itself, the French songs seem to concentrate overly on the gloomy aspects of Christianity and the founder's birthday.

We have now reached the grand *finale*, and our representative announces somewhat nervously, and in English, that the last carol is going to be a truly joint effort. If we turn to the last page in our song sheets, we will see that the song is to be 'O Come, All Ye Faithful'. To exemplify the Christmas spirit of reconciliation and togetherness, we will all join together in performing this traditional carol entirely in Latin.

During his translation for the benefit of the French congregation, I note that the curate adds a little to our man's address by exhorting his flock to give of their best and show their guests how well they can sing. He stops short of adding 'for the honour of France'.

The good curate of Fierville has apparently forgotten that at least half the English congregation are quite familiar with the French language, and there are some mutterings as the throat-clearing and coughing reaches a crescendo and the band strikes up.

All goes reasonably well for the first verse, then someone on our side breaks into English during the chorus. After the next verse, the entire British congregation joins the rebel, and there is an instant response from across the aisle. From this point on, every time we reach the chorus we sing in our own tongue, with each side triumphantly and joyfully taking on the old enemy. Meanwhile, the choir and the curate are sticking religiously to the Latin, and our man in the tweed suit is obviously wavering. The overall result of the friendly competition is that everyone is singing at the top of their voice, and the noise level seems enough to wake those villagers resting in eternal peace just beyond the vibrating oak doors.

During the final thundering chorus, I see the curate look up warily at the vaulted ceiling, and a faint shower of dust settles on his caped shoulders as we reach our ear-shattering conclusion.

The congregation is moving through the darkened streets of Fierville-les-Mines towards the village hall, and the silence is almost deafening. It is not so much that nobody wishes to speak, but that most are too hoarse to hold a prolonged conversation. Like battle-weary troops, we trudge wordlessly beneath the Christmas stars to where our differences will be forgotten as we share a festive drink.

Unfortunately, we arrive at the *salle* to find that the laying out of the food and drink has been as divisive as the seating arrangements at the church. At one end of the hall is the contribution from the English Goodwill Committee – traditional mince pies, a small Christmas cake and some punchbowls containing mulled and spiced ale. At the other end, the French table looks like the winning entry in the Paris Salon Culinaire, with every variety of sweetmeat, cake and exquisite delicacy artfully displayed.

On entering the hall, each of us goes instinctively to the French or English end, and we stand looking at each other like two opposing armies waiting for the off. Our man and the curate of Fierville are now stranded in the middle of no-man's land, and I do not help matters by suggesting a game of British Bulldog before we start on the refreshments.

Later, and the good food and drink have worked their magic, and past differences in the church are forgiven if not forgotten as the two sides come together to celebrate rather than dwell on our disparate cultures and attitudes. So far, none of our hosts has made even a single reference to the outcome of the World Cup, and we have begun to party in earnest as the musical entertainment begins. Fierville has its own disc jockey and he has an even wider collection of seventies disco hits than our own Néhou Kid. As my wife teaches the curate to dance the Shag, I top up my glass of mulled ale and take a breather from the fray.

Outside, a million stars jostle for attention in a crowded yet cloudless sky, and I find it hard to believe there is no life on a single one of them. Perhaps somewhere out there in the boundless reaches of the galaxy, a strange creature is even now looking at our tiny planet and wondering if life exists here, and what form it could take. I shall never know, but am sure of one thing. However vivid any alien's imagination might be, I think he would be very hard put to come up with as much as an inkling of what life is like for us here in our small corner of the universe.

I can speak French but I cannot understand it.
Mark Twain, American humorist and writer (1835–1910)

Eyes Down for a Full House

It could only happen to us.

When we arrived at the village hall in Néhou a week after the carol service, all seemed ready for the yearly Christmas knees-up. The temporary bar was fully stocked with a lethal collection of home-brew calvados disguised as lemonade, and our disc jockey, the Néhou Kid, was earnestly polishing his one-record collection of *The Greatest Disco Hits in the World Ever! (1969–70)*. Already the hall was jammed with enough tables and bench seats to accommodate the entire community, and the sturdy figures of freshly shaven and scrubbed villagers were busy laying claim to the best seats in the house. Their husbands were also dressed up to the nines.

But something was missing.

The tables were unlaid, and the kitchen doors firmly shut. And where was the usual fever of activity and delightfully conflicting aromas signposting the journey of culinary exploration we would be taking? Worse still, why was our legendary superchef JayPay blowing tentatively into the local DJ's microphone rather than on to a ladle of gently steaming *potage paysan*?

A hurried conversation with our new mayor revealed that we were here under false pretences. When Madame

Ghislaine asked us if we would be attending the village *bal*, we should have suspected something when she didn't lock us in until we bought our tickets. Proprietor of the local bar and grocery shop and president and sole member of the Néhou Retailers Association, Ghislaine is a ferocious fundraiser for the village school. She is also convinced that we, like all Britons mad enough to buy a ruin in France, are eccentric millionaires. Her sales pitch invariably comes at the close of our first Sunday morning session in the Bar Ghislaine after one of our own fundraising trips to England. With our euphoria level at its height and our resistance conversely low, Ghislaine knows that I will buy at least a dozen tickets for every raffle, draw and event in progress, and there are often as many as four a week. So far we have not been lucky in any of the sweepstakes, but came close to winning the hind quarters of a prematurely retired (due to the small matter of a missing leg) trotting pony last summer.

As the mayor now explains, I must have misheard Madame Ghislaine due to my unfamiliarity with basic French as it is spoken in this area. We are not gathered in the village hall for a *bal*, but to play the balls.

In other words, it is bingo night at Néhou.

Rather than looking contentedly at a full plate, it will be eyes down for a full *maison*. As our unofficial estate manager René Ribet observes when I tell him of the error, it seems as if we have made a real balls-up of the evening.

The session is now in full swing, and the atmosphere is far from *amiable*. It appears that the scale and level of prizes have attracted travelling pot-hunters, some from as far away as Valognes, which is all of ten miles distant. Apart from their unfamiliar faces and city-slicker cardigans, the visitors are instantly identifiable by their professional approach to the game and their state-of-the-art equipment. Our local players have handfuls of buttons and ten-centime coins to blank out the numbers on their cards, while René has persuaded me to buy a whole pack of beer so that we can use the bottle tops. The strangers are armed with little metal discs, which are picked up with a stylish magnetised wand after each game. Next to us is a serious-looking family of eight, each of whom has claimed the maximum of four cards per player. One of the children is still in his mother's arms, and there has been quite a to-do about whether he is qualified to take part. The mayor was called in to adjudicate before the games could commence, and he has reluctantly agreed that the advertising posters did not stipulate a minimum age. He has, however, refused to allow the family's fox terrier to play.

With the dispute settled, we start the first game, and I immediately realise we are going to have a problem in keeping up with the action. JayPay is our caller, and while he is the undisputed master of all things culinary, his microphone technique leaves much to be desired. Being a perfectionist by nature, he has taken an intensive training course from our local DJ, and is therefore almost unintelligible. Apart from adopting the nasal sing-song style favoured by disc jockeys everywhere, he is speaking at his usual machine-gun rate, and is using the local patois for the jokey remarks accompanying each call. Deciphering the numbers he is pulling from the drum is proving near impossible even for the locals, as JayPay is now affecting a pseudo-American accent. Neither my wife nor I would know the local equivalent of Two Little Ducks or Doctor's Orders even if we could understand what our caller is saying, and René is not proving much of a help.

Apart from the twelve cards he bought with my five-hundred-franc note, he has now ordered two more packs of beer so that we can use the caps as markers. My suggestion that we can re-use the same bottle tops for each game is turned down out of hand as tradition dictates this to be unlucky. René, known locally as the Fox, also insists on following his own traditions by emptying each bottle before using the cap.

As the evening progresses, the situation becomes even more stressful. The bounty-hunting family alongside us has already won a hand-axe, a pair of designer Wellington boots and a live chicken, and feelings are running high. For the sake of accord, I hope that the foreigners do not win the evening's star prize, which is an almost new chainsaw, complete with a bottle of lubricating oil and first-aid kit. Although all profits from the session will go to the school, the organisers and villagers like to see the prizes stay in the community. Our table is also the focus of additional hostility because René, having started on a third pack of bottle tops, is now querying every call that JayPay makes, and has even offered to take over the microphone. I have a feeling it won't be long before René the Fox takes to the table-top for his notorious Whirling Dervish routine.

I ease the tension by taking over René's cards and sending him to buy another pack of beer, and our fortunes change almost immediately. The next prize is a framed painting of the church at Néhou, and we appear to be well in the running as more and more of our numbers come up. We still cannot understand JayPay's transatlantic patois, but the ever practical Madame Ghislaine has come up with a solution. She has equipped herself with a marker pen and a supply of hastily assembled squares of cardboard torn from the prize packaging. Standing on a chair behind our caller, she is looking over his shoulder and noting the numbers as they come out of the drum, scribbling them on a card, then holding it up for all to see.

Unaware of the situation and hearing no further complaints from the audience, JayPay is reaching new heights of excess with his delivery. Sneaking a look at the pot-hunting family's cards, I see that the baby has only two uncovered spaces, while we are just my lucky number seven away from snatching the prize.

Having returned with our latest supply of bottle tops and appraised himself of the situation, René has gone round the hall with the news, and excitement is reaching fever-pitch. Although the villagers, being Norman, would naturally prefer to win any prize for themselves, a picture of the place they visit religiously every Sunday is not a great catch. However, they would obviously much prefer to see it won by honorary locals like us rather than total strangers.

As we wait in breathless silence, JayPay reaches a huge hand into the drum, rummages around to show fair play, then takes out a ping-pong ball. As he goes into overdrive with the build-up to his announcement, Madame Ghislaine writes swiftly on a card and holds the number up. It is, I see, a seven.

Caught up in the excitement, I leap to my feet and, after some rapid mental translation, shout, '*C'est moi – maison pleine!*'

At first there is no reaction, then seats scrape around the hall as almost the entire audience gets to its feet. For a moment, I think the villagers are going to give me a standing ovation, but soon realise they are merely taking the opportunity to visit the bar or toilets while my numbers are checked.

As an official takes our card for inspection and verification, René arrives from the bar to say that my triumphant full-house shout has been misinterpreted. The expression is unknown in French bingo circles, he explains, and predicts with grim relish that I will shortly be besieged as a result of my outburst. Having seen us spend a considerable fortune on changing a perfectly sound cattle shed at La Puce into a cottage and registered with disbelief the sums other settlers from the UK have spent on local houses, everyone in Néhou is convinced that all English people are completely mad when it comes to property speculation. According to our friend, a number of the audience will have taken my strangled shout as a cry for help and a plea for a further fix to satisfy my cravings to buy ruins at vastly inflated prices and throw lots of money at them. As a result, he says, at least six local farmers will shortly be approaching me with invitations to buy their unwanted outbuildings.

It later transpires that René has only been making a rather laboured joke, but it also appears that we have not, in fact, won the painting of the church. There follows an embarrassing moment as Madame Ghislaine goes through my card and discovers that I have not got a full house, or anything like it.

Half of the numbers covered by René have as yet to be called, as has my lucky winning number. In the excitement, I had forgotten that the French way of distinguishing a number one is to put a tail on the top of the vertical stroke, and had mistaken Madame Ghislaine's final card for a seven. I make a public apology, but worse is to follow as the interrupted game continues and the baby swiftly fills his two remaining spaces.

The *bal* is over, and we are walking back to La Puce. Normally, we would have been offered a lift in a passing car or tractor, but we are in disgrace. Because of the misunderstanding over my claim to the picture of the church at Néhou, the villagers seem to hold me responsible for the pot-hunting foreigners winning yet another prize. As if that were not bad enough, there was nearly an outbreak of violence when the head of family asked if he could swap the picture for something else. He said he thought the church particularly unattractive and the execution of the painting even worse. This double insult to the standards of local architecture and the skills of our resident artist was one thing; the revelation that the family are new residents of our rival village of St Jacques de Néhou was too much to bear.

After the mayor had calmed things down and convened the inevitable committee meeting, the foreigners were allowed to keep their prizes on the condition that they accepted the painting of the church, apologised to the artist and left before the game for the star prize. It did not help matters that the winner of the coveted chainsaw was our friend René Ribet, who had craftily taken over the cards abandoned by the pot-hunters.

We hurry across the main road and climb the broken gate to our top fields. In contrast to the angry scenes at the village hall, all is peaceful as we pause to look at the reflection of the buttery Norman moon on the calm surface of the big pond. Ronnie and Reggie Crayfish and their gang are safely banged up for the winter, and most of our other residents are sleeping or have gone off to warmer climes till spring returns. In the distance, an owl hoots as if in derision of our performance at our first Cotentinese bingo session, and I hear the unmistakeable buzz of René's moped as he weaves down the old cart track to our mill cottage.

Doubtless, our visitor will be in search of a nightcap and the opportunity to sell me his newly acquired chainsaw. As he will surely point out before closing the deal, we will need a newer model to replace the one that went missing from the tool shed at La Puce during our last visit to England.

The more I see of men, the more I like dogs.
Madame de Stael, French social leader (1766–1817)

On the Waterfront

I have been taking an early stroll around the estate, and find that an unexpected frost has turned La Puce into a Christmas card.

During the night, a giant hand has been sprinkling icing sugar across the fields, and the air is so cold and sharp that I might have been sucking a whole tube of Extra Strong Mints. Filling my lungs, I fleetingly consider the benefits of giving up the roll-ups, then regain my senses and sit by the jetty for a contemplative smoke.

One of the great pleasures of taking on such a sizeable amount of neglected land is that I have enough work not to do at La Puce to last the rest of my life. Although our dear friend the late mayor of Néhou kept the upper fields and hedges in immaculate condition, he left the unworkable land, trees and waterways in our hands, and we have left their care to Mother Nature. She knows much more than us about keeping things in order, and her labour comes free, so we are content to leave her to her work. The odd tree falls across the river, and we have an interesting new swamp at the end of the water meadow as a result of a huge beech branch causing the Lude to overflow. As Donella says, it would have cost a small fortune to build it ourselves, and will provide a new housing estate for the overspill from the big pond, where overpopulation and turf wars are becoming a major problem. There have been outbreaks of bloody violence all summer, and we are actually beginning to feel sorry for the normally ferocious crayfish gang.

When I first suggested introducing goldfish to the big pond to see if they would sink or swim, my wife was horrified. Though Trevor, the lone trout, has proved man enough to stand his ground, she could not bear the thought of providing bite-sized snacks for the Cray Twins and their mob. Consequently, I made a secret trip to the small pond one night and transferred Psycho the goldfish and a dozen or so of his harem to their new quarters. We originally inherited Psycho from friends who said he had killed off two of their very expensive Siamese fighting fish, and he has certainly lived up to his name.

Three years on, and there are now at least two hundred oddly coloured members of the *Carassius auratus* family living in the big pond, and all seem to have inherited the psychotic genes of their ancestor. Rather than swim aimlessly about on their own as other goldfish do, they cruise menacingly just below the surface in a spear-shaped flotilla. The whole tribe also seems to be utterly fearless and permanently ravenous, and I have long since abandoned my yearly dip in the big pond. Once undisputed lords of their manor, the individual members of the crayfish gang now seem loath to challenge the Psycho tribe's authority, and have even taken to going around in pairs.

As I stand to leave the tranquil winter setting, I hear a flutter from behind the giant gunnera plants lining the far bank of the pond and see that our overfed heron is regarding me reproachfully. Hector arrived at La Puce and the big pond two summers ago, and immediately became yet another non-paying guest. When I first disturbed him, he observed the niceties of the normal heron–human relationship and flapped off resentfully. Nowadays, he seems to spend all his time by the big pond, and to regard my appearance as an intrusion on his privacy. Within weeks of his arrival, I noticed that he was putting on weight and seemed to have increasing difficulty in getting airborne without a long and abnormally ponderous run-up. At first, I thought he was wreaking havoc among the goldfish and admired him for his bravery in taking them on. Later, I noticed that he seemed strangely reluctant to wade far enough into the water to get into striking distance, and his corpulence remained a mystery until I discovered a pile of rusting sardine cans hidden beneath a giant leaf in the gunnera rainforest.

As I turn to make my way back to the mill cottage, I nod sympathetically to Hector as he nervously eyes the shallows of the big pond. It's just as well that he no longer has to rely on traditional fishing activities for his daily intake. This morning I don't have the keys to the caravan with me, but will remember to tell my wife that a hungry resident is waiting for his breakfast.

~

It is Christmas Day, and I have been to see my darling Lucky.

He left us almost exactly a year ago, and it is the first time I have been able to bring myself to go and sit where my old friend sleeps beneath the Hobbit Tree on Hunters' Walk. The hollow oak was his favourite cool spot to rest after a long summer's day chasing imaginary rabbits in the water meadow, and is a peaceful place for him to lie for ever.

In the last months we shared our daily walk, I noticed that Lucky was slowing down, and one day he just sat in the car and looked at me when I called him. When he stopped eating, we took him to the vet already knowing what she would say, and leaving him there was the hardest decision we have ever had to make. As we held him in our arms, he looked at me and I knew that he understood. While I waited in the car afterwards, Donella cut some of the lovely golden feathered hair from his legs, and she says she will be happy to sell La Puce and everything we own to pay to have our dog cloned when it becomes possible.

I thought the pain would go away with time, but it has not. Sometimes, I wake in the night and think I feel his comforting weight at the foot of the bed, but he is not there. Of all the dogs we have loved over the years, he was somehow special, and I shall never forget him.

Good boy, Lucky. Sleep tight.

~

An almost surreal end to the day.

At René Ribet's suggestion, we had invited some of the unattached members of the community to a drinks party and buffet. As the Fox said, Christmas is a lonely time for those without family, and it would be a thoughtful way of showing the locals how people in my home country marked and celebrated the season of goodwill. As my wife said, if we wanted to introduce our Norman friends to a typical British family Christmas party, we would need to organise a selection of acrimonious arguments and even a full-scale punch-up.

Our guests arrived respectably late, in and on a selection of old cars, mopeds and even a donkey cart and a festively adorned tractor doubling as a charabanc. I stood at the door in my home-made kilt to welcome them to La Puce, and soon collected an interesting selection of empty cider, beer and liqueur bottles. When I asked René if this was some sort of Cotentinese ritual, he said that, on the contrary, my guests were merely trying to conform with what he had assumed to be another of our weird customs. I had told him that it was going to be a bottle party, but had said nothing about the bottles being filled. He had heard about guests bringing lumps of coal to New Year parties in Scotland, and had thought this was a further example of our strange traditions.

Another surprise was the lack of women guests, but as our estate manager said, if any of the men had been lucky enough to have female companions for Christmas, they would certainly not have brought them along to be leered at by the others.

After a stilted start as the guests stared bemusedly at the wooden floors and stone walls and obviously wondered why we had spent so much time and money in making an old mill cottage as uncomfortable as it would have been several centuries ago, my wife persuaded one of the more adventurous villagers to try the buffet. Approaching the table like a heretic being ushered into an Inquisition torture chamber, Jean-Claude Morel's face visibly blanched as he regarded the selection of party snacks, and I am sure his legs buckled when my wife asked if he would like to try a Scotch egg.

Eventually and as my special calva punch took effect, the atmosphere lightened and our guests overcame their trepidation. After expressing sympathy with Scottish chickens for what must be a painful daily delivery, Jean-Claude declared his egg almost eatable, and – being Norman – then began lecturing his fellow guests on the intricacies and variations of British catering.

The evening progressed, and as the drinks flowed even the most reticent of our guests got into the party spirit. My suggestion that we play some traditional British party games was met with enthusiasm, but once again the yawning gap between our cultures was made clear. Heated words were exchanged when our local postman refused to deliver the package on to the next player in Pass the Parcel, and René Ribet's attempt to pin the paper tail on to Mr Claubert's real donkey was not appreciated by its owner.

Then it was time for our guests to show us how Norman countrymen partied. By midnight, our estate manager was wearing my kilt and demonstrating his Whirling Dervish routine on the roof of the mill cottage, and I had lost my fifth consecutive arm-wrestling match. By four in the morning, the obstacle tournament in the water meadow had come to its inevitable conclusion and the tractor had been retrieved from the big pond. As dawn approached, our guests had drunk us dry and were finally ready to depart.

Standing in the mill garden beneath a canopy of stars, I shook hands with Mr Claubert and asked if he had enjoyed his taste of British hospitality. The old farmer considered my question for a moment, then gave a classic Gallic shrug. It was always interesting to see how foreigners celebrated significant occasions, he said, and he now realised why so many Britons choose to take their Christmas holidays abroad. Having said that, he thought the experience almost worth the two hundred francs that René Ribet had charged for the invitations.

Living in France is a bit like Marmite.
You either love it or hate it.
Daniel Hatcher, aged fifteen, British settler in Lower Normandy

Pension Plan

Another year has begun at La Puce and it is, as the locals say, duck cold. I have been on feeding duty, and on my way back to the cottage, I stop off at the postbox to pick up our latest batch of fan mail.

Together with the inevitable terse reminders from banks and other creditors, there is the usual selection of letters asking our advice or pointing out glaring errors in my writings about buying French property or moving across the Channel. But I am pleased to learn that we can now add another flag to the map of France on my study wall. A couple have written to tell us that they have just completed on a charming cottage in the Vendée, and wanted us to be the first to know. They have as yet to decide on a name for the new addition to their family, but write to thank us for the inspiration our books on the subject provided. At their darkest moments, they say, they only had to look at the disasters we had had to cheer themselves up and realise that they are nowhere near as incompetent as us.

We regularly receive this sort of back-handed compliment from readers as they pass through each stage of the journey to realising their dream of owning some corner of a foreign field, and the comments and criticisms are almost equally welcome.

We like nothing better at this time of year than to sit by the fire in the mill cottage and read how our correspondents are getting on. For us, it is a wonderful opportunity to re-live our own emotions and adventures in the early days, and there may be a practical bonus for our old age.

There are ninety-one *départements* in France. Most, with some notably French and therefore bewildering exceptions, are sensibly numbered in approximate alphabetical order. The department of Ain, for example, is number 1, while we in Manche are awarded a 50, and Yonne is number 89. The department of Belfort, for what I am sure are its own very good reasons, lays claim to number 90.

The map on my study wall bears a flag for every depart-ment where at least one of our correspondents has bought a home and settled, and been rash enough to offer us hospital-ity if we ever happen to be in their area. Little do they know that I have devised a foolproof scheme for taking advantage of their kind offers while spending the autumn of our years living and travelling in France for next to nothing. If my wife agrees, we will make out a carefully planned route, then turn up on the doorstep of the first with a bottle of wine and an overnight bag. Having worn out our welcome, it will be time to move on to the next host on the list. So far, there are fifty-seven flags sprouting from the map, which should mean we will not have to strain any individual host's tolerance for even a week.

Apart from the new addition to my pension-plan club, I also see that we have a letter from Moondance and Zak, the pen-names of two readers who have recently moved to France. They seem just the sort of couple to adapt, survive and even prosper in the new life they have chosen.

Like us, they would probably be called eccentric by most allegedly normal people, and like us, they would probably wonder why. This, I am told by psychologists, is the sign of a true eccentric, but what do they know about real life and real people? I like to consider myself a good judge of people and am full of confidence for Moondance and Zak's prospects. However, I have to admit that I find the accurate forecasting of which of our many correspondents will settle well on this side of the Channel a perennial problem.

Generally, a good rule of thumb is that I get it wrong and my wife gets it right. I believe it is something to do with women's intuition, while Donella says it is a matter of simple common sense, a faculty of which I am totally devoid.

There are, however, some general and broad categories into which various types of French property buyer or settler fit, and which have proved to give a fair indication of whether there is likely to be a happy outcome to the adventure.

The first category includes Lords of the Manor. These are people who buy property in France simply because it is so much cheaper than at home. They may not like the French or even France, but the nearest they can get to being landed gentry is by owning an impressive pile across the Channel. They are the sort of people who tell their friends that they own a chateau when what they have is really a biggish house with more than three bedrooms. Experience has shown that this type is not likely to make a go of their foreign adventuring, and are often people who know the price of everything and the value of nothing.

The second category in our rough guide includes Holiday Romantics. These sort of people are naïve enough to think that owning a property in France will be at least as much fun as their yearly three-week *gîte* holiday, with the added advantage that they will no longer have to pay an extortionate rental for staying there. They persuade themselves that they will be able to cover the running costs, insurance, rates, travel expenses and even restoration costs by getting someone else to pay to take the place for a few weeks each summer. Unfortunately, they will soon discover that a couple of thousand other owners in their region have had the same idea, and will actually end up letting friends use their French home for free.

Our favourite and by far the most successful category consists of would-be settlers who either genuinely want to live in France or in the countryside anywhere. They, like us, would never be able to afford even a modest country cottage in England, but can realise their hankering for rural life by adapting to their new circumstances.

So far, our settlers' guide has proved reasonably accurate, but life being what it is, there are always some notable exceptions, and that's what makes our little game such fun.

Of one thing we are sure: for the right sort of people, France offers endless opportunities and rewards. A simple visit to a shop can be an adventure, and unblocking a sewage pipe on a frosty morning can put life into a perspective of almost staggering clarity.

Un sot trouve toujours un plus sot qui l'admire.
(A fool can always find a greater fool to admire him.)
Nicolas Boileau, French critic and poet (1636–1711)

Close Encounters

No rain so far today, so I shall have a bath to celebrate.

This evening, we are dining with a couple of would-be settlers we met on a recent ferry crossing, and I am looking forward to giving them some sound advice on the best way of realising their dream. Having said that, I will add the standard disclaimer that whatever course of action they take, I will not be held responsible for the outcome.

Jackie and Tom seem a sensible couple, excepting that they are eager to meet with René Ribet at some stage of their weekend in the Cotentin. If they are not careful, he will sell them his cottage at a bargain price, which will not please the farmer who owns it. Our new friends introduced themselves while my wife and I were raiding the onboard duty-free shop, and Tom openly admits he was stalking us to see if we were who he thought we were. He had been reading my latest book when I shambled by en route to the shop, and he said it was extremely spooky to hear us discussing which economy-size bottle of Scotch we should buy for René.

Nowadays, it is unusual for us to make a crossing without being recognised and approached, and Donella says I love the attention. She claims that I always walk around the entire ship at least five times during the voyage, and that she has caught me standing by the book department laughing helplessly at the contents of one of my books and recommending it to anyone who passes by. To prove to my wife that all the attention is not turning my head, I have offered to stay in our cabin for the whole journey, or wear a false beard when venturing out. My wife, however, says that as I already have a beard, I am obviously not serious in my claims to wish to travel incognito.

When a close encounter of the boat kind does happen, whatever the situation, the approach will always be made by a male. Sometimes, it is the direct full-frontal attack, and in the past I have been nabbed during a meal, while asleep and even in the toilet. This can be embarrassing, especially if there are other passengers present. At other times, I will become aware of someone who has walked past me at least three times for no apparent good reason. Eventually, he will catch my eye, smile shyly or knowingly, then ask if I am indeed me. Occasionally, he will get my name right; more often he will ask if I am that fat bloke who made such a balls-up of buying a house in France.

The type of approach will also indicate the next stage, which will take one of three forms.

Sometimes, my reader will tell me how much he enjoys my work and go on to describe – sometimes in great detail and accompanied with notes, photographs and drawings – his own plans to buy a home in France. Sometimes, he will explain that he and his partner have already trod our path, and made a better or even worse fist of it. Always, he will say he found my writing much more or much less interesting and amusing than any other book on the subject. Very rarely I meet a real fan, and it is always disconcerting to encounter a stranger who knows so much about your life; especially when you have forgotten most of what you have written about.

Apart from our regular confrontations on the journey to and from La Puce, I occasionally meet a reader in the most unlikely circumstances, as happened once when we arrived at our house in Portsmouth some years ago.

We were ferrying cases of wine, cider, cheese and other delicacies from the car when I noticed we were being keenly watched by a very large man at the top of a ladder resting against the house opposite. For a moment I wondered if he might be an undercover revenue spy, but on closer scrutiny decided against it. He was wearing typical builder's summer rig of skimpy singlet and long shorts, sported a range of interesting tattoos, and had obviously practised painting himself before starting on the house. In my experience, few excise officers would have the initiative to create such an authentic disguise. But he obviously found us interesting for some reason, and after absent-mindedly painting a window pane on the house next door, he gave me a hail.

'I know who you are, don't I?' he shouted, shaking his paintbrush triumphantly. 'That's Victor the Volvo, isn't it?'

Smiling smugly, I shrugged deprecatingly at a passing traffic warden and waited for the revelation of my fame.

'I've read the books,' our distant admirer bellowed as he climbed down the ladder and crossed the road. 'You're that Fred West, ain't you?'

After I told him that I was not a mass murderer and that my wife was the concrete-laying specialist of the family, he apologised for the mistake and told us he was the proud new owner of a farm in Normandy, and had found my books most entertaining and helpful.

Over a glass of cider in the office, Jimmy-John explained how he had bought the cottage, five acres and assorted outbuildings as the result of a slight misunderstanding. Having a weekend break driving around the Cherbourg peninsula with his wife, he had dropped in to a tourist bureau to ask about a bed and breakfast stop for the night. Unsurprisingly, none of the specially trained staff spoke English, and Jimmy-John relied on sign language to indicate that they were looking for a house where they could sleep for the night. After much discussion with colleagues, the manager of the *syndicat d'initiative* made a couple of phone calls and replied with his hands and watch that the couple should return at seven that evening.

They did so, and were whisked away in the car of another non-English speaker. After travelling for an hour, they arrived in the gathering dusk at what appeared to be a derelict farmhouse. As Jimmy-John said, it was not a welcoming sight. Though used to the sometimes indifferent standards of French accommodation, he reckoned that glass in most of the windows should be a standard feature in any bed-and-breakfast enterprise, to say nothing of doors in the frames. Seeing his discomfiture, their guide called upon the translation services of an Englishman who lived nearby, and the confusion was cleared up. The farm was not on the tourist-office books as a *chambre d'hôte*; it was on the books of the local estate agent as a property for sale. After accepting the profuse apologies of the agent and before getting back in the car, Jimmy idly asked the price of the ramshackle building. It was, he discovered, going for slightly less than the cost of a couple of weeks in Tenerife. As a builder and used to working on garages that would cost more than the dilapidated but characterful property, Jimmy thought about it for all of five minutes, looked at his wife for approval and put in a bid.

It was accepted on the spot, and the couple who had gone to the Cotentin for a weekend break had become home-steaders. Jimmy and his wife were now halfway through a crash course in French and a complete restoration of their new home, and loving every moment of their adventure. He still wasn't sure if the tourist office and his estate agent contact had really mistaken his request for a night's bed and breakfast, but he and his family were more than happy at the prospect of spending much, much more time in the Cotentin than originally planned.

After hearing Jimmy-John's tale, we finished the bottle of cider, opened some moonshine calvados and decided to add his flag and details to the map of France in my study. Although Jimmy's farm is in our home region, he is very good company and, as any French-property owner knows, having a skilled, English-speaking builder on tap and just down the road is a real bonus.

Les yeux de l'étranger voient plus clair.
(The eyes of a foreigner see more clearly.)
Charles Reade, Victorian author (1814–84)

A Night on the Town

Donella having prepared a gourmet meal for her menagerie, we are off to Bricquebec for a budget meal with our new friends, the would-be settlers.

Tonight, they will have the benefit of my first-hand experience on the subject of making a new life in Normandy. I, my wife says, will have the pleasure of talking non-stop for several hours. As I point out, she will at least have the pleasure of not having to listen as she has heard it all before.

Before we leave, I visit the attic of our mill cottage to collect forensic evidence of yet another non-paying guest. Climbing through the tiny hatch to the void above the bedroom, I see that the Mouse family have refurbished their quarters with the remnants of the lagging from the cold water pipes. They have also made a start on the covering to the electrical cables from the immersion heater. Investigating further, I recognise a fragment of the only copy of an important article I had been working on, and which I thought was safely locked away in my desk drawer. With the aid of my torch, I can see that their *bijou* little home behind the water tank is looking ever more comfortable, and even modish. Perhaps the mice have been watching the latest series of DIY programmes on our satellite television. So far, they have not actually stolen any of our furniture, and use the wallpaper from the landing for bedding rather than decorative purposes, but I shall know where to look if any more of my carpentry tools go missing.

When we first converted the cattle byre back to its original function as a cottage, I set out on a campaign to rid the premises of all forms of wildlife, but my wife found the rat poison and made dark threats about adding some to my food if I did not get rid of it. From then on it was open house, with more species of animal and insect life to be found in the cottage than outside during the winter months. It sounds far-fetched, but I am sure that our beastly residents know they are welcome as far as my wife is concerned, and that she has the last word when it comes to visitors with more than two legs. I knew that I had lost the battle with the Mouse family when one of the younger members appeared while we were having an informal supper in front of the television. Not only did he clamber unconcernedly up on to the arm of my chair, but helped himself to a piece of Camembert cheese before settling down alongside me to enjoy a programme on the Nature Channel.

My visit to the Mouse household has also created a new natural history mystery, and I have the tangible evidence of yet another squatter safely stowed away in a Tesco carrier bag. Over the years at La Puce, I have become something of an expert in animal excretions of all types, sizes and textures, but this sample is a real mystery. The stool I stumbled on in the attic of the mill cottage is solid and tubular and mottled black and white, and too big in my judgement for a rat, yet too small for an owl. Either the constant supply of high-energy food from Donella has caused the Mouse family to produce a monstrous new species, or we have geese in our loft. I will take the sample to Bricquebec this evening and ask our friends for their expert opinions and conclusions.

~

We arrive at our favourite town, and park in what the locals claim to be the biggest market square in all France. It is certainly impressive, framed on one side by an imposing church and on the other by a Trappist monastery that is said to produce very fine *charcuterie* cold meat products (the finest in all France, naturally). Another side of the square is taken up with the castle of Bricquebec. It is said to date variously from the eleventh, twelfth or thirteenth centuries, depending on which of the locals is acting as unofficial town historian. I know it is true that Rommel used the place as his headquarters at some time during World War II, but draw the line at fanciful notions about Queen Victoria being a regular visitor for dirty weekends with her ghillie John Brown. Nowadays, the castle is classified as an ancient monument, though the hotel occupying part of it is owned by our good friends Hubert and Albine Hardy. Hubert is also the boss of the local tourist association, and naturally misses no opportunity to promote his hotel and the attractions of the town. The continuing operation to maintain the fabric of the castle is funded with Euro money, and the town fathers make sure that Bricquebec gets its fair share of any grants going. There is always a team of local craftsmen working on some part of the building, and I am sure that some of the immaculate walls and towers have been painstakingly restored at least three times in the past year.

As we leave the car and walk across the square to meet our dinner companions at the Café de Paris, we hear what appears to be the screams of an animal in great pain, and the dreadful noise appears to be coming directly from our local. I fleetingly wonder if Freddo the proprietor has taken to staging his regular hunting parties actually inside his bar to save the customers from having to venture out into the rain and cold of winter.

On our entry to the bar, the source of the din is resolved. Our local wide boy and very general dealer, Dodgy Didier Bouvier, is at centre stage, attempting to get a tune out of a set of Breton bagpipes. He is also wearing a plaid skirt. Thinking for a moment that we have stumbled across a particularly weird Saturday evening fetish party, I then see a huge haggis on the bartop and realise that this is some sort of dress rehearsal for next month's Burns' Night celebrations. Freddo has joined in the spirit of the evening by wearing a paper tartan bonnet on his head, and has a large paintbrush hanging from a string round his waist. After greetings are exchanged, our host confirms that he and Didier are testing the popularity of foreign theme nights, and that the occasion will also give him a chance to shift some of the Scotch whisky he has recently acquired from certain quarters. Looking around, I see that the regulars are watching the proceedings with typical Norman detachment, while our bemused new friends Jackie and Tom are being taught handy patois sayings and phrases by our latest exchange student, Ken Barnes.

A former master carpenter, Ken is approaching retirement age, and has taken advantage of one of the benefits of our twinning arrangement. Officially, Bricquebec is matched with the quaint and historic country town of Arlesford in Hampshire. Unofficially, we have twinned the Café de Paris with our local pub in Portsmouth, and there have been several goodwill visits between the two establishments and their customers. After learning that he could buy a cottage in Bricquebec for about the same annual rent he pays for his terraced home in Hampshire, Ken is staying with a local family for a month while house-hunting, and is already well on the way to going native. Being a thoughtful man with an enquiring and open mind and a liking for a smoke and drink, our friend fitted in well from the start of his visit, and has been taken to the community's heart. But before he arrived in Bricquebec, I cautioned him not to tell his new friends that his job for thirty years has been in the Portsmouth dockyard, using his skills to maintain the sails and spars of Nelson's flagship, HMS *Victory*. It is a curious fact that while the Cotentinese seem to bear no malice towards German visitors, they have long memories when it comes to more ancient encounters.

Before joining our friends, I have a word with Didier, who explains that he brought the haggis back from a recent business trip to Scotland, and has made it his concern to educate the patrons of the Café de Paris on the traditions of the Burns' ceremony and the history and habits of the animal itself. Freddo has shown great interest in the idea of organising a hunting trip to the Highlands of Scotland during the open season on the beast, but the regulars have been put off sampling the dish because of the presence of so many vegetables on the giant platter. Didier has responded by reminding them of France's traditional friendship and links with Scotland, and then there is the Norman connection. It is well documented, Didier assures his potential customers, that haggis herds once roamed free across the Cotentin landscape, and were introduced to Scotland by Bonnie Prince Arthur after one of his periodical flights to the peninsula during the English Civil War.

Finally reaching our table, I see that our new friend Tom is showing Ken a large plastic bottle with a name and some dates on the stopper. The bottle, Tom says, was given to him by an elderly friend who had heard about their visit to Normandy. Her husband, she said, had been involved in the evacuation at Dunkirk, and it had been his dying wish that his ashes be scattered on the surface of the English Channel. Though he had died some twenty years before, his widow had a morbid fear of the sea, and the urn had remained on her mantelpiece ever since. Now that Tom was going to France, would he be so kind as to tastefully sprinkle the contents over the side as the car ferry reached mid-Channel?

As Tom said, he could hardly refuse the request and duly went on deck during the crossing. Unfortunately, he was not a seafaring man, and had naturally chosen the side of the boat with the fewest people at the rail. It was only after emptying the container that he realised that the other passengers had sensibly chosen the sheltered side of the ferry. Rather than gently settling on the choppy waters of the Channel, the ashes had immediately been blown aboard. Most had disappeared harmlessly in the general direction of the funnel, but a sprinkling had found their way on to an ice cream being enjoyed by a toddler standing nearby. He had bought the child another, said Tom, but had thought it best not to explain to the mother exactly what the gritty stuff was. Especially as the youngster had eaten a couple of mouthfuls before he could make amends.

We look at the empty bottle and reflect on the unpredictability of life and death, and my wife consoles Tom with the thought that the former sailor will now be able to cross and recross the Channel for all eternity, and totally free of charge.

To change the subject, I compliment Ken on his beret, and learn that he has already seen a most suitable retirement home. The tiny and dilapidated cottage is on the outskirts of Bricquebec and not officially on the market, but Ken's hosts say that an offer in excess of thirty thousand francs may persuade the owner to part with it. As to property details, the important particulars are most encouraging. The cottage has a widow of an uncertain age living next door, and open fields as a neighbour on the other side. Even better, the distance to the Café de Paris has been timed as precisely six minutes at a gentle stroll. Apart from the developments with the cottage, Ken reports that he is making great progress with his French, and I take the opportunity to ask why he keeps calling out the name of a cartoon character as regulars leave the premises. He explains that I am obviously not as handy with the local lingo as I ought to be. As I should know, it is basic good manners to say 'See you later' when parting company with a friend. After another couple of puzzled regulars leave, I understand, and tactfully point out that the local way of saying cheerio is pronounced 'plutar' as in 'later', and not 'pluto' as in Mickey Mouse's friend.

As we talk and the Burns' Night rehearsal gathers momentum, we are joined by one of the handful of expatriates who have become fixtures in the town. BBC Charles is of a similar age to Ken and, like many English settlers with their own reasons for living anonymously abroad, he is an interesting and unusual character.

We first met in the nearby Donjon restaurant last year, when he heard my wife and I talking English and came over to introduce himself and point out the local tourist attractions. He was, he explained, a former foreign correspondent with the British Broadcasting Corporation, and was biding his time in Bricquebec till the terms of his pension and annuities were sorted out. For an hour or so he enthralled us with tales of his exploits in the Congo and other exotic locations, and then introduced us to his partner. A genuine Russian princess, the lady was a direct descendant of the Romanov dynasty. We were disappointed to learn that Madame did not speak Russian, and later agreed that her huge sunglasses and flowing scarf made her look more like Biggles than the long-lost daughter of Anastasia, but she was a pleasant enough person. After accepting our invitation to join us for a bottle of wine, Charles told us all about a local celebrity who had written a book about the area, made a couple of million and retired to a water mill down the road. Such were his powers of oratory that it was not until we had left the restaurant some hours later that I realised he had, in fact, been talking about me. I had also been too entranced to notice that he had added his restaurant bill for the evening to ours.

From what Charles tells us as I stand him a couple of beers, his BBC pension has still not come through. Sadly, his princess has gone back to Mother Russia, and he is reduced to living in a cell at the Trappist monastery. As he touches me for a few francs until his cheque arrives from the BBC, he explains that his little room is quite comfortable, and his hosts are very kind. Being part of a silent order, however, conversation is not their strong point. On the plus side, the good brothers serve a liberal glass of wine after every devotional meeting, and there are no fewer than twelve a day.

If past form for his sort of expatriate adventurer is anything to go by, one day we will notice that Charles is not around, and learn from various debtors that he has moved on to quarters new or simply not woken up one morning. When that happens, we shall miss his engaging company, dry wit and fortitude, and our little community will be the poorer for his passing.

The practice Burns' Night is now in full swing, but I have had no luck in identifying our mystery resident. The carrier bag containing the animal droppings has been passed repeatedly around the bar, and everyone has given an opinion on who or what is responsible for the contents. While admitting to not knowing what the animal could be, Freddo has offered to come to La Puce in the morning and shoot it.

As the bag continues its round of new arrivals, I return from the toilets and note that we have been joined by our undercover police officer. Gilbert *le flic* has lived in the town all his life and is seen by all the townspeople by day as he goes about his desk job at the local *gendarmerie*. By night, however, he disguises himself with a leather jacket and a change of parting, and haunts the nightspots of the town to observe any evil-doing and write down the names of those responsible. Freddo says he is far from a harmless eccentric. His favourite trick is to drink with the locals then be waiting outside at closing time to invite drivers to blow into his soufflé, or breathalyser.

Pretending not to recognise the undercover detective, I nod coolly, rescue my carrier bag from a couple who are about to taste the evidence in the interest of solving our mystery, and retire to our table.

Much later, and the party crowd is thinning out. Outside the bar, the legendary Cotentin wind soughs through the vast square and chases departing revellers to their homes. Inside, the haggis has been eaten and pronounced surprisingly good, and we seem to be under special scrutiny from the undercover cop. I order another round, and continue to enjoy a memorable evening in good company.

The talk now turns to my attempts to tell the world about our adventures in the Cotentin, and Jackie asks me why I choose to spend my life writing about this small corner of France. To begin with, I explain, it is far better than working for a living, and it is a delight as well as a privilege to be invited into my readers' minds to paint pictures of real life in real France. It is also a constant fascination to reflect that, at any time, someone far away is reading about our friends in Néhou. They may never have sought it, but I am proud to have given them some small measure of acknowledgement – and even a sort of immortality.

As I warm to my theme, my wife tells me I am becoming maudlin and suggests we return to La Puce for a bedtime coffee and calvados. We say goodnight to our host, and Ken bids all the regulars 'pluto', then we climb aboard Victor for the drive home. Turning back for a final farewell wave, I see through the window of the bar that Gilbert the undercover cop has crossed to our table and is investigating the contents of our abandoned Tesco carrier bag.

I think about returning for the bag or explaining to him what is inside, but decide against it. With any luck, the tireless sleuth will send the strange droppings to the Paris headquarters of the Sûreté for analysis as a suspicious substance, and we will finally discover the identity of our mystery resident at La Puce.

Boy, those French. They have a different word for everything.
Steve Martin, American actor and comedian

Speaking in Tongues

I arrive at Madame Ghislaine's for the traditional Sunday morning aperitif, and am surprised to find René is not among the company.

When I ask after him, one of the customers explains that he is away fishing for ormers. I find this even more surprising, as I know this rare and highly prized truffle of the sea is found mainly around the Channel Islands and is only taken during spring tides.

After I innocently remark that I did not know my friend was a diver, there is general and somewhat coarse laughter in the bar, and someone remarks that the Fox would not be getting even his feet wet as he would be fishing for his ormers at low tide. Later, JayPay joins me on a visit to the *pissoir* and explains delicately that the remark about the delicious shellfish that we also call the sea-ear or abalone was actually code for another sort of popular leisure activity. Though I have never seen one, the fleshy fruit inside the shell is said to look remarkably like a very private part of the female anatomy. My friend the Fox of Cotentin is, it seems, on a visit to the house of the Widow of Négreville.

JayPay also explains that if René had been intending an encounter in the open air this fine morning, he would have been said to have been chasing lobsters in the gorse.

As we zip up and return to the bar, I wonder once again at the peculiarities of the *lingua franca*. All these ridiculous euphemisms and expressions seem a very strange kettle of fish to me.

~

It's all very well people going on about how disgraceful it is that so few Britons speak French and how everyone in France is fluent in our language, but in my experience, it just isn't true. Nobody in our village speaks a word of English, and I can't imagine them wanting to. In Bricquebec, our notary and bank manager pretend not to. We have long been aware of this tendency by certain sections of the French middle classes to feign ignorance of our language when it suits them, but we can usually tell by their eyes when they are listening in on our private conversations to see if they can gain some advantage. A good test is to say something outrageous about French food, driving, football teams or Napoleon, and watch to see if they blink.

Closer to home in our commune of Néhou, the locals not only ignore foreign languages, but also prefer their own patois to standard French. This puts visitors at a considerable disadvantage even if they are from another department of Normandy, or sometimes even another area of the Cotentin. Particularly afflicted by the problems of making themselves clearly understood are the occasional government officials from St Lô on a mission to discover why the people of Néhou seem so incompetent at filling in tax returns and other official documents. Recently, I was present when one such visitor tried his hand at irony by suggesting our village go the whole hog and declare itself a separate republic. He was unaware that we have already looked into the pros and cons of separatism, with the Jolly Boys Club proposing that we approach Monaco with a request for tips on how best to go about the process of establishing a principality. The motion was eventually defeated when we got into a fractious debate about who was most entitled to take on the title of HRH of Néhou.

～

A notable exception to the general language rule at Néhou is Didier, our local entrepreneur. Being a much travelled and sophisticated businessman, he claims to have not only visited every part of England, but also to be fluent in the language and familiar with many aspects of that most peculiar country. Much given to airing his knowledge of the latest overseas fads, fashions and developments, his dress code reflects his knowledge of all things foreign. Today, he is wearing a white suit with huge lapels, which he claims to be all the rage in London, and is predicting that Mrs Thatcher will soon abdicate from her position in favour of Prince Charles. We have thought about enlightening him in the past, but don't want to embarrass a friend or threaten the regular supplies of English delicacies he allegedly buys from British lorry drivers at the ferry port in Cherbourg.

This morning, it was our turn for a visit from Dodgy Didier's van. The Bar Ghislaine was packed with those wishing to find a real bargain, and the few who like to know what has been going on in the outside world. In full attendance today was the Néhou Jolly Boys Club, of which I have the honour to be an overseas member. Though having no written constitution or membership regulations, rules governing full entry to the club are very precise, and include having lived in or on the outskirts of the village since at least birth, having an above average consumption rate of alcohol and an understanding of all things to do with the countryside and the nature and true meaning of life. And, of course, being free to attend at least five meetings every week at the Bar Ghislaine. Another requirement is to be of an age when one has learned that just waking up each morning is a good start to the day. I am by far the youngest member, and our president is Old Pierrot. So far, I have not been able to discover exactly where he lives or how old he is, but it is whispered that he predates the village thanks to his secret elixir of life and special dietary regime, which seems to consist almost entirely of home-brew calvados. I have also heard it claimed that he has magical powers and was on first-name terms with William the Conqueror. Whatever the truth about his age and mystic powers, Old Pierrot has become the Merlin to the court of the Jolly Boys Club, and hardly a meeting goes by without him making a mysterious prediction or pronouncement. Last week, he even put a curse on René Ribet for laughing at his yearly forecast of the worst flooding in living memory. It was the talk of the commune when René fell off his moped and broke his wrist on the way home from the meeting. The more superstitious of the villagers credited Old Pierrot's black arts with the accident, but I think it more likely that Mr Johnny Walker was to blame.

Apart from such entertaining diversions, pure philosophy reigns during our sessions at the Bar Ghislaine. I can think of few pleasures that surpass a gathering of the Jolly Boys Club on a wet winter afternoon in the Bar Ghislaine, with the single log in the grate at least smouldering, a bottle of calvados on the table and our minds ablaze with the possibilities of restructuring the world and its ways. Since being given the honour of becoming the first outsider admitted to the ranks of the JBC, I have tried to introduce refinements to the rules from time to time, such as other members buying the occasional round, but my motions have been rejected without a vote. Membership of women even as associate members is, of course, unthinkable.

Today, other members present included JayPay the chef, Old Pierrot, Marcel Bernard and, of course, René Ribet. But the main event today was Didier's weekly visit.

Didier began his traditional story-telling session with the topical tale of President Clinton's excuse that he actually asked Monica Lewinsky to sack his cook and she misheard him, but it fell rather flat as the play on words does not work in French, let alone patois.

~

Apart from these occasional confusions over common usage, one thing all my French friends are agreed upon is their opinion of my standard of French. The sound of me speaking their precious language, as one friend rather unkindly put it, is enough to make any true Frenchman wish he was deaf.

Regardless or perhaps because of this attitude, many French people still take every opportunity to pretend they don't know what I am talking about, even when they patently do. I have written before about this peculiar and irritating trait, experienced on my early visits to France. But it still happens, even nowadays.

A typical example of misinterpretation arrived today with our weekly communiqué from Moondance and Zak, who report that they are settling down really well in their new home in Mayenne. This is quite a relief, as Moondance likes cuddly animals, is a strict vegetarian and only found out on moving-in day that their neighbour is a veal farmer. Apart from the bloodstained clothing, she says, he seems to be quite a friendly man and wants to make them feel part of the community. They have, however, politely refused his offer to go with him to the local abattoir for a day out.

In their fax, our post-hippie friends also say that they have been having some communication problems with their other neighbour, a man who lives alone and speaks his own version of patois that cannot be understood by even the local people. When they first moved in and invited him over for a drink, virtually the whole evening was spent in achieving the exchange of names. As they got to know him, he became more friendly and set about advising them on the ways of the countryside, including an often repeated warning about the problems of finding crap in their shoes in the morning. At first, thinking he was warning them of the nocturnal habits of his cat, our friends would carefully put their footwear on top of the wardrobe before going to bed. Once, however, after a particularly enjoyable evening entertaining friends, they forgot the routine. The confusion over the mystery shoe-shitter was solved next morning when they found a large brown toad, or *crapaud*, snoozing contentedly in Moondance's left slipper.

Selling Out

Monday morning and a treat is in store. Today, we shall make our weekly visit to the market at Bricquebec. As if to mark the occasion, it even stopped raining for ten minutes earlier today.

Before making ready for our trip to town, we venture into the mill garden and stand beside the thundering cascade to look out across the flooded water meadow. It is certainly living up to its official name of *le réservoir*, and the big pond is getting bigger by the day. Donella expresses concern about the wellbeing of the fish, and I ask if she is worried they may drown in the constant downpour. She is not amused by what she calls my callous remark, and says that if the big pond continues to overflow, Psycho and his tribe could be washed into the neighbouring fields. I make a mental note to warn the local farmers to move their livestock to higher ground if the flooding worsens. I have heard that the deadly Amazonian piranha fish can strip a fully grown horse to the bone in twenty minutes, but I bet Psycho and his chums could do it in half the time.

Before returning to the cottage to put on our going-to-market clothes, we sit on the bench and look at the cascade, and I wonder rather smugly just how many people can boast of a waterfall in their back garden.

Arriving in the square at Bricquebec, we receive the predictable black looks from a huddle of small men in big boots. Civilians are not particularly welcome when the farmers gather to conduct what they see as the real business of the day. Hard bargaining is the norm at any traditional animal marketplace, but here the Cotentinese farmers take every centime made or lost on a deal very seriously indeed. Allegedly, the damp red patches found dotted about the square are not always the result of an unfortunate animal being despatched on the spot for easier transportation purposes. This occasional bloodletting is the main reason we always arrive after the animals have gone and the stallholders have descended on the square. It's not that Donella would be frightened by the sight of a punch-up, but I fear for the safety of anyone she might think is mistreating an animal.

An hour passes as the ancient paving slabs are hosed down, the pens and cages removed, and the farmers depart to the various bars where they will celebrate or mourn their morning's dealings. Already the square is filling up with dozens of stands and stalls in various stages of assembly, and we wander among them to enjoy the atmosphere. Ours is one of the largest and liveliest markets on the peninsula, and hardly a soul from the surrounding villages and hamlets will miss the traditional start to the week. It was not until we settled in a fairly remote area and got into the rhythm and pace of country living that we realised the real significance of any rural market. After a week spent working in relative and sometimes complete solitude, the soul cries out for a regular opportunity to rub shoulders with other human beings instead of livestock. Companionship by proximity is the real reason country people go to market. At least, that's my view. My wife says it is actually because visitors can get a whole week's worth of gossip in one glorious hit, and it is certainly true that as much tittle-tattle as money is exchanged at Bricquebec market. Whatever the reason for the gathering, I would rather be at a Norman market than any air-conditioned shopping mall or precinct in Britain.

We take our time strolling through the lines of stalls, and I divert Donella's attention from a row of crates containing some very unhappy-looking turkeys. There are at least a dozen stands offering the local equivalent of hot dogs. The spicey merguez sausages are more than delicious on a cold December morning and when eaten in a crisp baguette with lashings of Dijon mustard and a huge portion of chips. Other snacks include the French version of Welsh rarebit and very un-Italian pizzas, filled pancakes and giant mugs of thick Normandy potato and cream soup. Nearby, whole ducks, chickens and joints of lamb and beef are sizzling on mechanical turnspits above oaken logs. The combined aroma of these delights is irresistible, and munching on a hot sandwich of goat's cheese and olives, I drag my wife away from a stall selling chainsaws and try to interest her in something less expensive as a souvenir of our day at market.

Later, we venture into the lair of Madame Lefarge. There are a dozen bars in Bricquebec, each catering for a particular type of clientele, but the proprietor of the Café Bon Accueil appears to cater for none. A large and intimidating woman with a small and understandably nervous husband, she bears down on those who dare trespass on her territory like a galleon in full sail. If she eventually approves of you and your manner and dress code, it is possible she may take your order. Madame obviously considers customers an inconvenient interruption to her daily duties of haranguing her husband. Every other bar in Bricquebec will be packed this morning, with farmers trying to get their bulbous Norman noses into tiny glasses of liqueur, and housewives resting from their bargaining encounters with the stallholders. But here, we will find no problem in getting a seat, providing we pass the threshold audition. As we walk across the square, I see that the patch outside the Lefarge lair is once again occupied by the least successful traders. Whether this is because the market manager places them there deliberately as a sort of punishment, I do not know, but today is no exception. Approaching the darkened bar, I am amazed to see a woman actually trying to sell mistletoe. Even more astonishingly, she is not a new English settler with what she thinks is a bright idea. In an area where the plant grows like weed and farmers will almost pay you to take it away, the obviously dejected local trader must be either doing it for a bet or be employed by Madame Lefarge to frighten prospective customers away.

Inside the Good Welcome Café, we are met by the formidable Madame, who listens to our application for a brace of coffees with calvados, then grudgingly sweeps off to shout the order at her husband, even though he is only a yard away on the other side of the counter.

Choosing seats by the window, we enjoy the activity outside, then take stock of our fellow customers. There are only two. Both male, they sit in utter silence opposite each other, taking occasional and tentative sips from their coffee cups as if they were tasters in Lucrezia Borgia's research laboratory. Like Madame's husband, both men are small and aged beyond their years. In a whisper, I ask Donella why she thinks they come to such a place, and she says they probably feel at home here.

Our drinks arrive, and Madame Lefarge towers over me till I produce the necessary coins. She does not actually spit in our coffee, but it is obvious that she would rather we took our custom elsewhere, which is another reason my wife likes to come here. We first visited the Good Welcome when on an introductory pub crawl of Bricquebec with René Ribet, and immediately got off to a bad start with the proprietor. Before we entered, René told me that it would tickle Madame if I used the patois when ordering Donella's coffee, and the correct term would be *jus de chaussettes*. After her husband had ducked beneath the bar and Madame had retreated to her private quarters to recover from the insult, our new friend explained that I had asked for a cup of her best sock juice. To be fair though, I do not think we are being singled out for special treatment on our visits to the bar. As we have seen over the years, Madame treats all her customers just as badly.

After watching the bustle of activity beyond the window, I look around and wonder yet again why all Norman bars are, in essence, the same bar. The floors are always tiled like a public toilet, and the walls always seem to bear the same shade of dead-fish wallpaper. There will always be too much window and not enough wood, and what there is will have its natural grain and hue hidden beneath layers of custard-yellow paint. As I have said before, we love virtually everything about our adopted homeland, but there are some British institutions, products and establishments that we sorely miss, and a proper English pub comes high on the list.

We finish our coffee and calvados, nod goodbye to the other customers, and thank Monsieur Lefarge for his hospitality. Although Madame is elsewhere, he does not reply, and averts his eyes in case she appears like the wicked witch in a pantomine and catches him fraternising with the enemy.

Outside in the square, business at the weekly market has reached its peak, and we see that our friends Alan and Sally Offord are doing a roaring trade. This is a huge credit to their entrepreneurial skills and judgement of what British foodstuffs the French can be tempted to buy, as so many settlers have tried and failed their hand at this form of niche marketeering. The number of normally dour Norman farmers we have seen self-consciously wearing post-season Father Christmas hats and masks this morning is further evidence of the couple's trading skills.

We spend a few pleasant minutes with Sally and Alan,

and in between customers, they tell us about their progress in bringing a taste of Britain to the Cotentin. Apart from Branston Pickle, a very popular line at the moment is jars of humble sandwich spread. Apparently, it is all the rage in Paris, with hostesses putting dollops in silver salvers for use as a chic salad side dish, and Sally makes me promise not to spread the word about its relatively low status in England to our more sophisticated French friends.

Walking back to the car, I comment on the general merriment my Father Christmas mask is occasioning. My wife gently reminds me that anyone less in need of a disguise to look like a fat man with a white beard would be hard to imagine.

If the horizon is grey, stay at the buffet.
Norman proverb

Wet, Wet, Wet

It is still raining. We have not ventured out for days, and I am worried about the integrity of our eighteenth-century roof. I made a return visit to the loft today and was relieved to see that the Mouse family has made a workman-like job of repairing a particularly bad leak above their quarters. They used a couple of pages from the manuscript of my latest book as caulking, but I have a spare copy, so all is not lost.

With a bit of luck, the weather will break soon and the ground will have a chance to recover, but all the auguries are bad, and the impending disaster is now the main topic of conversation at the Jolly Boys' meetings. Older members are talking with grim relish about the winter that the val de Néhou was declared a disaster area, and Didier is taking bets on how many cows will be drowned this winter. It has not helped the general mood of doom that the local carpenter recently started work on a redundant fishing boat he took in settlement of a bad debt, and some wag sneaked into his yard one night with a pot of paint and renamed it the *Ark of Néhou*.

Even if the rain stops soon, I fear that the clay soil of La Puce will take a long time to drain off. The big pond has now joined the little pond, and the water meadow has become one huge lake. My wife continues to worry about the residents of both ponds, but I cheer her up her by pointing out that now they have so much more space, the incidents of violence between the Cray gang and Psycho the goldfish and his tribe should hopefully diminish.

Although I am striving to treat the threat of flooding lightly, I am quite worried about what may happen if the water reaches and covers the stone wall dividing the mill garden from the water meadow. On our side of the wall, it is all downhill to the cottage. When the lord of the manor chose the site and built the Mill of the Flea all those years ago, he spared no effort or expense to ensure that the water would go past the buildings, but he could not have envisaged these conditions.

Climate and prevailing weather patterns in France are subjects with which many English settlers have a problem. Most people base their ideas on a touchingly simple calculation that France is further south than Britain, so the weather must be generally better wherever you are in the country. This is, of course, not true, as anyone who has experienced a winter in Provence will confirm.

In fact, the micro-climate in the Cotentin is virtually the same as it is in southern England, and just a degree or so hotter in summer and colder in the winter. As we are on a peninsula, it also rains often. Being mostly from the town and used to having central heating in their houses and pavements under their feet, English people are shielded from the effects of the weather, and many of our visitors seem to think that it is our fault when the skies open, and that mud is an avoidable inconvenience caused by our sloppy land management. They also seem to think that our winter dress code is based upon eccentricity rather than experience. Last winter, a trendy reporter from a posh woman's magazine turned up to do a piece about the delights of living a sophisticated rural life in a restored Normandy mill. Despite our advice on sensible footwear, she arrived wearing white stiletto-heeled shoes, and one of them inevitably went missing when she took a gentle stroll in the spongy area around the septic tank. I explained about the cracked sewage pipe and offered to root around for her shoe, but she said not to bother. Our PR exercise was all a waste of time anyway, as the proposed article never appeared.

~

Now I have seen it all.

This morning, I squelched into the cottage to find a large lizard taking its ease on a rug in front of the stove. Even my wife draws the line at inviting serpents into our home, so I can only conclude that it is sheltering from the incessant rain. Tomorrow, I shall ring the carpenter at Néhou to ask if his ark is up for sale.

Friends and Neighbours

Beechwood fires burn bright and clear,
If the logs are kept a year.
Store your beech for Xmastide,
With new cut holly laid beside.
Chestnut's only good, they say,
If for years it's stored away.
Birch and firwood burn too fast,
Blaze too bright and do not last.
Flames from larch will shoot up high,
Dangerously the sparks will fly.
But ashwood green and ashwood brown,
Are fit for a queen with golden crown.
Oaken logs if dry and old
Keep away the winter's cold.
Poplar gives a bitter smoke,
Fills your eyes and makes you choke.
Elmwood burns like churchyard mould,
E'en the very flames are cold.
Applewood will scent the room,
Pearwood smells like flowers in bloom.
But ashwood wet and ashwood dry,
A king may warm his slippers by.

                    'The Firewood Poem', Anon.

In spite of the weather, or perhaps because of it, we have decided to go on a foraging expedition. The wood stove has been eating into our fuel reserves, and the log pile behind the cottage is getting uncomfortably low. The good news is that Donella has spotted a new and ready-made supply of fuel in one of the top fields, and we must harvest it before someone else does. Another bonus is that if the worst does happen and the floods arrive, we can always lash the biggest of these mystery logs together and make a raft for emergency use. We climb into our waterproof gear, collect an axe and saw from the shed, and set out on our hunter-gathering expedition in high spirits.

In an area where most homes are heated by log-burning stoves, the value placed on quality firewood cannot be overestimated. To our Norman neighbours, a tree is valued not so much for its beauty as its worth when cut down and chopped into stove-sized logs, and I have to admit that we are beginning to adopt this mentality. With a mature tree providing enough fuel for cooking and heating for the best part of a winter, it has become increasingly easy to look at a stately oak and see only a hundred hot dinners in every bough. And La Puce is a veritable treasure trove of fuel. Due to neglect over the years, our roadside copse is littered with fallen trees. Age, storms, infestation and the odd badly driven tractor regularly provide new corpses for us to feed upon. Last autumn, a giant beech came crashing down in Hunters' Walk after a gale, and we fell upon the carcass before the leaves stopped quivering.

Today, it appears that we have a gift from an unusually conscientious neighbour rather than the elements. While badger-spotting in the larger of the roadside fields yesterday, my wife discovered a huge pile of neatly trimmed and stacked logs alongside the hedge marking the boundary of our land. Investigating further, she saw that severe surgery had taken place on a sturdy ash tree growing on our side of the hedge, and a ladder was still resting against the trunk.

All the branches had been lopped off, and there was another, even larger pile of logs on our neighbour's terrain. Obviously, my wife said, old Mr Moineau had been at work, and had left the branches on our side of the hedge as our fair share. I have my doubts that our benefactor is Mr Moineau. He must be over ninety years of age, and even in the Cotentin this is a good age to be shinning up trees with a chainsaw. Besides, we have not seen him for several years, and this is quite a space between sightings.

Another thing that visitors and settlers find hard to accept about the way of life in our area and, for all I know, throughout rural France, is that people like to keep themselves to themselves. With his ramshackle roadside cottage no more than a quarter of a mile from our house as the crow flies, Mr Moineau is our closest neighbour, and he seems to think we are too close for comfort. When we first arrived at La Puce, we called at his home several times, but he was either out or pretending to be, and our friends in the village say he is not a great one for visitors or social niceties. Like most reclusive people, he is the centre of much conjecture, and said to be enormously rich, spending all his time counting his fortune in the cellar. I don't know if this is true, but he has certainly not wasted any money on DIY in the past half-century or so.

As we are anticipating a good haul of logs, we decide to take the car, so I go to tell Victor he is on tractor duty today.

Of all the cars we have ever owned, Victor has been the most versatile and valuable. Over the years, he has helped us ship many tons of goods across the Channel, and is now in semi-retirement at La Puce. I read somewhere that more than 70% of all Volvos are still on the road, and Victor has certainly left a good percentage of his bodywork and bits on the highways and byways of the Cotentin. 'It's not expensive when you consider what goes into it' was the Volvo slogan when Victor was born, and I think the advertising people who dreamed that up would be amazed if they knew what he had carried since joining the family. Nowadays, though, he is beginning to show his age, and his duties are restricted to taking us on relatively short journeys or working on the land. I know that one day he will either conk out in the middle of a field or simply refuse to wake up on a chilly morning, and that will be the best way for him to go. We have already discussed a suitable use for his remains, and I favour the pragmatic approach of our friends in Néhou who find that dead cars make ideal chicken coops. My wife refuses to contemplate the thought, and has been talking about a dignified burial in the water meadow. I think she is overreacting, but at least this would be less costly than her original idea of staging a Scandinavian warrior's farewell, with Victor drifting into the sunset off Utah Beach on a fire-raft.

Fortunately, Victor appears in good health and spirits despite the constant deluge, and we are soon lurching up the cart track towards the road that runs alongside La Puce. We park by a convenient hole in our roadside hedge and climb through to investigate the situation. Just as Donella has described, the newly shorn ash marks the spot, and for the next hour we drag logs from the pile across the field, through the hole in the hedge and on to Victor's roof rack. Occasionally, a car screams by with a wail of protest at our position just around a dangerous bend in the road, and I have some good practice at verbal and visual insults. Donella is by now worried about the weight of the load, and points out that Victor's back bumper is almost touching the ground. But the fever is on me, and I insist we can clear the pile. Dusk is gathering, the rain is falling even harder, but I want to be sure that we collect every scrap of firewood rather than leave it to a passing predator.

Finally, the last log has been eased on to the giant pile aboard the roof rack, and we are about to set off, when a small car rounds the bend and screeches to a halt along-side. A stocky individual of around my age jumps out and approaches us with much stylised arm-waving. At first, I think he wants to buy some logs from us, and then I real-ise that he is very unhappy and claiming that they are all his.

Eventually, when he has calmed down a little and spotted that I am carrying a felling axe, he identifies himself as the son of Mr Moineau. His father is hardly cold in his grave, he says, and here we are plundering his possessions like thieves in the night. As the eldest son, he is the rightful owner of every log, faggot, branch and twig that we are stealing, and he will help us move them from our car to his. Now. While sympathising with his loss, I point out that the logs in ques-tion have come from my tree, which is growing in my field on my land, and are now destined to travel on my car to my log pile, and from there to my stove to heat my home and cook my dinners. Furthermore, I could bring into question his right to lay claim to the logs on his side of the hedge, and the ladder against our tree shows that he has clearly been trespassing on our land. In the sad circumstances, however, I am willing to overlook the matter, and he can even keep the wood on his land.

By now, at least a dozen cars have pulled up, and their owners have arrived to remonstrate with us for blocking the highway. Discovering the nature of our dispute, however, they immediately forget all about continuing their journeys while there is a confrontation in which to become involved. A committee is quickly sworn in, and the members take it upon themselves to lecture us about the lores and laws of tree ownership. The self-appointed deputation visits the former site of the log pile, and the traffic jam continues to grow. Finally, the committee reaches its decision, which is that they cannot reach a decision. Half of them say that the logs are mine, and half say they are the property of my neighbour. One old farmer says that the tree itself belongs to Mr Moineau Jnr, even though it has stood contentedly on my land for many years.

As more and more passers-by arrive to weigh in with their verdicts, it is clear that we are at an impasse. Then, I am thankful to see help arrive in the shape of a fellow Jolly Boy. The ancient lorry of Marcel Bernard rattles up and our wise friend is quick to calm the situation with a compromise. His proposal is that we take the matter to arbitration in a much more civilised situation and location. Tomorrow, he suggests, we will meet at the Bar Ghislaine to resolve the dispute in the light of day. In the meantime, he will convene a meeting of the village elders, while I will promise to leave the logs on Victor's roof, and Mr Moineau will move his car so that everyone can go about their lawful business.

Grudgingly, my opponent agrees, and after pointedly counting the number of logs on Victor's roof, roars off. The roadside committee goes happily on its way to report the details of the dispute to the rest of the region, and Donella, Victor and I continue our slow journey down to the mill cottage. Tomorrow will bring what it brings, but I am no longer the green townie that some of the villagers take me for. As my wife busies herself preparing our evening meal, I spend an hour with Victor, busily swapping the bottom layer of the pile of ash on the roof rack for an identical number of firwood logs.

If the verdict of the court goes against me tomorrow, I shall find some future consolation in toasting my feet in front of the ashwood logs I have managed to salvage. As the countryside poem has it, they will make a fire fit for a king. If my substitution is not spotted, Madame Moineau will also have more than a few words to say to her husband about the holes in her hearthrug that will inevitably result from burning the inferior and volatile pine logs.

Have the French for friends, but not neighbours.
Nicephorus, Byzantine emperor (AD 912–69)

Called to the Bar

The ancient and eccentric church clock at Néhou is striking thirteen, and I am in the Bar Ghislaine drowning my sorrows.

In spite of being heavily rigged with fellow members of the Jolly Boys Club, the special tribunal has found in favour of my neighbour in the matter of ownership of the log pile on my land.

It also seems that all my hedgerow trees belong to someone else.

According to ancient countryside law (according to the committee, that is), not only does Mr Moineau have sole wooding rights to all the trees along our party line, but they all belong to him. Worse still, all the trees on my side of the other three boundaries at La Puce belong to my other neighbours. When I asked how it could come to pass that trees growing on my land could belong to someone else, the chairman went into a complex and long-winded explanation that would defy credibility if I had not had some experience in French rural customs, especially when applied to foreigners. Basically, what it boils down to is that everyone in the countryside allegedly owns one metre of their neighbour's land, and my misfortune appears to be that all the trees are on my side of our boundaries; if they were on the other side of the hedge, they would be mine. It is as simple as that. As our chairman says during his summing-up, not only was Mr Moineau the Younger not trespassing on my land by stacking his logs on my side of the hedge, it was I who had been committing a heinous act by crossing the invisible line marking my land from his. Without question, Mr Moineau is the aggrieved party, and his logs must be returned. As I half expect the chairman to don a black cap, the sentence is passed. Being a reasonable man, my neighbour will accept my plea of ignorance of the law, and will not press charges. He will be content with my apology and the return of the logs, though the chairman adds pointedly that a small token of my true contrition and remorse in the form of a bottle of Scotch or two might not go amiss.

I accept the ruling with the best grace I can muster, then go outside to ceremonially hand the disputed logs over. Thinking quickly, I reject Mr Moineau's offer of assistance and tell him I will shift the pile from my car to his as a further demonstration of my remorse. Now completely mollified, he joins the Jolly Boys Club for some mutual backslapping while I start work. The job is made more complex by my having to unload the huge pile of logs from Victor's roof rack and put them on the road before reloading them on to the roof of the Moineau car, but it is a necessary chore. The inferior pine logs I swapped for the ashwood were at the bottom of the pile on Victor's roof, and must be loaded first on to Mr Moineau's Peugeot if he is not to spot my ruse immediately he emerges from the bar. By the time he has uncovered my deception, there will be no witnesses and it will be my word against his. It is a small victory, but better than none. We Brits may not know much about Revolutionary countryside law, but it is not for nothing that we have earned the title of Perfidious Albion.

Finishing the job and ensuring that the ropes securing the load are dangerously but not obviously slack, I return to the bar to smile at my neighbour and scowl at my fellow

JBC members. Apart from my subterfuge with the log sub-stitution, my mood has also been improved by hearing the springs of Mr Moineau's Peugeot groan ominously towards the end of the loading process. I do not think that any small French car is man enough to bear the sort of loads that Victor the Volvo finds nothing more than a trifling incon-venience.

By mid-afternoon, my spirits are fully restored. After mend-ing our broken fences over a few drinks, Mr Moineau and I are getting along almost famously. I have promised to present him with a freshly shot haggis as well as a bottle of Scotch after my next visit to Scotland, while he has prom-ised to give me regular lessons on countryside etiquette and land management. Elsewhere, the regulars are settling down for a relaxing afternoon. By the fire, our resident celebrity chef JayPay is enthralling his audience with a blow-by-blow account of a recent experiment with some fine herbs, dan-delion leaves and broiled badger loin. At the bar, René Ribet has been unwise enough to take on the giant Mr Janne in a friendly arm-wrestling match, and Marcel Bernard is hap-pily playing with the Rubik's Cube he bought during Dodgy Didier's last visit. All the squares are the same colour, so he has solved the puzzle at least twenty times in the past hour. Hearing a crash, I turn away from my conversation with Old Pierrot to see that our host Bernard has measured his length on the bar floor. This is not unusual, as Madame Ghislaine's husband always knows when he has had enough, and marks the achievement of this state of grace by simply falling down and resting till he is ready to start again. What is unusual about the incident is that Bernard has performed his party piece on home ground, and while his wife is on the premises. Within seconds, Ghislaine has appeared through the door-way separating the bar area from the grocery department, and we scatter like field mice when the combine harvester hoves into view. Madame Ghislaine, as we have all learned to our cost, disapproves of men in general, and men drinking in particular. Expecting to see her either step over the recumbant figure of her husband to get at us or deliver a swift kick at his body while she has the opportunity, I am amazed to see her rush into her back room and telephone the fire brigade. I know, of course, that the local *pompiers* squad doubles as paramedical emergency cover, but had forgotten that she has never seen Bernard make his celebrated dive for the floor. Madame Ghislaine obviously believes that her husband is ill, not merely legless.

Given that the traditional three-hour lunch break is barely over, less than forty minutes passes before the giant fire brigade tender screeches to a stop outside the Bar Ghislaine with lights flashing and siren screaming. Although the crew know they are attending a medical emergency rather than a fire, they are obviously determined not to miss out on the dramatic possibilities of the situation and are in full regalia of helmets and oilskins; some are actually wearing oxygen tanks and face masks. One is waving an axe as he leaps down from the tender, and seems disappointed to find the door to the bar wide open. The entire population of the village has naturally turned out to enjoy the spectacle, and there are even some small children waving American and British flags left over from the fiftieth D-Day celebrations. Dogs bark, geese honk, and crows flutter irritably from the church tower as the village cheers the highly trained squad into action. Unfortunately, the man with the axe of office leads them through the wrong door, and he and his team are soon packed shoulder to shoulder in the grocery shop alongside the Bar Ghislaine.

After apologising to the customers for the inconvenience, they leave in an orderly and even subdued fashion, then psych themselves up again for the assault on the bar. They are to be bitterly disappointed as they arrive in a mêlée of shouting and shoving to find that Bernard has got his second wind and is standing by the bar quietly enjoying a glass of the house red.

Protracted negotiations take place, and our host is finally persuaded to resume his position on the floor so that the paramedics can show their paces. Apparently, they have a wondrous new piece of electronic equipment, and it will be a shame not to try it out in a real-life situation. Within minutes, Bernard is recumbent, still carefully holding his glass of wine as he is hooked up to the machine. As the specially trained officers of the medical unit study the dials and blinking lights intently, their colleagues remove their face masks and helmets and take the opportunity to have a smoke and a drink. To nobody's surprise, Bernard is eventually declared alive, but the paramedic team are loath to miss out on the opportunity for continued drama. There may be complications or some delayed reaction, they argue, so it is necessary for their patient to be rushed to hospital for a more comprehensive check-up. This cheers up everyone except Bernard, but having seen the look on his wife's face, he obviously realises that the hospital at St Sauveur will probably offer a safer refuge than the back room at the Bar Ghislaine. Grudgingly, he agrees to play along providing he is allowed to take his drink and cigarettes with him, and the paramedics spring into action once more. A stretcher of the type used for mountain rescues is brought into the bar, and Bernard is strapped safely in. Still carefully balancing the glass of wine, he is carried triumphantly aloft from the bar. Flags wave, spectators cheer, and the heroes of the hour smile modestly as they clamber aboard the tender, their jobs well done.

A serious bout of handshaking then takes place as their leader apologises to Madame Ghislaine for the delay in attending the emergency. He explains that the problem was caused by a blockage on the road to the village as some fool had made a rotten job of loading logs on his car. He was obviously a townie, the fire chief said scathingly, as half the load was made up of worthless pine faggots.

I like Frenchmen very much, because even when
they insult you they do it so nicely.
Josephine Baker, singer and *Folies Bergère* performer (1906–1975)

On the Road

Spring has returned to La Puce.

As I opened a downstairs window at the mill cottage this morning, a small bird brushed me aside and flew in with an air that could only be described as proprietary. It circled the room a couple of times, paused to make a special inspection of the kitchen area then, apparently satisfied, left the way it had arrived.

Donella was delighted to hear that the tiny wren has booked in for another season. She tells me that it is very unusual for a bird to return to the same nesting site year on year, and is sure the creature somehow knows that she and her future family will be comfortable and safe with us.

I agree, but do not see anything unusual or surprising in a visitor deciding to return to a bed and breakfast establishment where not only are the food and accommodation of five-star quality, but they are also absolutely free. I resign myself to losing the rind from my bacon and the cream from my cornflakes each morning for the foreseeable future. The only consolation is that I will be able to take a lengthy break from the expensive restoration work on the ruined end of the mill. Our guest, as my wife points out, favours a certain niche in the south-facing gable wall, and must not

be disturbed by a gang of rough workmen clattering about
in their heavy boots.

Having been relieved of my immediate building responsibilities, I suggest that this would be a perfect time for our
long-awaited visit to Brittany, where we shall continue the
search for Donella's ancestors. My wife agrees. She is keen
to see how far we can go along the branches of her family
tree, and I am just as interested. Not being able to trace my
paternal forebears back further than three generations, I am
enjoying our search for my wife's ancestors.

Our interest began when a distant relative got in touch
to say that she had discovered that the family roots lay
in Breton, not Welsh, soil. So far, we have been able to
establish that Donella's mother's great-great-grandfather
was born in Guingamp, and was the illegitimate son of a
butcher. Now we will visit the town to see what else we
can dig up, and we shall have some valuable assistance.
Skimming through a magazine last year, I saw an article by
the Scots wife of the pastor of Guingamp, and have enlisted
her aid. When we spoke on the telephone, the pastor's wife
said that many Bretons fled to Wales to escape religious
intolerance at the end of the eighteenth century, and there
may well be some interesting archives in the Guingamp
library. While I do not see how anyone would choose to go
to Wales to escape intolerance, I agree that this is a good
lead. I will not, however, tell our friends at Néhou about the
trip and the reason for it. Though they have come to accept
us in spite of our being English, learning that Donella has
her roots in a foreign country like Brittany could well be
too much of a hurdle for the most open-minded Norman to
overcome.

I set about preparing for the trip, but am still puzzled
by my wife's willingness to leave our latest avian visitor to
fend for herself. The mystery is solved when I hear Donella
on the telephone to Madame Ghislaine. She is not only
putting in a large order for cream, bacon and cheese, but

is also arranging to have the provisions specially prepared and delivered on a daily basis by Ghislaine's son to the guest wing in the ruined end of the mill. Thus, my wife has broken new ground by extending the facilities at our animal B&B to full room service.

Before leaving on our journey of discovery, we make a tour of inspection of the grounds, and I have a bracing encounter with a human intruder. Like an oversized garden gnome, he is sitting comfortably on a tree stump with his line dangling in the foaming waters of the cascade, and has the cheek to bid me a cheery good morning. He also comments that he is having a problem casting his line, and it might be helpful if I were to trim back the branches overhanging his favourite spot. When I recover the power of speech, I ask him if he would also like me to fetch him a cup of tea and a piece of cake. My sarcasm is lost on him, and he says no, but a cup of proper French coffee would not go amiss.

After he departs to dry out his clothing, I fish his rod out of the water basin and call our local *notaire* to ask which methods of killing trespassers are acceptable in this region of France. Predictably, I discover that the laws of the land are not in my favour. Any French fisherman, I am informed, is entitled to cross private terrain to get at a river or stream running through it. Worse still, in the same way that I do not own the trees bordering my land, it seems I do not own the water running through La Puce, or even the fish eating the weed on the river bed. In fact, as the landowner, I (unlike my recent visitor) will have to apply for a permit if I want to enjoy a spot of angling from my river bank. If the person I have just seen off my land had been merely walking across it, I would have been at liberty to maim him in the manner of my choosing. But as he was a true sportsman enjoying his inalienable right to indulge his passion for hunting, I may consider myself lucky if he does not have me arrested.

I thank the *notaire* for the information, and ask him if it will be all right for me to pick the mushrooms in my woods later this year. He laughs and says of course I may, but only if I get to them before he does.

~

We are well on our way to Brittany, and I have discovered that it is not only in our neck of the woods that drivers are completely mad. Although Victor the Volvo is bowling along at a reasonable rate of knots, his rear bumper seems to exert a magnetic attraction to every French car behind us, and most seem to want to join our luggage in the back. What is particularly galling about this obviously widespread Gallic fetish is that they only do it when the road ahead is perfectly clear. Our tormentors sit for miles on our tail like dogs sniffing a bitch on heat, ignoring all my invitations to pass when there is nothing coming the other way. Even my final gambit of slowing down to a walking pace does not shake them off. Then, just as we reach a blind bend or a juggernaut lorry comes steaming towards us, they overtake with a wave of contempt and a blast on the horn. Dicing with death on the roads is obviously a national sport throughout France, and my fellow motorists are probably spicing up a long journey by playing this dangerous game. After being overtaken by a tractor while we were doing at least fifty miles per hour and approaching a narrow hump-bridge already fully occupied by a milk tanker, I lose my nerve and pull off the road for a calming cup of coffee. While at the stop, we phone our daughter, Katie, in England and gain more evidence of French driving habits and skills at the wheel.

Clearly not wishing to spoil our break in Brittany, Katie tells us the bad news in a roundabout manner. Our car in England has apparently starred on the front page of the local paper. In a recent edition there is a large photograph showing it parked inside a friend's new takeaway shop. The headline writers have had great fun, Katie says, and captioned the picture as showing the first truly drive-in fast-food shop in the city. The good news is that our friend Jean-Marie Guedeney is, unlike the car, relatively unmarked by his experience.

One of our closest friends, Jean is a Burgundian who runs a number of highly successful takeaway food shops in Portsmouth. Being French, he refuses to believe that English flour and water can combine to make anything resembling a proper piece of bread, so expensively imports the dough for his filled baguettes. Being Burgundian, he also believes that his region produces not only the best bread, cooks, businessmen and lovers in the world, but also the best drivers. Having demonstrated his prowess in all the other areas, he shows off his driving skills by racing around the countryside at weekends and turning every track and lane he visits into a quagmire. During our last visit to England, I could not help but notice that his left leg was encased in plaster to the hip, and innocently asked if he had done the damage while indulging his passion for off-road racing. Outraged, he came up with a rather lame excuse about being kicked by a horse in Hungary, and said that the most painful result of the accident was his inability to drive his car. His right foot was still able to perform wonders on the accelerator and, on the rare occasions it was needed, the brake, but even a driver of his capabilities found engaging the clutch with his plastered left foot more than an inconvenience. Apart from the taxi fares costing him a fortune as he toured his small empire, he was sorely missing being behind a wheel and in full control of his destination and destiny. As he said this, he looked meaningfully at my old Granada automatic, and the penny dropped. As I would not be needing it while in Normandy, I replied, he would be welcome to use it till his leg got better. If, I cautioned, he was sure that he could handle such a powerful British car. When he had recovered his composure, my friend reminded me that I of all people should know that the only guaranteed method of enraging a Frenchman was to imply that he was a bad cook, lover or driver. He would be happy to supply me with a detailed list of several hundred witnesses as to his prowess between the sheets in his pre-marriage days, and would gladly produce a copy of his bank balance to demonstrate his abilities as a *cuisinier*. As to his driving skills, the cups and medals vying for space on his mantelpiece should be evidence enough.

As I feed coins into the telephone box, Katie comes to the denouement of the story of how our second car has become an overnight celebrity in Portsmouth. Apparently, Jean had driven it to make a final inspection of his latest outlet on the eve of the official opening and check that all was well. The advertisements had been booked, the guests invited, the area circulated with leaflets, and the shop completely refitted. Arriving outside and noting that the expensive display counters were also in place in the shop window, and the signwriter was delicately finishing his task, Jean was pleased to find a parking space in the series of bays facing his new premises. Forgetting in his eagerness to buy a parking ticket and having been warned of a traffic warden in the offing, he had returned to the car, and noticed that the front tyres were pinched against the gutter. A considerate person, he had taken the trouble to lever himself behind the wheel again so that he could reverse a few inches. According to Jean, his mobile phone rang just as he was about to engage the automatic shift into reverse, and his attention was distracted. Probably due to a fault in my car, he claimed, the engine somehow became stuck in a forward gear. Matters were not helped as his plastered left foot somehow became trapped between the brake and the accelerator, and the car rocketed forward over the pavement and through the plate-glass window. As the signwriter crawled from the wreckage and odd pieces of the shop front settled on the roof of my car, Jean finally answered the call from his wife, Kathy. Having told her that he was in the new shop, he then had to tell her that he was also still in my car, and the official opening would have to be delayed for a little while. His mood was not helped by the arrival of the press photographer to discuss the best shots for the opening ceremony the next day. Nor by the somewhat heavy humour of the traffic warden who encouraged him to look on the bright side, as by moving the car off the road he had avoided a stiff parking fine.

I wonder what the French say when they get déjà-vu?
Hattie Hayridge (Holly in *Red Dwarf*)

Meet the Ancestors

Going strictly on first impressions, Brittany is exactly the same as our part of Normandy, only obviously more affluent and not afraid to show it. A sort of Cotentin with attitude.

Guingamp is like any prosperous market town in our region, but with a number of imposing civic buildings where the budget obviously allowed for embellishment as well as the basics. There is also a particularly impressive gothic cathedral, which dominates the centre of the old quarter. But if the architecture of Brittany seems familiar, the road signs and public notices do not. A frequent visitor to Wales, I am used to seeing English directions subtitled in Welsh for the exclusive benefit of the 0.05% of natives who need to be told in their own language where the motorway is. Here, it is even more bizarre to see signs in a foreign language with an even more foreign translation beneath. What is particularly puzzling is that, unlike the other European languages that have their roots in Latin, Breton seems to have been made up deliberately to spite and confuse the rest of France.

If the language is so patently different from French, however, the inhabitants of Guingamp look remarkably similar to our Norman friends. Everyone we see as we park near the square and take a stroll is very dark and very short. The main difference lies in the relative neatness of their features and, interestingly, most of the males we see seem to be as long in the body as they are short in the leg. I have a regular correspondence with a settler in the Lot who is Welsh and a former head teacher in Newcastle, and he has carried out a study of this condition. Neville has an interesting turn of mind and a huge intellect, and has formed a theory that evolution and natural selection have resulted in any mining area having more than its fair share of stocky men with long bodies and short legs. He has taken and collated inside-leg measurements and other vital data in mining regions in Britain and is now convinced that his theory has, as they say in the academic research business, legs. I am a prime example of the condition, which my wife describes as duck's disease, and can see his point about this being the ideal shape for working below ground in confined spaces, but I don't know of too many mines in Hampshire, Normandy or Brittany.

Another basic difference between Normans and Bretons seems to be in the character of the people. We have already passed several Guingampians who have actually smiled at us for no good reason, and Donella says she heard the sound of laughter and people generally enjoying themselves in a bar we passed earlier.

Deciding to investigate, we retrace our steps and enter what looks like a typical PMU betting shop and bar. Inside, there is the usual throng of punters with faces wrinkled in concentration as they fill in their forecasts for the day's racing, but there the similarity with our home region ends. The décor is lavish in comparison with our local betting shop, and all the chairs and tables appear to have a full complement of legs. At the far end, there is an even more incongruous sight. The lady busily taking bets and paying out the winners from her seat at a space-age computer is operating through a window in what appears to be a perfectly preserved late-mediaeval wall, complete with gothic gargoyles and flying buttresses.

Right alongside a wonderfully executed arched entranceway is a shiny green door leading to the toilet facilities. After looking at this meeting of the new and old worlds, I ask a customer about the feature. Barely pausing to look up from his calculations, he explains that we are looking at the sole remnants of the ancient town wall. When application was put in to build the betting shop, permission was granted as long as the wall was left unharmed. It was a good way of bringing culture to the people, he says with the air of a man whose logic is indisputable, as many more locals visit the betting shop at Guingamp than would otherwise bother to make a dedicated journey to traipse around a ruin.

Refreshed by our visit to the PMU, we leave the car and go to meet our guide in the search for my wife's Breton ancestors. Christine Monclair proves to be another interesting addition to our collection of settler friends. From the east coast of Scotland, she has various degrees in history and language, and an obvious and infectious enthusiasm for learning about other cultures, people and their past. Soon, we are taking coffee and enjoying a whirlwind summary of Brittany's long and troubled history from Christine's husband, Alain. A true Breton who can trace his own ancestors back for the best part of a thousand years, the Protestant pastor of Guingamp has the typical sturdy build and colouring of his race. He also has what we are to discover is a typical passion for all things Breton, and very little enthusiasm for anything remotely French in origin. Over the next hour, he tells us a story of betrayal, annexation and foreign interference with a zeal and fire that would make the most rabid Welsh National Party activist appear quite moderate. He is speaking in Breton with Christine translating, and I get the feeling that she is, if anything, toning down his views on past French dealings with his region. At the end of a fascinating hour, I thank him and apologise for my lack of command of the French language, which he seems to find more pleasing than offensive. I also persuade Donella to sing a verse from 'Land of My Fathers' in Welsh, which puts the seal on our friendship, as he says the language is very similar to Breton and therefore far superior to any other.

Later that day, and we find ourselves sitting in the Guingamp library, poring over the town records of births, marriages and deaths for 1751. Despite the entries being in ancient Breton and made in the idiosyncratic hand of a long-dead curate, we have made remarkable progress.

Already, we have traced Donella's ancestors back another three generations, and the Le Cornec family appear to have been substantial and respectable members of the community. Christine Monclair has had to leave us to carry on the research alone, but has been invaluable in showing us the key words and phrases to look for. *Illégitime* seems to be the word most associated with my wife's ancestors and their activities, but Christine has assured us that this was quite normal for these times. More impressive has been our discovery of not only the name but the address of one Henri Le Cornec, master butcher and husband of a Marie Le Moal. As it will be dusk in an hour and we cannot resist the idea of searching for Donella's ancestral home, we thank the librarian and share a smoke with her before setting off on our pilgrimage. It would be too much to hope that we can find any traces of the original butcher's shop, but hopefully, the rue Montbareil may still exist.

Though neither my wife nor I are particularly prone to a belief in the supernatural, we both agree that strange forces seem to have been at work from the moment we arrived in Guingamp. Returning to our car after our session in the library, we go into a nearby *tabac* and ask the owner if he has heard of Montbareil Street. He looks at me rather oddly, then takes me outside and points at the plaque on the wall above his shop. He has not only heard of the street, he says, but he and his family before him have lived and traded in it for many generations. In fact, we are standing in it now. Unfortunately, his local knowledge of other traders does not go back two centuries, but he is sure there are no butcher's shops in the vicinity. Undeterred, we walk along the pleasant street, and stop to take photographs of the monastery and brewery standing in a row of imposing townhouses. We are obviously in a wealthy quarter of the old town, and my wife is already beginning to adopt a slightly patronising air when the discussion turns to my own humble roots in Glasgow's notorious Maryhill district. With the light fading, we make our way to the nearby cathedral, and I pose Donella in front of the giant doors for a final snap. As I look through the viewfinder, the name on the plaque above her head comes into focus. The street is named for Henri Le Moal, after the chief architect of the restoration of the cathedral in the sixteenth-century. Inside, we find more plaques and tributes to the Le Moals and, acting completely out of character, my wife begins accosting passers-by to tell them of the family connection. At one stage she poses beside a statue of an eighteenth-century Le Moal and asks if I can see the likeness. With difficulty, I persuade her to leave, and we go off to celebrate the day's work.

~

Before exploring the fleshpots of Guingamp, we decide to buy the makings of a picnic to eat in our hotel. Most of the food shops are still open, and the budget hotel we are staying in boasts neither a restaurant nor room service.

Having window-shopped the length of the high street, we select an appropriately lavish patisserie and enter. As with many places of this nature, the lady behind the counter looks like a beauty consultant on the perfume counter of a department store. Her face is as brightly and artfully deco-rated as the cakes on display, and her imposing bouffant hairstyle is like a reflection of the spun-sugar confections on the counter between us. She is also wearing the inevitable tailored suit, and her fingernails look as though they have been dipped in fresh blood. As usual, there is now an embarrassing interlude while my wife tries to decide upon the few cakes and pastries she does not like. While I try to engage the manageress in a conversation about the interesting architectural features of the betting shop along the road, Donella finally makes her agonising choice, which includes some interesting-looking bridge rolls stuffed with all sorts of exotic meats and cheeses. Rather than be pleased that we will have virtually cleared her stock of leftovers, however, the woman gives the all-too-familiar Gallic shake of the head and says that we cannot have the rolls – they are to be thrown away at closing time. I ask if they are past their sell-by date, and when she understands what I am talking about she looks shocked and says certainly not. The fact is that the rolls must be eaten hot and the ovens have been turned off for the day. I then ask if there is not a microwave on the premises, and her bouffant appears to swell and crackle at the insult. Trying to placate her, I say that we are only English, and will be quite happy to eat them cold. With a withering look, the woman agrees that, being English, we would probably not mind the insult to their creator, but she would. With that, she takes the rolls from the display case and carefully puts them out of sight under the counter. Not wishing to lose the rest of our supper, I submit, but get my own back by asking if she has any HP brown sauce to give her veal and wild goose *vol-au-vents* a little more flavour.

We arrive at the hotel, and are greeted by an almost surreal spectacle in the reception area. A number of large lorry drivers and weary commercial travellers are slumped in their chairs looking with complete mystification at a television set on a shelf in the corner. I hear the rapid French dialogue interspersed with canned laughter, and at first think that the viewers are all Breton and pretending not to understand the foreign language. Then I look up and see that they are numbly watching a dubbed version of the British sitcom *'Allo 'Allo*. As we climb the stairs to our room, we discuss the entertainment value in Brittany of a comedy programme about a café in Occupied France where nearly all the jokes are puns that depend upon the characters apparently mispronouncing French in English.

~

Our midnight feast at the Guingamp Kwik-Stay is over, and we have voted it the best hotel meal we have had since our visit to the south last year. We use hotels rarely, preferring to stay above bars or in *chambres d'hôte* when we cannot impose ourselves on an English settler in the area. In our experience, food in French hotels is usually overpriced to make up for the low cost of the rooms. But there are some notable exceptions, and we cherish them.

Early last year, we were on our way to visit friends in the deep south. As usual, I had underestimated the journey time, and overestimated the availability of accommodation in the depths of winter. As per our marital agreement, I had blamed Donella's poor navigation for the situation, though it had been my idea to go by the scenic route rather than stay on the motorway. Now, dusk was falling, and we were hopelessly lost in a strange and increasingly desolate place. Irritatingly, all the names on the map seemed to end with -ac, but none of them agreed with the road signs we occasionally passed. As it grew darker, it began to snow, the road narrowed, and the signs petered out altogether. The petrol gauge had been hovering on zero for some time, and I was promising Victor the Volvo anything if he would just last out till we arrived at the next service station. Overall, the situation was getting serious. Then, just as my wife said she thought she could hear a wolf howling, we emerged from a pass between two gigantic slabs of rock, and saw, on a hilltop, the brooding outline of an ancient *bastide* town, its grim walls and towers standing out against the silvery night sky. As far as I could see, there were no suspiciously large bats circling the battlements or villagers with flaming torches laying siege to the keep, so in our situation it looked almost welcoming. And it was only a mile away. At least, it was only a mile away as the bat flies. As we crawled upwards in an ever decreasing spiral, the road got narrower, the snow fell with ever increasing intensity, and the precipice alongside the road got steeper.

Then, as Victor was beginning to fight for breath and I was contemplating ending our misery with a quick wrench upon the steering wheel, we limped through a giant stone archway and into the cobbled square, where we found the town completely deserted and we seemed to be in another, stranger world. Either we had entered a different dimension and time zone immediately after leaving the motorway or the entire community was at a goat-sacrificing ceremony in the next town.

After making a crude crucifix from my car jack and lever, I led the way through the empty streets. Eventually, we saw a single light dimly filtering through the closed shutters of a gaunt stone building. An old van stood outside, and there were steps up to a pair of double doors and what looked like the outline of a human body on a faded sign above the entrance. Either it was a hotel or the town mortuary. Looking at each other, the desolate streets and snow-filled sky, we silently considered our alternatives and entered.

Inside, we found a huge vaulted room with flagged floor, a cat with three legs, several trestle tables and a selection of customers who looked at us as if they had run out of goats for next week's coven meeting. Crossing the floor to the sound of our own footsteps, we smiled weakly, and I tried not to look for a bolt through the giant barman's neck as I ordered our drinks. As I spoke, the muttered conversation in the room ceased and the atmosphere became, if possible, even colder.

Unable to summon up the nerve to ask about accommodation, I led the way to a corner seat, put my back to the wall and started drawing up an escape plan. Swiftly finishing our drinks, we got up, and staying close together, sidled back to the bar to pay. As I debated waiting for the change or making a break for it while his attention was diverted, I saw the barman frowning at the money I had given him and realised it was a twenty-pound note. Holding it up to the light, he looked at it and then me, and asked suspiciously if we were English. Thinking quickly, I explained that I was actually more than half Scottish on my father's side, and my wife's mother came from Wales. In our travels I find this is usually the safest bet in a strange and hostile setting. To my knowledge, neither Scotland nor Wales has ever colonised, occupied or been at war with any foreign power except the English. However, the way things were going, this could be the one town in Europe invaded and conquered by an away team from the Cameron Highlanders.

For a moment, the giant scratched his head where his left ear should have been, then bared his teeth in what could just have been a smile. From then on, the atmosphere was to change dramatically. Our new friend barked a few words at the customers, gave me back my banknote and asked us if we had anywhere to stay for the night. As we relaxed over another drink, he explained that my size and our strange accents had given the impression that we were Germans. Every man in the bar had lost a relative to local atrocities during the war, he went on, and return visits from the Boche were not exactly encouraged. Hearing that we were lost, he insisted that we stay for the night, and shortly showed us up to a surprisingly comfortable room.

Hungry but at least having found shelter for the night, we were preparing to go to bed when a heavy knocking rattled the solid-oak door in its frame. Opening it tentatively, I was confronted with a man who looked like the barman's bigger and uglier brother. He was dressed in grimy chef's whites and, more importantly, carrying a large cleaver. As I began to babble that we had never even visited Germany, he interrupted me to tetchily enquire if we were coming down for the gourmet evening. There were only two seats left, and the aperitifs would be served in exactly twelve minutes.

We were downstairs in less than five, and found the bar transformed. The trestle tables had been dressed with white linen tablecloths, and the customers and cat had obviously gone to the goat barbecue. In their place, a throng of smartly dressed diners were sitting in obvious anticipation of the treat to come. Hurriedly, we found our places and joined them.

Over the next three hours, we were to be transported to culinary heaven. I am the first to agree with my wife that I am a gourmand rather than a gourmet, but even I could tell that we were in the presence of an eating experience as unique as our surroundings. There were a full five courses, each accompanied by a different wine, and each based upon a central theme of the fruits of the local streams, fields and forests. There were mushrooms the size of parasols, and cheek of wild boar with a skin that crackled and echoed around the hall like gunshot fire. There was hare, trout and other mysterious animal titbits, which I relished but chose not to have identified. There were even five different textures and types of local bread, some stuffed with crisp golden nuggets of walnut. After each course came an oral examination, conducted by the giant chef, who visited every table to demand frank comment on his offerings. He said he would accept praise and constructive criticism equally, and it was a mark of the quality of the meal that not a single diner complained or even made a helpful suggestion for future reference. In my experience, this is almost unheard of in France. I like to think it was because our table could not find a single thought as to how the feast could have been enhanced, but it might have had a little to do with the fact that our *chef de cuisine* was still carrying his cleaver.

Next day, the snow lay deep and crisp and fairly even upon the cobbles of the square as we drove contentedly through the giant archway. Reaching the road at the bottom of the hill and heading back to civilisation, we swore that we would return one day.

If only, that is, we would ever be able to find the place again.

～

It is to be our last morning in Brittany, so we decide to stock up on local delicacies. They will make ideal gifts for the settlers we shall be staying with during our journey back to La Puce. It is only a little more than three hours from Guingamp to north Cotentin, but we have several readers and correspondents in Brittany who have been rash enough to invite us to drop in any time we are passing. I believe that a bottle of reasonable wine and a round of cheese is more than adequate exchange for a night's accommodation, given that our hosts will also have the gift of my company and sparkling conversation. My wife believes they will get the worse side of the deal, and forecasts that, after an initial visit, many of my fans will move home and not tell us.

We spot a specialist grocery store and wander in. As we breathe in the heady aroma of huge rounds of cheese stacked like wheels in a tyre-repair centre, the shopkeeper emerges through a beaded curtain and looks us up and down. Apparently, we pass muster. I know this because he enquires as to our needs with a fractional jerk of his head and miniscule movement of the eyebrow, which can say or ask a hundred different things in French. He is small and dark with a long body and short legs, so obviously on home territory. I open the proceedings by apologising for speaking French like a Spanish cow, which always breaks the ice in Normandy. Here, it has little effect. The proprietor scratches his goatee beard and looks out of the window as if to see what interesting activities are occupying other people's lives. Flustered by his lack of response, I say the first thing that comes into my head and ask if he has any cheese. Now both eyebrows come into play, the beret is removed, and the bald head scratched while the shoulders lift a full centimetre to register his incredulity at the question. Rising to the bait, I then employ a little English body language by narrowing my eyes, straightening my shoulders and puffing out my chest in preparation for the battle ahead. It is a pity about my moustache, because I can't also show off my rapidly stiffening upper lip.

Some time later, and we are sharing Victor with more than twenty painstakingly wrapped and tied packages of cheese, each no more than a few grams in weight. The whole process of my careful study, sampling and final purchase took more than an hour, and I made sure that nearly all of our selections came from giant cheeses at the bottom of each pile. With any luck, the sour-faced shopkeeper will have a sore back to remember us by, if not a lot of money in the till.

As we wave goodbye to the town of her ancestors, my wife fishes around in the box to find the morsel of Morbihan cheese that was my final choice. About to unwrap the package, she stares at the wrapper, then silently holds it up for me to see the name of our cheese specialist. Of all the shops in Guingamp, we have somehow been steered into the premises of one Henri Le Cornec.

My wife is overcome with emotion, and wants us to return to the town so that she can tell Mr Le Cornec that they must be related, but I persuade her against the idea. Probably, I gently point out, Le Cornec is the Breton equivalent of Smith or Jones, and the disappointment would spoil our visit for her. Much better to write and ask Christine to pursue any family connection. We drive on in silence as I mull over the possibility that my wife and the sulky shopkeeper are, in fact, related. Now I think of it, Donella's mother was, for some reason, rather taciturn with me, and also short and dark. I consider asking Donella if any members of her family apart from her great aunt ever sported a beard, but decide against it and concentrate on my driving.

We must believe in luck. For how else can
we explain the success of those we don't like?
Jean Cocteau, French artist and writer (1889–1963)

Rain Gods

Above us, the Brittany sky is an untroubled azure, but a single dark cloud lies anchored directly over the valley ahead. Les Miserables and his wife, Ono, must be at home.

As we are in the region, we feel it our duty to call in on this unfortunate couple. Les Miserables and Ono are not their real names, of course, but should be. Les has been in the depths of despair since making the crossing to settle in Brittany. We have rather cruelly dubbed his unfortunate wife 'Ono' because this is what she says when their latest mishap occurs. As we have found over the past year, she says it very often.

We first heard from the Miserables when they wrote to ask our advice about moving to France. They were fed up with their undeserved misfortunes and betrayals at the hands of so-called friends in England, and planned to sell up and escape to where life was simpler and people more trustworthy. Their idea, they said, was foolproof. They would, quite literally, go back to their ancestors' rural roots. Having sold their apartment on the south coast and invested half of the profit, they would buy a picturesque cottage with a lot of land somewhere deep in the heart of France. They would have a cow for their milk, chickens for their eggs, and grow acres of organic vegetables. The surplus would be sold to or traded with the local baker, butcher and even bank manager. In his spare time, Les would build a holiday cottage or two for summer letting. With the experience gained from her window boxes in Brighton and evening-class sessions in flower arranging, Ono would grow orchids and other exotic blooms for sale at market. They had visited France on several occasions, and enjoyed themselves immensely. It would all seem just like being on holiday for ever.

The Miserables had had the good fortune to meet a man in a pub who was, he had told them, a top financial consultant. He would secure them the maximum return on their money, and leave them to get on with living the good life. All they needed now was to decide on exactly where in France to settle. As they both suffered from incipient arthritis and would need plenty of sunshine, they had decided to plump for the deep south, and liked the idea of Brittany. Did we think that Bretons would be keen on organically grown British onions, and did we not agree that their carefully thought-out plan of action was a sure-fire winner?

I had heard all this before, and could usually predict the outcome with pinpoint accuracy. While not wanting for one moment to put them off turning their dream into reality, I finally responded, asking them whether they had really thought it all through and suggesting that their ideas could perhaps benefit from further examination.

For instance, would Les's undoubted ability in DIY equip him to build a couple of houses from the ground up? Also, Brittany was not exactly in the deep south of France, and we had found that most of the inhabitants already knew their onions, and were keenest on the home-grown variety.

Predictably, my letter received a chilly reply, and the next we heard was a rather triumphal phone call to inform us that the Miserables were now settled happily in a cottage in the heart of the Côtes d'Armor. That is, they would be settled happily as soon as the property was truly theirs. Les explained that they had agreed to buy the first house the local agent had shown them because it was a snip (or at least the agent had said it was a snip), and a minimum of four other English buyers were in a race to buy it. There was also a considerable amount of land surrounding the property, and the house had been scrupulously restored by the owners. The rusty corrugated-iron roof, their agent had pointed out, was actually a strong selling feature, as this was one of the few remaining examples of traditional Breton craftsmanship in the area. Anxious not to miss the moment, the Miserables had signed all the necessary papers, sold their apartment in England at a cut price for the sake of expediency and moved to their dream home in France. Les added that they had been particularly impressed with the way their agent had casually given them the keys and invited them to move in with all their furniture even before the final contracts had been exchanged. It was all so French, informal and trusting.

The next call came less than a week later. According to the Miserables' agent, a long-lost daughter of the vendors had appeared and was proving reluctant to agree to the sale. Thoughtfully, the owners were not insisting that the Miserables move out of their future home, but of course they would now have to pay a fair rent until the matter could be resolved.

From then on we received at least one call a month, each bringing more bad news from Brittany and finally convincing us that the Miserables were not merely exceptionally unlucky, they were rain gods. Whereas a little rain must be expected to fall into every life, the Miserables seemed to be spending theirs in a permanent downpour.

Approaching the Miserables' house, I switch the lights and wipers on as we enter the rain zone starting at their front gate. My wife remarks rather unkindly that at least they are assured of plenty of water for the vegetable plot.

We park Victor next to a car with a broken axle and run

to the front door, which I notice has been hung upside down. Looking at the bare wires behind the bell-push, I settle for knocking, and take care not to dislodge the one hinge which is holding the door roughly in place. Ono appears, and is obviously trying to be brave. She welcomes us in with a caution to avoid the brimming bucket in the passageway and the holes in the floor. Shouting above the relentless drumming of the rain beating down on the tin roof, I comment on the weather and she says that it is not as bad as when they arrived. Donella then makes the mistake of observing that their cat, Claude, must be enjoying his new-found freedom, and there is a painful scene as Ono breaks down while telling us that he has gone missing and it is said he has been shot by local hunters. It is not that they would have mistaken him for a legitimate wildlife target, she says. Cats are routinely despatched on sight for having the temerity to kill baby rabbits before they grow large enough for shooting by the human hunters.

Awkwardly, we enter the living room and are greeted by our host, who apologises for not being able to shake hands properly due to the bandages. As we take coffee, he explains that their plans for building the rustic holiday cottages in the garden have had to be put on hold. Not because of his accident with the electric saw, but because they have nowhere to build them. The field alongside the cottage that they thought was theirs was apparently not included in the sale agreement, and the owners want a premium price for it because of the rich and fertile soil it offers. Ono sniffs and says it must be more fertile than the plot in front of their house, where the earth only goes down for two inches, after which it is solid rock. This discovery has put paid to their vegetable-growing plans.

After an embarrassing silence while we refrain from posing any further questions for fear of what the answers might be, my wife asks where their toilet is. Les responds rather bitterly that she will find it in a showroom in St Malo, with the rest of the bathroom they have had to order. He goes on to explain that when the previous owners told them that they were taking the bathroom fittings with them, he had thought that they were referring to the towel rails and medicine cabinet. The Miserables had arrived back from the *notaire*'s office on the day of the exchange and found an empty room with pipes sticking up from the floor. They had also found that the pipe from the former toilet pan led no further than the outside wall of the cottage, where what they had assumed to be a septic tank has turned out to be merely a shallow hole in the ground. The problem of fitting a proper disposal system will be compounded because of the solid rock just beneath the surface.

Later, Les takes me on a tour of the house, and when I ask about the prospects for providing bed and breakfast facilities, he says that they will first need some bedrooms to put the beds in. They had not visited the upstairs of the house when the agent showed them round, or they would have realised that it is nothing but a windowless loft. He had not then understood the French tradition of using spare rooms on the ground floor as bedrooms, and the owners counting the living room, coal hole and even a corrugated-iron lean-to in the tally had given a completely misleading impression.

Later that afternoon, we make our excuses and leave. We cannot bear to hear of any more catastrophes, and besides, Donella does not want to force the Miserables into the coal shed for the night so that we can have their bedroom.

As we leave, Donella presents Ono with a colourful pot of myrtle we had bought in a market earlier that day. Ono examines the flowers, then shakes her head sadly. The tiny scarlet blooms, she says, are not real flowers. They are pieces of material cunningly wired on to the stems to give the appearance that the plant is in bloom. It is not uncommon practice in this part of France, she says, and unfortunately we have been gullible and been conned into paying out for something that is not what it seems.

We nod sombrely, then beat a hasty retreat up the muddy track, making a pact not to return. As my wife says, while sympathising deeply with their misfortunes, the myrtle incident must make one wonder whether such a degree of bad luck can be catching.

Nature has always had more force than education.
Voltaire (François-Marie Arouet), French philosopher
(1694–1778)

Educating Rita

We are on the last leg of our journey from Brittany, and will pop into our favourite English local in France.

We turn off the coastal road and head for the Lobster Pot pub and restaurant, and I narrowly avoid a flock of crows squabbling over a grisly collection of skin and fur in the road. On reflection, the crows are more likely to be rooks. There is a saying in the Cotentin that if you see a flock of crows they are probably rooks, and if you see a solitary rook it is probably a crow. It is a mark of my level of acclimatisation to the way people think in this region that I can follow the logic of this argument with no difficulty.

Mike and Rita have been running the Lobster Pot for more than a year now, and have done much, much better than anyone who knows anything about running a small business in France would have predicted.

Owning a bar and restaurant in France is one of the most popular fantasies for the sort of Britons who like entertaining at home and think that doing it professionally would be just as pleasurable, and profitable to boot. Luckily for them, the vast majority never get to learn the huge difference between cooking for friends for fun and customers for cash. For those who go on to turn their dream into reality, it almost always proves to be a fatal attraction. It is hard enough running a pub or restaurant in Britain, and the catering industry comes above even the building trade in the small-business bankruptcy lists each year. Add the difficulties of trying to succeed in the countryside and in a country where they think that foreigners, and especially Britons, have a problem boiling an egg, and you have a recipe for disaster. Even the French find it difficult to make a rural bar or restaurant pay, and the Lobster Pot is not only isolated but is in a coastal area where summers are short and winters very long.

When our mutual friend Madame Lynn told us that Mike and Rita were taking over a defunct premises near the west coast and planning to combine an English pub with a French restaurant, we thought they had gone completely mad. To our knowledge, neither had even cooked as much as a Pop Tart for profit, and neither could speak more than a few words of French. In bookmaking terms, the odds on their coming through the first year intact would make a bet on Elvis Presley being found alive and well and running a chip shop in Doncaster look attractive.

However, our gloomy forecasts had obviously not allowed for the couple's combined qualities of enthusiasm, imagination and that most useful of attributes for anyone wishing to make a go of a business in France – sheer bloody-mindedness. The layout of the Lobster Pot is a perfect example of their flair for combining the best of both worlds and appealing to all sorts of potential customers. The small and cosy bar gives more than a flavour of an English pub, with wrought-iron tables, suitably nautical knick-knacks on the wall, and there is even a carpet on the floor. This inspired accessory is unknown in Cotentin bars, and is a novelty that has attracted sightseers from miles around. Most importantly, the couple have ensured that they have not created a gimmicky Brit theme pub, which would appeal only to homesick expatriates.

Another inspired decision was to leave all traces of

Englishness at the door to the restaurant. Within, the style is of a typically unpretentious French eating house, and the menu and kitchen are entirely in the hands of a local chef.

Over the past year, the couple have also learned the importance of providing their regulars with more than the range of services an English pub would expect to offer. As we enter, we see a farmer sitting with a glass of wine in one hand and a large new bandage on the other. Nurse Rita has obviously been at work. When we settle down to catch up on their progress, Rita explains that a vital part of the adaptation process was to educate herself in the various roles and skills necessary for the running of a small pub in the countryside of Normandy. As well as becoming the landlady of the local bar, she has learned to be a counsellor, fortune teller, dispute arbitrator, bank manager and even a bookie's runner and surrogate physician. She places bets and picks up prescriptions on her regular runs to town, and it is clear from the attitude of the customers that she and her husband have won the hearts of the locals in a very short time.

But, as they tell us, getting through the year successfully has been a two-way educational process, with some interesting breakdowns in communication occurring on both sides of the bar.

These early hiccups included several of the locals confusing a designer pedal bin in the refurbished toilets for a new-fangled urinal, and the chef asking Rita if she would like a little nookie when discussing a forthcoming Italian theme night. He was, she discovered with some relief, merely seeking her opinion on the wisdom of including *gnocchi* pasta dumplings on the menu.

But more than a few mistakes have also been made on their side of the linguistic fence. On a special fruits of the sea evening, the chef had been close to tears when not a single diner ordered his signature dish of *filet de dorade*, or sea bream. Investigation beyond the kitchen doors eventually revealed that Mike had been practising his French in the bar by boasting of the chef's choice, but pronouncing the dish not 'dorade' as in fish, but 'de rah' as in rat.

On another occasion, a French holidaymaker had come into the bar and announced he was on a special tour, tracing the footsteps of Guillaume le Conquérant in the area. As the village licensee, did Mike have any special knowledge in the matter of where the great William had been seen locally? Mike apologised and said he had not heard of anyone of that name in the area, but advised his visitor to try the village grocery shop. They, if anyone, would be sure to know Mr Conquérant's home address.

> *A true friend is the greatest of all blessings,*
> *and that which we take the least care of all to acquire.*
> François de La Rochefoucauld, French classical writer
> (1613–80)

After the Fox

It is good to be home again.

We have been on a book-signing tour around Britain, and Donella is in a very bad mood. As usual, our disagreement has started over something trivial, in this case my innocent question as to why women always slam car doors. Within minutes we had moved on to the issue of why men never put the toilet-seat cover down after use, and I have not helped matters by pointing out that it would surely be much worse if we didn't bother to lift them before use.

I do have some sympathy for my wife, because I know that she hates our occasional round-Britain tours as much as I enjoy them. The highlight of this trip has been the major French property exhibition of the year, and I relished virtually every moment of it. Staged at a hotel in London, the exhibition attracts tens of thousands of visitors, and I take a delight in meeting as many of them as possible during the weekend. The event is also a suitably impressive occasion at which to meet the nation's travel writers and book critics and persuade them to give my work some free publicity. At the show last week, I devised an inspirational marketing ploy, although my wife thinks I may have got carried away and bitten off more than we can both chew.

Surrounded by various regional and national newspaper

hacks, I proceeded to tell them that they were missing a golden opportunity to unearth a rare treasure. All they ever wrote about, I argued while topping up their glasses with some specially imported home-brew calvados, was what I contemptuously dismissed as tourist France. Why did they not break new ground and come to real France and see just how much the Cotentin has to offer? Warming to my theme and the calvados samples, I challenged them all to come on an all-expenses paid voyage of discovery to my home region. Unfortunately, at least half of the reporters present were so enthused by my rhetoric that they agreed to my proposal on the spot. When I woke up in our hotel room the following morning with a hangover, my wife reminded me that all we had to do now was (a) find the money to pay for the event, and (b) think of somewhere to take our guests that would live up to my glowing description of the Cotentin as the undiscovered jewel of Normandy.

It is the day of the press pack's visit, and I am feeling somewhat nervous about the outcome. We are in Cherbourg, awaiting the arrival of the cream of newspaper and magazine travel writers from around Britain. All we need now is some decent weather and a successful conclusion to the day, which is to take the form of a novelty treasure hunt. After spending a few sleepless nights and some long days with a map of our region, I have come up with an idea, which, if all goes well, will promote both the attractions of the Cotentin as a short-stay holiday destination and bare-facedly plug our books about our adventures here. Theoretically, our guests will arrive on the overnight boat, take breakfast in the terminal, then race off in their cars with a map of the peninsula and a sheet of paper bearing cryptic clues and directions to places of interest in the area. If they don't get lost, break down or become stuck behind a herd of cows in a lane somewhere along the way, they will arrive at the Café de Paris in Bricquebec in time for a glass or two of calvados and a meeting with all the local characters featured in my books. My touch of inspiration was to call the event a Fox Hunt, and arrange for René Ribet to be on hand to sign copies of my book about him. Best of all, the cost of the trip is being met by a somewhat bemused Cotentin Tourist Board, and P&O Ferries have kindly pitched in to provide the crossing and prizes for the first hacks to pass the winning post.

As we wait at the quayside, it starts to rain, and my wife points out that it is quite possible that René Ribet, the actual quarry of the so-called Fox Hunt, may decide to visit the Widow of Négreville instead of Bricquebec this evening. He has a pocketful of spending money I gave him for expenses, and even if he is at our rendezvous, he may well be incapable of speaking to the journalists if and when they arrive. Then there is the possibility of the press pack wandering into the sights of a real hunt, or even being shot by a farmer if they get my clues wrong and trespass on private land. Worse still, what if they are unfamiliar with driving customs in the Cotentin, and think they will be safe if they obey the rules of the road as they apply to the rest of France? There could, she says grimly, even be a fatality.

I think about the possibilities, then point out that her worries are needless. The one thing that everybody knows about the publicity business is that no news is bad news. An accidental death or even murder of a journalist would guarantee acres of newsprint, and could account for thousands of extra copies of our books being sold this year.

By mid-morning, I find myself lying belly down in the rolling dunes at the seaside resort of Carteret. If all has gone well, the press pack will have collected specially marked mussel shells from the fishing village of Barfleur, scaled the heights at La Pernelle in search of the smallest town hall in Normandy and be well on their way to Carteret to find the next clue, which is in a bottle I have secreted in the seafront toilets directly below our observation point. With my binoculars trained on the toilet block to watch for their arrival, I am heavily disguised in my Father Christmas mask, with dark glasses and a giant beret for good measure. Beside me, the elegant public relations lady from P&O Ferries is dusting sand from her designer coat, and wearing the look of someone who is wondering what the implications are for her future if the day gets any more bizarre.

～

It is the early hours of the next day, and Donella, the ferry lady and I are sitting on a low wall in the square at Bricquebec. A cold rain is falling but we are oblivious to its sting. Against all odds, the press-pack hunt has gone better than we dared hope, despite an unfortunate incident when one of the journalists had been arrested for looking under the doors of the cubicles in the gents' in search of the bottle with the message in it. After we had effected his release, the hunt was on again, and the journalists had virtually all fallen in to the spirit of the chase. Between them, they had also fallen in to at least one river, a pond and a forest of brambles as they scoured the countryside for clues before arriving bloody but unbeaten at Bricquebec to beard the Fox in his den. To my wife's surprise, René was there and on his best behaviour. He was also wearing his best suit and had shaved and combed his hair especially for the occasion, which rather spoiled the characterful rustic effect I had been hoping for. Later, there had been a splendid dinner at the hotel in the castle, a long speech of welcome from a representative of the Cotentin Tourist Board and a much longer selection of traditional country airs from a man with a guitar and a very untraditional pork-pie hat.

After the singer had been persuaded to take his final bow, it was time for the prizes to be awarded and our guests to put on the strings of onions and silly hats I had persuaded the PR lady they would enjoy wearing. Then it was off on a tour of the nightlife of Bricquebec, which did not take long. Our night ended spectacularly at the bar that is the haunt of the local bikers we have dubbed the Wild Bunch, but who in reality are a group of overly polite youths who spend the evenings looking admiringly at each other's mopeds.

Next morning, we stood at the hotel doors and saw our guests off. Some were still wearing their silly hats and onion strings, and all looked slightly dazed as a result of their wild weekend. Each of them promised to do what they could to tell their readers exactly what the Cotentin had to offer the sophisticated traveller, and one took the trouble to tell me what an unforgettable and rewarding trip it had been. Normally, he said, he and his colleagues would be whisked away on a jet to some exotic location where they would be put up in five-star accommodation and force-fed gourmet delicacies. I was obviously a master in reverse marketing, and it had made a real change to have been our guests. When his sprained wrist got better, he would certainly do his best to do justice to his story about their weekend in pursuit of the Fox of Cotentin. In the meantime, he was looking forward to becoming the owner of the charming little cottage that René Ribet had agreed to sell him. It seemed a real snip at the ten thousand pounds he had beaten our friend down to after the rest of us had gone to bed. He hoped that the transaction wouldn't be seen by the local people as a worldly-wise newspaper man from London taking advantage of a gullible countryman, and that René will be able to find somewhere else to live with not too much trouble.

I tell him not to worry, and hope that he will write the piece publicising our book and the area before he finds out that René's cottage actually belongs to the farmer on whose land it stands.

After all the fuss and excitement of the Fox Hunt, we are visiting friends for a relaxing weekend by the seaside.

Ste-Mère-Eglise is an otherwise unremarkable town on the eastern coast of the peninsula, but was the scene of some of the fiercest fighting during the D-Day landings. Most people may not remember the name of the place, but will know of the bizarre incident when an American paratrooper snagged his parachute on the church steeple and hung there for hours before being rescued. He was deafened by the church bells, but escaped death in spite of hundreds of Germans taking pot shots at him from below. To commemorate the liberation of the town and remind people of the sacrifices made to win freedom, a parachute is draped from the steeple of the church at Ste-Mère-Eglise on special occasions throughout the year.

As we pull up in the square, I see that the parachute is in place, and try to imagine what it must have been like to be trapped up there with people shooting at you like a china plate at the funfair.

We walk across the cobbles towards the bar where we are meeting our friends and the church bells begin to ring the Angelus; I hear music coming through the open window of a car parked outside the café. It is the jaunty film theme from *The Longest Day*, and I feel the hairs on the back of my neck bristle. Somewhere in my head I hear the sound of bullets and people screaming as madness and death visited this peaceful square. I had forgotten that today is 6 June.

I cannot stop the French being French.
Charles de Gaulle, former French President (1890–1970)

Party Pieces

The final moments of another year of our lives in Lower Normandy are ticking away, and in the past hour I have learned another important lesson in life: it is very difficult to play 'Way Down Upon the Swannee River' on the spoons while dressed as a carrot.

We have spent the past six months in England trying to drum up interest in my books about our small adventures in rural France, while at the same time trying to persuade a procession of obdurate bank managers and finance houses that they should invest in our future here. So far, there has been little enthusiasm from either publishers or money-lenders, and we are closer to financial meltdown than ever before. But life goes on, and we are gathered in one of our favourite locals to see in the New Year and forget our pecuniary troubles.

Because of its affably eccentric landlord and the sublime cooking talents of his wife, the Flaming Curtains is one of the most popular bars in the area. Tonight, the bar is as full as our doctor's waiting room when rumours of an interesting new virus are sweeping through our community.

While I attempt to wave my empty glass in the direction of our host, Coco, I engage Morton, the pub dog, in conversation and explain that I am wearing a carrot suit because of yet another small but significant communication problem.

When Coco telephoned this morning to ask if I would be doing my usual party piece with the spoons and kazoo, I thought he said that all the other foreigners – by which he of course meant British settlers – would be wearing fancy dress. On arrival, I realised he had meant formal dress, and found myself a lonely giant vegetable among a monochrome forest of bow ties and black dresses. It says something about the local people's view of the British community that nobody has commented on the costume I shall be wearing at this year's Carrot Festival.

During our time in rural France I have often observed that most local people think all British settlers are rich and either harmlessly eccentric or completely barking. To be fair, they often have good reason for coming to that conclusion.

A little later, and despite the chill, our group has moved on to the terrace. We are gathered at the rickety table that Coco calls the British Embassy. In her less generous moments, my wife calls it the overseas branch of Alcoholics Unanimous. At other times, she says it should be known as King George's Round Table because it is where I most like to hold court. It is true that the table is a favourite meeting place for our informal club of settlers and locals, and that I like to talk. This, I often tell Donella, is why I am a writer. I think I have something to say and want people to listen. Besides, as in any half-decent pub, drinking and talking go naturally together.

As well as being a gathering place for debate and discourse, scandal and intrigue, our special table is also distinguished by the apple tree growing through its centre. According to legend, the tree sprang from the remains of an English Cox that a French farmer tried and then discarded after one tentative bite. Impressed by the tenacity and determination of the sapling and rather than going to the bother of rearranging the seating, Coco simply cut a hole in the table top. Although it has not borne fruit in the decade I have been sitting beneath its branches, the tree is now a sturdy growth, and if it could speak it would have some interesting tales to tell. And each year as the trunk gets bigger, Coco simply enlarges the hole.

The alleged history of how the tree came to be here is also a perfect example of why we choose to live in rural France. If the tale is true, the apple came from Britain, was initially treated with suspicion and ignored, but hung on, spread its roots and bided its time until it was accepted as part of the community.

As we sit and drink and think about the dying year and how it has treated us, an impish wind explores the high street and hurries yet more revellers towards the bar, which lies in the shadow of what is said to be the oldest church in Normandy (if not all France, of course). This arrangement is most convenient, as the people of the town still cling mostly to the old faith. Coco's wife, Chantal, also serves the best and cheapest food in the area, so nobody has far to travel to satisfy soul or stomach or both. Having such a broad church of clientele, the Flaming Curtains, or Rideau Cramoisi, is also the official information-exchange centre for the town and surrounding area, and the high proportion of British expatriates among the regular customers ensures there is always a juicy story about foreign and therefore bizarre activities to hear and pass on.

After a warning howl, the loudspeakers lining the high street blare into life and we decide unanimously to return to the crowded bar rather than sit through yet another replay of the town's favourite seasonal pop songs. Though accomplished in so many other areas of creativity, the French do not seem to have quite got the hang of most forms of modern music. The big hit this year in our area is a lament about a boy whose dog is run over on Christmas Eve as his mother lies dying of consumption. Other tunes and themes are even less life-affirming.

We squeeze into the bar just as the church clock strikes midnight, but know this is a false alarm. Like many of the townspeople, the clock seems to run on its own time. Rival bar owners allege that our host at the Flaming Curtains has an arrangement with the verger so that the clock goes forward when Coco wants an early night or backwards when he scents a profitable session, but I know this is not true. Like all good Frenchmen, Coco Lecoq is a great believer in liberty over licence, and opens and shuts the bar regardless of the official hours of trading.

While fighting my way to the bar counter, I explore Donella's purse and see that our supply of old money should just last out the evening. This thought evokes a pang of nostalgia as it will be the last occasion in forty years that I shall be buying my drinks with French francs. Although the rest of France has been trading in euros for some time, Coco declared the Curtains an independent financial state on changeover day. He explained that, like Britain, he was waiting for more favourable conditions before officially adopting the euro. Apart from being another example of the sort of attitude that attracts us to life in this country, Coco's refusal to conform was also a shrewd business move as it allowed local farmers to launder their hoards of undeclared and thus tax-free francs while enjoying a break from the demands of market day.

Waiting at the bar, I feel a friendly nudge and turn to see that my friend Jean-Claude Goulot is out on the town, and that he is not wearing his trademark brown overalls. A defiantly individualistic personality even by rural Norman standards, Jean-Claude is acknowledged as the best producer of bootleg calvados apple brandy in the area and said to be a very competent carpenter in his spare time. I can vouch for the quality and strength of his calvados, but I do not know much about his abilities at working with wood, as we have been waiting for him to fit a door in a hole in the mill cottage since he first gave us an estimate in 1994. Over the years he has become a good friend, and calls in at least once a week to see if the hole is still there.

When I ask how business is going, Jean-Claude says he has decided to abandon the demands of carpentry to set out on a new career path. While I buy him a whisky, he proudly takes out and shows me his new set of dentures, then announces that he has decided to become a leg of lamb. When he has put his teeth back and enlarges on his plans, I realise that he has decided on a lifestyle as a *gigolo* rather than a *gigot*. Although he is certainly small enough to qualify as a toyboy, he will never see sixty again and is also not handsome in the conventional sense, even for rural France. Whatever his qualifications, my friend is obviously dressed for his new role. Apart from the new teeth and a rather obvious wig, he is wearing platform-soled shoes and a suit that even the most extrovert character would have been embarrassed to wear at a small-town seventies disco during a power cut. In a subtle shade of tangerine, it is at least two sizes too big and the ultra-flared trousers cascade on to the floor like a set of badly made Austrian blinds.

After some adjustment of his dentures, Jean says the idea of his new business venture came about, somewhat predictably, after spending an evening in the bar with Didier Bouvier. It does not surprise me that our local entrepreneur and rogue trader lies behind the scheme, or that Jean bought his ill-fitting teeth and clothing from Dodgy Didier.

While I get Jean-Claude another drink, he explains the *raison d'être* behind his new enterprise. It is a fact, he says, that the local freesheet is always full of advertisements placed by single women in search of male company and even marriage. The big idea for the New Year is to set up business as an escort agency with himself as the sole escort, and split the profits with Didier. He also believes that he has got one over on Didier for a change, as he will have all the pleasure and Didier will only get half the money resulting from his assignations. Also, if he meets a rich widow, he will marry her and he will be able to retire. As a final and unarguable argument for the Cartesian logic of his business plan, my friend points out that the notorious Widow of Négreville is never short of customers. She is marginally less attractive than the rear end of a cow suffering from the runs and has a bigger moustache than most of her visitors. It is also surely time, he concludes, that the modern craze for gender equality reached our area.

Asked for my opinion of his New Year resolution, I settle for making vaguely approving noises and decide not to ask what Madame Goulot thinks about her husband selling his body rather than his carpentry skills.

While Jean-Claude is practising some of his conversational gambits on an elderly lady who has obviously turned off her hearing-aid, Coco climbs on to the bar and calls the house to order. Anticipating an acknowledgement of our contributions to his retirement fund during the past months and an invitation to refill our glasses and toast the New Year in, the crowd presses forward eagerly. But gasps of disappointment mingle with the grunts of crowded discomfort when Coco's invitation to drink up is followed by the announcement that the Flaming Curtains is closing a full quarter of an hour before the New Year arrives.

Mass shrugging breaks out as the customers discuss this development. To appreciate the scene, it is important to understand that the Gallic shrug is infinitely more sophisticated in style and significance than its lacklustre British equivalent. In its kaleidoscopic variety of manifestations, the French shrug not only makes full use of shoulders, arms and hands, but also mouth, nose, eyes, eyebrows and even, in extreme cases, ears. In a deft combination of twitches, jerks and spasms, the shrugger can convey an almost limitless range of emotions, concerns and comments to the shrugee. There is even claimed to be a shruggers' convention held in Paris each year, with the finest exponents meeting to compare and evaluate new and previously little known techniques and styles. I do not know if the event actually takes place, as being a foreigner I would not of course be allowed access to such a gathering, and by the very nature of the event there can be no written reports. Voltaire said that we invent words to conceal truths, so he may well have had the French Shruggers' Association in mind when he wrote his thoughtful essays about the eternal search for *vérité* and how best to find and demonstrate that precious virtue.

Slaloming my way through the maelstrom of gesticulating limbs and jerking heads, I catch up with Coco as he opens the door to admit the cold night air and expel his customers. I ask him if there is a particular reason for his decision to shut the bar at this particular time. With the insouciant shrug he reserves for drunks, rude foreigners and tax inspectors, my friend explains that he has been invited to a New Year's party at the home of a friend and that it would be very bad manners for him to turn up after the midnight hour has struck, and it will be nice for him and his wife to be guests rather than hosts for a change. While mildly aggrieved at this sudden change to our plans for seeing in the New Year, it is a sign of the time I have been living in Lower Normandy that I understand and even appreciate the logic of his actions. It is not the sort of situation one would expect to encounter at a typical British pub, but represents another of the reasons why we choose to live in this very special part of France.

As Coco and Chantal see us off the premises, I attempt to express my best wishes and thanks for a year of friendship with a carefully orchestrated shrug, but Coco merely looks at me bemusedly and asks if I have trapped my private parts in the carrot suit. Obviously, and despite my best efforts over the years, we still do not even speak the same body language.

Regrouped in the street outside the Flaming Curtains, my wife and I decide to make the best of our situation and demonstrate how Britons traditionally usher in the New Year. After explaining the basic rules, we link arms and lead the singing of 'Auld Lang Syne'. Though the lyrics in their traditional form do not translate well into Norman patois, our friends join in enthusiastically and shutters soon begin to open along the high street. They have not been opened by the owners so that they may complain, but rather to see what is going on and then to tell us how we should be singing the song they have never before encountered. Honest curiosity and frank criticism are two more Norman traits I love well.

Our circle is joined by more and more residents, and soon it seems the whole of St Sauveur is joining in the celebrations. Miraculously, the church clock begins its unsteady chimes just as we reach the crescendo of the fifteenth chorus, and the participants need no instruction or invitation to exchange embraces. As he emerges from the crowd after apologising to and retrieving his new dentures from the wife of the town's principal baker, Jean-Claude comments that there are at least some English customs that are sensible and enjoyable. The mass kiss-in has also been good practice for his new career. He can now see the logic behind the final orgy of embracing as New Year's Eve is probably, from what he has heard, the only time that English men get around to kissing their wives or any other woman.

An hour has passed, and we are sitting on the ramparts of the town's castle. Milly, our new cross-collie, is contentedly exploring the graveyard where our famous local writer rests, and from our elevated position, I see that St Sauveur is now virtually deserted.

Looking out across the River Douve and the great flood plains beyond, my wife and I consider the promise of the coming year and review our situation. It has been another year of struggle, and we yet again came close to losing the Mill of the Flea as we continued our battle to make a living from my writing. Our bank account is as low, as they say in this area, as a toad's testicles, and my plans for bringing in money with imaginative business ventures have all failed. But my wife has been as steadfast, uncomplaining and tirelessly supportive as ever, and we have somehow managed to survive another year at the home we love.

The only shadow on our unexceptional but contented life at La Puce is money, or the way it seems to melt away when I come near. But, as my wife reminds me, we are still here, and we are living a life that millions would envy.

I take my wife's hand and wonder again how I could have been so lucky to find someone like her and how she manages to maintain her calm but boundless optimism and faith in me, my abilities as a writer and our future. I whistle for Milly and we begin the long walk back to the Mill of the Flea.

Nothing has changed in France.
Comte d'Artois, later Charles X of France (1757–1836)

Culture Club

Dawn has long since arrived, but at this time of year sensible people in our area go to bed early and rise late, and I am presently occupied counting holes in the oak beam that spans the bedroom of the mill cottage. There is little to do on the land as we wait for spring, and the rhythms of the seasons dictate our movements and moods. It is one of my favourite rituals at this time of year and day to think about all the jobs I will do when the weather breaks. This pleasant routine also wins me another few moments with my wife, cat and dog in bed. I have been promising myself for at least ten years that I will do something about the wood-worm problem, but when I asked our carpenter-turned-gigolo friend Jean-Claude, he said the best solution was to let my great-great-grandchildren's children worry about it. He reminded me that the giant and largely untrimmed tree trunks straddling the walls of our home had been doing their job quite well for three hundred years, and even Norman woodworms will not make much of an impression on them for another century or so.

An impatient call from the hen-house reminds me of my responsibilities, and I look at the bathtub, consider my op-tions, then dress quickly and go downstairs to set about my first task of each day between October and March. In our old life, the central heating woke with us and double-glazed windows insulated us from what lay outside our comfortable terraced house in England. Now and here, the old wood-burning stove must be laid and lit and fed to take the edge off the cold and heat the water for a skimpy wash.

When we first came to live in the Cotentin countryside I thought my romanticised middle-class urban notions of the joys of making a real fire would soon wear off, but the pleasure has stayed with me. Perhaps it is a genetic echo from a time when a real fire represented survival, or just my small conceit, but I like the simple physicality of laying and lighting a fire; when I eventually grow resentful of the effort on a cold morning, I will know it is time to think about leaving La Puce.

The Mill of the Flea is now comfortably warm by rural Norman standards, and most of the smoke from the stove is finding its way through the tin drainage pipe that serves as our chimney. Donella is preparing our breakfast, and Cato has gone off in search of hers. I pity any living creature smaller than a cow that crosses the path of our werecat this morning as she is in a particularly bad mood. I have already fed the chickens, fish, muskrats, crayfish, geese and other freeloading residents of La Puce, and am further working up an appetite by collecting wood in the copse by the road.

On one side, La Puce is bounded by a steeply sloping road where drivers test their brakes and nerves, while on the other, the tree-lined Hunters' Walk overlooks hundreds of acres of small fields mostly left to pasture or nature. We know those of our neighbours who farm their land for a living, but many of the smaller fields are owned by townspeople who do no more than visit them occasionally. The love of land lies deep within the Norman soul, and the ownership of a distant plot can be more of a status symbol than a new car. Ownership of woodland and the fuel it provides is even more of a status symbol, and I have to make regular patrols to frustrate raiding parties in search of easily harvested fallen branches, or sometimes whole trees.

Hearing the testy and familiar popping of a moped, I disguise my pile of wood with a covering of dead leaves and hurry to intercept our postman. As well as saving him the discomfort of bumping down the heavily rutted track to the cottage, I will also avoid inviting him in for a breakfast of two cups of coffee, three glasses of home-made apple brandy and at least six cigarettes, which is the standard fee for learning the latest rumours circulating the area. There will also be news of Patrick the Post's latest collection of rare and cruel ailments, and a blow-by-blow account of how he has survived another night despite the demands of the sexually voracious Madame Megère. Normally I enjoy these early morning briefing sessions, but today I am anxious to get on with my work.

Rather than suffering from the writer's block that has plagued me in the past, the words have come tumbling almost unbidden from my mind as I sit at my table in the caravan by the big pond. We are as ever desperately in need of income, and a new book will hopefully generate interest in my past works. With the ever increasing appetite in Britain for buying a home in France, there is also the chance that a major publisher will at last decide to make a significant investment in bringing out my stories.

Our postman has buzzed away to complete his rounds, and we are at breakfast. Today, we humans are having fried black pudding with apple slices and cream to set us up for a busy day, and having left the official-looking envelopes (i.e. bills) for Donella's attention, I read her some carefully selected extracts from a week-old copy of a tabloid newspaper a friend has sent from England. A few moments with any British newspaper and we are reminded of what we are missing in modern Britain, and some additional reasons why we choose to live in Lower Normandy.

As the paper was published at the beginning of January, it contains lengthy astrological forecasts for the coming twelve months, and I see that my wife is due for what could be a traumatic year if she does not take resolute action. Warming to a general theme, the celebrity astrologer says Donella is being held back by an unrewarding and restricting relationship with someone who does not appreciate her. It will be much better for her future fulfilment if she ditches the encumbrance of this dead weight and at last realises her own true potential.

Noting that the four million people born in the same month as me are all going to move home, travel across water and experience bitter disappointment and financial problems in the coming months, I conclude that Mystic Morganna is having a bad air-signs day and move on to the healthy-living supplement. This section is almost beyond satire as it even includes a cosily intimate article entitled 'Me and My Operation'. The main item explains the importance of the ratio between height and weight, and even predicts readers' life spans based on their size and shape. Idly jotting down my statistics and doing the necessary calculations, I see that I have apparently been dead for at least five years and ask my wife to add another slice of fried bread to my plate so I can recover from the shock.

I now turn to our satisfyingly thick pile of correspondence and find a jolly letter from a widow of a certain age who says she has developed an interesting and potentially valuable relationship with the owner of the hardware store near her holiday home in the Dordogne. Arriving at the end of last summer to find the loft had become an insect mortuary, she called at the shop and said in what she thought was reasonable French that she had a plague of flies in her attic and was probably in need of a good fumigator. After looking at her thoughtfully with his good eye (the other, she says she could not help but notice, was glass, ill-fitting and of a strange hue), the man had pointedly wet his lips, twirled his moustache in a decidedly lascivious manner and suggested that he call round personally to attend to her needs. It would be best for obvious reasons, he said, if her husband were not at home. Later that day, she told her English-speaking neighbour about the conversation and how helpful the man had been, and the lady explained why. The news of the English woman's visit to the shop had raced around the village after the shopkeeper had visited the local bar to tell his story. He had, he said, always believed that English men were by nature and temperament sexually repressed, with the women being consequently starved of their due marital rights. It was thus, he said, not a complete surprise to be propositioned by the attractive, if mature, new owner of the old Dupont place. She had arrived at the shop that afternoon, used what was obviously an English euphemism about having flies in her attic, then openly told him that she was in need of a good fornicator.

Surprisingly, my correspondent says that rather than causing a problem, her mistake in pronunciation had worked to her advantage. When the shopkeeper had called in his best overalls and clutching a bunch of flowers, she had told him that her husband was due to arrive from the ferry port at any moment and suggested that he fix her leaking tap in the kitchen as an excuse for being in the house. He had made an excellent job and so far called on ten other occasions, and had been persuaded each time to do several useful jobs around the house as a cover for his visit. At the time of writing, she had managed to avoid being alone on the premises when her would-be conspirator in fornication arrived and, if her luck and nerve held, she estimated that her holiday cottage would be completely restored within the year.

My creative session in the caravan at the end of the water meadow is done for the day, the manuscript for the new book is nearly finished, and I am off to a meeting of the Jolly Boys Club of Néhou.

Donella is happy to see me go, as she appreciates that I need some time to relax in male company. She also knows that our regular gatherings are ideal sources of material for my book, and I know that she is keen to have me safely out of the way so she can begin her latest assault on the acres of bramble in the no-man's land beyond the big pond.

In recent years, the bramble has advanced relentlessly, and my wife does not like being denied access to a square metre of her land, so as a special late Christmas present I have bought her an appliance that should be more than equal to the challenge. I had seen Donella looking wistfully at the new and very expensive scrub-burners in the local garden centre, and asked a fellow JBC member if he could find one for me at wholesale price. Dodgy Didier runs his business from a barn in Néhou that he likes to call his European headquarters, and claims royalty and foreign governments among his list of regular clients. Although I do not know if this is true, anyone who can make a living from selling blank Rubik's Cubes to canny Norman countrymen could teach the average British double-glazing salesman a thing or two about closing a deal. He is a likeable rogue, and if not always up to official specification, his goods are always much cheaper than list price. This, of course, is the key factor in selling people things they don't really need or want. Didier also likes to intimate that his wares have fallen off the back of a lorry passing conveniently through Cherbourg ferry port, which is a further inducement to buy for any self-respecting Norman.

A week after I told him about our problem with the impenetrable bracken, he arrived at La Puce with a large, government-issue crate in the back of his van. Unlike the smaller commercial devices in the shop, the device he unveiled was khaki in colour and looked not unlike the sort of thing I have seen in newsreel footage of the D-Day landings. After admitting that it was, in fact, a government-surplus flame-thrower, Didier assured us it was unused and therefore as good as new. He closed the sale by pointing out that the prototype had been field-tested in the jungles of Vietnam, so should be more than equal to a confrontation with even the most overgrown areas of La Puce.

I have safely emerged from the mill track and on to the road that runs past the eastern boundary of La Puce. Once upon a time, what is now the D900 was used by little more than the grain carts servicing the Mill of the Flea, local people on their way from outlying hamlets to and from the village and parties of pilgrims on their way to Spain to pay their respects to St James. In those times, the holy route would have been marked by scallop shells, but nowadays, the old route is light on pilgrims, and in the short time we have been custodians of La Puce, the D900 has become a busy trunk route. To leave the tranquillity of our ancient and sheltered home and take to the high road is to become a time traveller and appreciate more fully how the internal combustion engine has changed all our lives.

Later, turning off the main road and taking the winding route to our village, I toot my horn as I pass each of the outlying houses and am rewarded with the occasional wave from a doorway, window or garden. Though it is January, it has not rained all morning and many villagers are taking this unusual opportunity to spend some time outdoors. People here still leave their front doors open in all seasons and seem to like fleeting contact with passers-by. Perhaps it is the natural desire of those living in isolated situations to feel somehow more in touch with what is happening in the rest of the world, or perhaps the owners just want to know who is going by. When we lived in a Hampshire city, I knew little about our immediate neighbours other than their names. But then, there were more people living in one long road than in the whole of Néhou. Parisians are not noted for their communication skills and warmth, so population density may have more to do with neighbourliness than culture.

Rounding the bend leading to the heart of the village, I see a figure on the roof of a cottage that is dilapidated even by rural Norman standards, and decide not to sound my horn. Madame Cochet is obviously doing some running repairs to the rusting corrugated iron, and I do not wish to distract her and cause an accident. Although she has a fit husband and three hulking sons, Madame, like my wife, prefers to do all the maintenance work on her property and is acknowledged as one of the most skilful general builders in the area. She is also said to be the finest cake-maker in the region, and some of the villagers claim her experience with the ancient family cement-mixer helped hone her technique for creating the perfect consistency and texture of her *gâteaux*. As she sees me and waves her hammer cheerily, I think about stopping to ask if she would be interested in giving us an estimate for the complete restoration of the ruined end of the Mill of the Flea, but decide against it. Until the new book comes out and our financial situation improves, we could not afford even Madame Cochet's modest rates, and I do not know if Donella would approve of another woman taking over the heavy work at La Puce.

Parking outside the Bar Ghislaine, I sit for a moment to hear the completion of an earnest discussion on Radio Four. The programme is *Woman's Hour*, and the debate is about a recent survey. The researchers asked women of varying ages how satisfied they were with their lives and, in broad terms, found that despite ever increasing independence from their traditional home-making role, greatly enhanced career prospects and salaries, the younger women were much more dissatisfied with their lives than the older respondents. The panellists have different theories on why the young women are all so unhappy, but agree that, whatever other interpretations are made of the statistics, men must be to blame. Although I am no expert in these matters, it appears to me that this situation is a fine example of the Law of Unintended Consequences swinging into action. Though nearly all the women in our village lead what might seem an underprivileged and even repressed life when viewed from the other side of the Channel, it seems to me that while they may not be happier than most British women I meet, they are certainly no unhappier.

Before joining my friends, I stroll across the pavement to make use of the *pissoir* alongside Madame Ghislaine's bar and grocery shop. As the bar has no other toilet facilities for male customers, it will save me a journey later and at a time when I might otherwise have to leave the gathering at some vital point in a debate or, more importantly, miss my share of a round of drinks. Now that I have persuaded our members that we should adopt the English tradition of taking turns in buying the drinks, some of our less generous members have adopted the ploy of ordering their rounds at opportune times.

My time facing the old metal poster and guttering pipe will also allow me to window-shop for lunch. As I aim at the worn spot on the enamelled Gitanes placard while leaning sideways to look at an interesting display of pig's trotters in aspic, the door to the shop opens and two elderly ladies emerge. With my free hand, I lift my Mickey Mouse cap, and the two women nod in formal response. Small matters of courtesy are important in our community, and I would not wish to cause offence by ignoring the niceties.

Despite the proprietor of the Bar Ghislaine's opinion of men, there is something about her and her customer service philosophy that I find appealing. She can be sharp of tongue and acid in wit, but this somehow enhances rather than detracts from the atmosphere. There is no other bar within five miles of our village, so the locals do not have much of a choice as to where they do their drinking, but I know that, despite their grumbles, they enjoy using the Bar Ghislaine. René Ribet says this is because exposure to the proprietor is like having a tooth pulled. The experience is painful, but you feel so much better when it is over. Other members of our club say that our hostess's treatment makes them feel at home, while the single members of our club say that she makes them appreciate how lucky they are not to be married.

For myself, I enjoy my daily encounters with Ghislaine. She may be small of stature and sharp of tongue but has, as the local saying goes, more guts than a Breton abattoir. She also has a heart as big as the Norman sky. While a village bar and store is almost a curiosity in our area nowadays, Ghislaine has managed to keep her business going and is tireless in her efforts to keep the traditional village spirit alive. I once asked her why, as well as all her work in the bar and store, she dedicated so much time to organising all the community events. After a moment's thought, she shrugged and said she did not know, but someone had to do it, although she often thought she must be mad. I replied that France and the rest of the world would be a better place if there were more mad people like her, and before bustling away she almost smiled.

Arriving in the bar, I see that Madame Ghislaine is already filling my beer mug and testing the bicycle bell attached to its handle. I also see that our club is in full session, that we have visitors, and that one of them is sitting in my seat. The male half of the couple is standing at the bar, and I conclude that he is English, comes from the Home Counties, is middle-class and voted New Labour in the last General Election. I make this deduction like Sherlock Holmes by first considering all the evidence. The first clue in the evidential chain was the new and fashionable four-wheel-drive vehicle parked outside, and the British number plate and North London parking permit on its windscreen. I also noticed a faded sticker on the bumper assuring readers that things could only get better under New Labour. There was also a placard in the back window commanding drivers to keep a safe distance as there was a 'Small Person On Board'. For some irrational reason, I find these signs immensely irritating, and suspect they have the opposite effect to that intended.

Further evidence of the vehicle owner's class, character and voting predisposition is that he has a fashionably cropped skull, rimless glasses and a sulky expression that makes him look like a myopic and irritable baby. He has obviously worked very hard on his expensively casual appearance, and is equally clearly a fan of *serge de Nîmes*. His denim bomber jacket is worn over a pre-faded working shirt with no collar, and on his feet is a pair of designer suede workboots that have clearly never seen an hour's work. He wears no ornaments except a thin wedding band and an even thinner watch. Altogether, he looks like a man trying hard to look like he is enjoying the egalitarian company and surroundings, but would much rather be in a wine bar in Fulham telling his friends how wonderful it is to be in rural France.

The woman sitting in my seat is an attractive thirtysomething, but her carefully composed features do not completely mask occasional flashes of the irritated and exasperated expression commonly worn by the sort of woman who is usually married to a man like her husband. She is dressed in similarly expensive and *faux* workaday clothing, and is doing her best to impress my fellow club members with her familiarity with their language and culture. As I pass the table, I realise she is talking about her admiration for the works of the great French writer and philosopher Albert Camus, and each time she mentions his name she stretches and emphasises the last syllable till she sounds like a cow in labour. This affectation is clearly lost on my friends, who will not know how their language should be spoken in intellectual foreign circles.

I nod a general greeting to the table, then move to the bar to discover if my evaluation of our visitors is correct. I introduce myself to the man and find out what it must be like to shake hands with a dead halibut. Our visitor tells me his name is John but without the 'h'. He is obviously concerned about this, so I console him for the loss, and as I take out my tobacco tin, he cringes away like a vampire catching sight of a freshly sharpened stake. I take the hint and move along the bar, but offer my tin to Madame Ghislaine so we can catch him in the crossfire.

Before too long, I realise that Jon and his wife are prime examples of that division of the chattering classes that likes to think of itself as *bien pensant*. Invariably, I have found that people who claim to be right-thinking do not think too much at all. While his wife – who he says is to be known as Franny – moves on to eulogise what she calls honest and earthy rural French cuisine, Jon explains that they have stopped off in our part of Normandy to look for a new home after selling their cottage in the better part of Provence. In recent years, he says, they have been horrified to see what he calls the colonisation of their region of France by Britons. As he laments the loss of the traditional way of life caused by this invasion of unsuitable and insensitive foreigners, I reflect that it will be pointless to remind him that he and his wife are also colonists and that they are probably suffering from the Not-in-My-Adopted-Country syndrome.

As with many country-dwellers in Britain who have got what they want and are now eager to pull up the drawbridge, the attitude seems to be flourishing in the circles of middle-class Britons who own property in France. They have found their favoured part of France and do not want to share it, especially with other Britons. The affliction also appears to have a terminal effect on the sufferer's ability to recognise irony, as immediately after saying how the dramatic increase in property values in rural France is preventing young local people from buying a first home, our visitor cannot resist telling me how much he and his wife made on the sale of their cottage just outside Avignon. He adds that they are hoping to find a modest *manoir* in our area, which they hear has not yet been flooded with British buyers and will still retain communities of real French country people for them to mix with.

I assure him that nowhere in Normandy – and possibly nowhere else in all France – will he meet people who are more real than in and around our village, and particularly so among the membership of the Jolly Boys Club of Néhou.

Afternoon has become evening, it has begun to rain, and our visitors have departed. They are on their way back to the ferry, and I do not think that they will be continuing their search for a second home in Lower Normandy. After Jon and I moved to the table, our club chairman insisted on introducing our visitors to Madame Ghislaine's best farm-brewed calvados, and the couple were also introduced to the bill for all our drinks when they left. This is one local tradition at least that they did not seem to appreciate. They were also visibly unimpressed by an offer from René Ribet to sell them a time-share in the barn attached to his cottage, despite his assurances that the cattle would be moved out before each of their yearly visits.

Our visitors gone, the weekly meeting is now in full session. At the head of the table is Old Pierrot, and at his side is the giant JayPay, who is our secretary, youngest member and local celebrity chef. Beside me sit our president, Jacques Délabré, and my special friend René Ribet.

When we arrived at La Puce, René was one of our first visitors and he soon became my mentor in the ways of living in and off the Norman countryside. Through him, I have learned much, and at little cost beyond money. In local circles, my friend is often treated with suspicion and known to the more respectable members of our community as the Fox of Cotentin; but as I have come to appreciate, who better to teach a newcomer about the lie of the land than a fox?

I learn that Patrick the Post and Michel le Scabeuse have sent their apologies. They are speaking at a symposium in Paris on the rare tropical diseases both claim to have contracted, despite never travelling further than Cherbourg in their lives. Our local general dealer and social events organiser Didier Bouvier is, according to a note he has sent, away on urgent business. His usual seat has been taken by a new member who is, even for our club, an unusual character.

Luc Voiron, like most of our older members, is of indeterminate and undeclared age. In our area, this means he could have witnessed anything from seventy to ninety summers. Also, like most of our members, he is not a slave to the concerns of fashion or image, and claims that too much attention to personal hygiene is an unhealthy and pointless preoccupation for a man of the countryside. Although this is not an unusual attitude among elderly men in our area, Luc is a special case, which explains why a seat nearest to the conveniently open door of the bar is always reserved for his visits. According to club records, which are purely oral, Luc lives alone in a near-derelict cottage on the marshes outside Carentan that would be condemned under the Public Health Act if anyone knew it was occupied.

What makes Luc particularly unusual is his claim to be a direct descendant of Nostradamus and to have inherited the sixteenth-century seer's gift of second sight. Although he is highly respected in our area, I have noted that virtually all of his most dramatic predictions have already taken place by the time he makes them. His claims to notable examples of second sight include the forecasting of the D-Day landings a year to the day after the invasion occurred, and naming the winner of the first Prix de l'Arc de Triomphe immediately the race was over. Strangely, his habit of making post-dated predictions has not diminished his status among our members and much weight is given to his pronouncements, especially when he is looking into the future to predict who is going to buy the next round of drinks.

As ever, the main and final item on today's agenda is progress with our continuing battle to plunder a significant grant from the relevant department of what used to be called the European Economic Community. Having learned of Italian farmers winning huge sums by inventing groves of olive trees, and Spanish farmers claiming subsidies for imaginary fields of rape, our club members are naturally anxious to ensure that rural France should not be outclassed in such creative thinking.

So far, we have made representations for a grant to turn the largest silage clamp in the area into a tourist attraction along the lines of the Millennium Dome, for all members of the club to give up gardening and therefore qualify for set-aside grants, and to make the local moustache-growing competition an official Olympic event and thus qualify for Euro-sponsorship. Today, we are discussing our latest application. At a recent meeting, I mentioned that farmers in Cornwall are now being paid to plant saplings rather than cereal crops in their fields, and there was an immediate motion that we should ask for parity with England on this issue. Although I pointed out that the Cotentin and its countless miles of *bocage* and vast forests is hardly in need of more trees, the funds committee persuaded me, as a local landowner, to draw up an initial letter of enquiry and send it off. Astonishingly, I have received a reply saying that my

request is being considered and a response will be forthcoming. This ends our weekly meeting on a high note, and
I am officially invited to buy a final extra round of drinks to
celebrate the good news.

Don't count your chickens before they are hatched.
Anon.

Counting Your Chickens

I came upon a colourful harbinger of spring this morning. A blanket of crocuses has appeared in the roadside copse. Individually, they are small, exquisitely formed and appear somehow tentative like guests at a dinner party who fear they have arrived too early for good manners. While others go about their business of preparing their land for the season of growth, I am sitting at the grotto trying to calculate how many gallons of water are cascading into the tree-ringed basin as our river makes its eternal way to the Douve and on to the open sea. I am also trying to devise a way to harness the power of this thundering torrent. For centuries, past owners of the Mill of the Flea made a good living from the natural power of running water, yet I still dread the arrival of electricity bills; sitting here, it seems a bad joke that we have to actually pay for what comes out of our taps.

I give up trying to estimate how many bathtubs of water are passing through the grotto every minute, and start my daily trip to the top of the track to wait for the arrival of Patrick the Post. I have met him there so often during the past week that I think he realises I am trying to avoid giving him breakfast, or he thinks I'm worried about catching one of the communicable diseases he claims to have picked up during his visit to Paris for the tropical diseases symposium.

Yesterday, he made a sarcastic and reproachful remark about lepers, and I noticed he was wearing a pair of cotton gloves when he handed me our mail.

But the real reason I am so anxious to get my hands on our post before it reaches the cottage is more prosaic. What our postman brings in his sack could be of vital importance to our future and have a direct influence on whether we shall be able to spend the rest of our lives at La Puce. The new book finished, I sent copies of the manuscript to four leading publishers at the end of last month. I know it is too soon to expect a reply, but still I wait each morning for Patrick's arrival.

It is more than thirty years since I sent my first submission to a publisher, and I have become an authority on rejection in all its literary forms. Sometimes a curt response will arrive within days, and sometimes it will be attached to the manuscript. For a writer with a script on offer, there is no more unwelcome arrival than a bulky package. Sometimes a standard letter will confirm that the script has arrived and that someone will be looking at it in the near future. Sometimes a personal letter will arrive promising that the sender will look at the manuscript in due course and let me know what he or she thinks. This response is both good and bad, as it will mean weeks or months of alternate bouts of unrealistic optimism and black pessimism until the bulky parcel appears, or does not.

But this time, I believe it could be our time. For millions of Britons the idea of living in France has never been more popular, and books on the subject which have been promoted by major publishers have sold more copies in a week than all mine have sold in a decade. The modestly published and promoted books about our small adventures in Lower Normandy sell well, but at a fraction of the rate they would if I were taken on and promoted by a top international publishing house.

This is why I have been waiting at the postbox at the top

of the track each morning. If the news from London is bad, I shall not tell Donella until I must; if it is good news, I want to watch my wife's face as I deliver it.

Patrick has made a sullen departure, and I am equally unhappy as one of the publishers has returned my manuscript, and another has sent a card saying that they do not publish fiction.

~

In our part of France, this is the time of year we call the rainy season. Some visitors to the Cotentin peninsula would claim that every season here is the rainy season, but this is unfair. With an average of twelve metres of rain every year, Mawsynram in north-east India is said to be the wettest place on earth, and this is one record that not even the most patriotic Cotentinese would wish to claim. In truth, it often rains here because we are on a peninsula and the warm air of the Gulf Stream runs by the western coast. This is why the grass is so green and lush, and we like to think we produce the finest dairy products in all France, if not all the world. Today, the deluge has eased to a mild downpour, and I am on the roof, conducting a fingertip search for entry points.

When we bought La Puce, one of our first concerns was to have a passably dry roof over our heads. After trying to find a local company that would re-roof the cottage for less than we had paid for the property itself, we considered doing the work ourselves. Then, one frosty January morning, an ancient moped came clattering down the track. The rider introduced himself as René Ribet, and said that he had been told we were in need of his expertise. He claimed that re-roofing old properties was his special *métier*, and that he could do the job much better and more quickly than any of the so-called professionals in the area. He would also charge a tenth of the best price we had been quoted. The conditions were that we would need to pay him in cash, not tell anyone he was doing the work for us, and the only materials we would need to supply would be two cases of beer a day for the duration of the job. As we were English, he would obviously bring his own lunch.

The deal was struck, I paid in advance, and when we returned from a week in England, I was delighted to find our new friend on the cottage roof cementing a clay figurine of a wounded pigeon on what remained of the original chimney. A moment later, he came sliding down the ladder, declared the project completed and said that the pigeon was traditionally placed on a finished roof to ensure that there would always be food in the house. It was his personal gift to our future at La Puce.

When I mentioned that the new *couverture* seemed to be identical to the old one even down to the patches of moss and surface cracks on the tiles, he smiled and said he was sorry that I had not appreciated the significance of what he had done, or the skill it had taken. Rather than destroy the character of the cottage by using new, mass-produced tiles or (even worse) imitation slates, he had actually (and at no extra charge) gone to the trouble of taking each eighteenth-century hand-crafted slab off, marking the underside with a number, then painstakingly replacing it on the brand-new structure of joists, lathes and other woodwork. The beauty of it all, he said, was that the roof was now as good as new yet looked as if it had not been touched since the original tiler had done the job almost three hundred years before.

I agreed with him that, apart from the wounded pigeon, the roof certainly looked exactly as it had before. Climbing in to the tiny attic, I also pointed out that all the ancient woodwork looked the same, even to the undisturbed cobwebs and dust. With an expression teachers reserve for particularly slow pupils, the Fox of Cotentin explained that, as with the outside, he had wanted it to look as if the roof had not been touched so had replaced all the old slats and lathes over the top of the new ones. Such was the care he had taken in replacing the old wood, he had even managed to keep the dust in place. If I was not satisfied, he would give me back my money and write the job off. I apologised for offending him, and it was not till it rained inside as well as outside the cottage next day that I had to admit to myself as well as to my wife that I had been had.

When I confronted René in the Bar Ghislaine, he admitted that he had done little more than fix the wounded pigeon on the roof, said he had needed the money to pay a pressing debt and had therefore been a desperate man. I was English and therefore rich, and a newcomer to his country and region. Experience always came at a cost, and I had now at least learned never to trust a fox. We looked at each other for a moment as I considered my options, then suggested he bought me a beer while we came to an arrangement. One drink led to another, and at the end of a long session, an amicable agreement was reached. René would fix the roof properly when the good weather came and make up for his trickery by becoming my consultant and agent in all future dealings with local craftsmen. As he pointed out, former poachers make the best gamekeepers.

That was twelve years ago. The roof still leaks, and the Fox is still waiting for the good weather. But in the way of country people, he often spends hours helping on the land for no reward other than a cold glass of beer and my friendship. He also nominated and seconded my admission to the Jolly Boys Club as the first overseas member and has taught me much about the way of life here, and about people everywhere. Despite our occasional differences, he is my oldest and firmest friend in the Cotentin. All things considered, I think I have mostly had the best of our many and sometimes irregular dealings.

The rain has stopped, so I lean against the crooked chimney stack, roll a cigarette and survey our little empire.

A harsh cry echoes across the water meadow as two rooks settle a disagreement high above Hunters' Walk, the avenue of lofty beech trees alongside the River Lude. Because of the rich pickings at La Puce, the waterside rookery is now as crowded as an inner-city tenement block, and family and neighbourly disputes are frequent. Watching the squabbling pair is our new grey heron, who sits on a branch of the Hobbit Tree patiently waiting for the coast to be clear for his mid-morning visit to the big pond. He is a much bolder bird, and I turn a blind eye to his fishing trips as long as he rations himself to no more than a dozen fish a day. I don't suppose that he maintains his side of our agreement, but even a Norman heron would have a job to keep up with the birth rate in the fertile waters of the big pond.

The trout we originally dug the big pond to contain have long since been poached by the fishermen who think they have right of access to every drop of private water in their area, but even they will not catch and eat goldfish.

Apart from the heron and each other, the only other mortal danger threatening the fish comes from our feisty female duck, Hen, and her companion, Ermintrude the goose. As with many members of our sometimes dysfunctional extended family, Ermintrude is not as other geese. Our balletic and good-natured goose is what the Chinese call a gift from the gods, and was waiting to greet us when we arrived at La Puce after a long absence. We do not know where she came from and did not make too many attempts to find out. After some fruitless attempts to find her a mate, she settled down to become a contented companion to Hen, and is obviously happy to think that she is a duck rather than a Loire goose.

As I survey the bucolic scene, my wife comes out of the caravan to give Hen and Ermintrude their mid-morning snack of maize niblets. The two friends squawk and honk in anticipation, slide off the islet in the middle of the pond and swim swiftly across to the bank. They clamber out and waddle up to the bench where my wife is sitting, then Hen flaps up and on to Donella's lap. Alerted by the noise, Fred the cockerel and his live-in lover, Gert, emerge from their hut alongside the grotto and take the path towards the pond. A moment later, Barney the bantam and his mate, Big Daisy, emerge from their luxury accommodation in the mill garden and set off in pursuit. Now Milly appears from inside the cottage and joins the race to get the best seats for a second breakfast, and I see the bulrushes by the middle pond shudder as Cato emerges from a covert hunting operation. From my position, I have a pigeon's eye view as the cavalcade arrives and clusters round my wife. She seems to sense that someone is watching, and turns to look up at where I sit. I wave, and she responds. Even at this distance, I can see that her face is radiant with delight. Her husband is safely out of the way and at a distance, but within sight and getting up to no mischief, and she is tending to her brood. Not every woman would envy the life she leads here at La Puce, but I think all would envy her deep contentment at this moment.

~

The sound of a labouring engine distracts me from my pleasant reverie, and I turn to see a most interesting vehicle lumbering down the track. The ancient Renault delivery van has seen better days, but contained within and lashed to a low railing on the roof is a teetering stack of wooden cages, and in them is a selection of hugely plump, glossily feathered and somehow haughty-looking chickens. From the sides of the van hang a miscellany of closed crates, buckets and feed bins, and as it clanks to a halt in the turning circle I see that a bicycle that must predate the van is strapped to the back. The last time I saw anything like this was when thumbing a lift from a bus in a rural province of India, but as the door creaks open and a sprightly figure emerges, I realise that we are to be honoured with a visit from the legendary Chicken Georges.

I climb down from the roof to greet the founder and chairman of the Cotentin Chicken Fanciers Association, and reflect that what is said about people growing to look like their pets certainly has some substance in Georges Culin's case. He is short and wiry, and as he approaches me he puffs his chest out, holds his shoulders back and sticks his head out in an almost pugnacious fashion. His rolling gait is jerky, and he lifts his feet unusually high as if he were hesitantly picking his way through a field of high grass or delicate crops. When he comes closer, I see that his sallow skin bears the pockmark reminders of youthful acne and that his prominent, beak-like nose is bright red, though I think this might be more to do with his well-known affection for home-brew calvados than his lifelong association with chickens. The small and bright eyes are sharp and beady, and the overall similarity to an old but still sparky bantam is enhanced by the loose skin around his chin and neck, which age and gravity have helped form into an almost perfect simulation of wattles.

Although he is a familiar figure around the local marketplaces, this is the first time I have met Chicken Georges formally, as he is known to prefer the company of chickens to people. I know he lives on a smallholding at the end of a long track on the outskirts of St Jacques, but I have never met anyone who has been invited into his home. His land is said to be surrounded by a high and impregnable wire fence made from the leftovers of German beach defences against the D-Day landings, and his cottage is said to resemble a giant chicken coop. Some village wags even claim that he has no bed and spends his nights dozing on a broomstick fixed to the cottage walls. Georges emerges from his giant chicken run only to buy feed, chair the weekly meetings of his club at the *salle des fêtes* in Bricquebec, attend shows and sell his eggs at market. He deals in neither live nor dead chickens because, it is said, he cannot bear the thought of anyone eating his friends or of sending them to a possibly bad home. He is a devout vegetarian, and as he has never been seen in a grocery shop or supermarket, it is thought he lives solely on what he feeds his pets.

As I invite him into the cottage, there is an excited clucking and squawking and Fred, Barney, Gert and Daisy come fluttering through the gate to the water meadow and crowd around Georges like fans mobbing a pop star. He bends and gently strokes each of our birds, then issues a series of clucks and throaty squawks as he reaches into his pocket and produces a handful of grain. Whatever he says has an immediate effect, and our normally belligerent chickens stand quietly as he feeds and then examines them like a fussy judge at a dog show. As he ruffles then smoothes their feathers, turns their heads from side to side and gauges their posture and stance, he grunts and nods approvingly, and I notice he pays particular and lingering attention to Big Daisy, our monster hen and undisputed ruler of the roost. Daisy was a gift from a retired English geneticist who lives in a nearby village and spends his days experimenting with the possibilities of dramatically improving the size and yield of farm animals by selective cross-breeding. For the past decade he has specialised in chickens, and Big Daisy is almost twice the size of an average hen, and sometimes lays three eggs a day. She also makes twice the mess of an average hen, and one can see why the manic breeder's wife and neighbours dread the day when he moves on to experiment with cows.

Having finished his examination, Chicken Georges explains that he has a proposition to make to us. Donella and Milly join us as we enter the porch, and I am astonished to see that our chickens follow us. Although I have never been keen on the idea of allowing farmyard animals into the house, I know that Donella has been secretly and unsuccessfully encouraging them for years. Now, they calmly strut into our living room and gather round the chair in which Georges sits. I put the kettle on the wood-burning stove and quietly drape a tea cloth over the meal we were intending to have for dinner. When one has visitors in our area, it is customary to ask them to share your meal, but although it is a very popular dish throughout France, I do not think Chicken Georges will be interested in sharing our classic *poule au pot*.

Our chickens are back in their own homes, and Georges has returned to his. We dined on bread and cheese out of deference to our guest's presence – the chicken stew will keep till tomorrow. It has been an interesting afternoon, and Donella is flattered to have received a visit from such a renowned fancier. She is even more flattered by the reason for his visit, which was to suggest that we might like to take part in one of the most popular and prestigious events in the region.

When we came to live in the Cotentin, I thought that I might become bored with the lack of social activities in the winter. I knew that the region was in apparently permanent *fête* during the summer months and that I would find it hard to keep up with the demanding roster of celebrations at every town, village and hamlet. What I had not realised was that virtually every date in the Cotentin calendar has some special significance, and thus is an excuse for a celebration of some aspect of country and coastal living. Throughout every year there are milk fairs, cheese conventions, flower shows, oyster and fish convocations and even a whole weekend spent celebrating the carrot and its contribution to the local economy and spiritual wellbeing of the area. I sometimes suspect that there is a regional conspiracy to finally arrive at the no-day working week.

As Georges reminded us, the major events of next month will include Cotentin Chicken Week. During those seven days, the region will enjoy marking the worth of the chicken and its place in our history, daily lives and especially on our tables. Few rural households do not have at least a pair of hens scratching around the yard, and many people in our area pay almost the same level of regard to the chicken as the Huron Indians accord the salmon. That ancient nation so appreciates the fish's contribution to their lives that they pay lavish honour to their main source of protein before cooking and eating it. In the Cotentin, we do not erect totem poles or hold services dedicated to the domesticated fowl, but there will be chicken-themed functions in village halls across the region; schools will hold chicken painting and story competitions; parades will be led by men and women dressed as roosters and hens; and many shops will devote window space to a special fowl-flavoured display. Above all, the legend of the Cotentin Black will be told and retold.

Every region of any country likes to have its own claim to a superior and singular animal or dish. Yorkshire has its puddings, Bakewell its tarts, and Hampshire its hogs. In northern France, Calvados has its eponymous apple brandy and its racehorses, Alsace its *choucroute* and guard dogs. In the Cotentin area of Lower Normandy, we have our weather, apples and their by-products, our history and our dairy produce – and the giant and conveniently extinct superchicken with legendary laying powers.

Although I have never seen or heard of any solid evidence, the Cotentin Black was allegedly once common in our area. Like the central characters in all legends, its feats, capacities and adventures have grown with the telling, and some stories claim that the Best in Breed at the Barfleur Chicken Show of 1066 actually sailed with William the Conqueror to England and inspired him to win the Battle of Hastings. I have seen photographs of the Bayeux Tapestry that are said to show the great Cotentin Black accompanying William into battle, but to me it looks more like a badly embroidered charger with its hind legs hidden behind a provisions cart.

Regardless, the Cotentin Black is the model to which all breeders aspire, and Georges Culin believes that Big Daisy is a natural candidate for the competition at Cherbourg. He had heard rumours about our giant hen and so decided to visit us and see for himself if they were true. Although he is officially a resident of our rival village of St Jacques de Néhou and will be entering his own birds in all classes, he is above petty concerns of rivalry when it comes to chickens. He will not be popular with the fanciers in his own village, especially as it is a St Jacques bird who has held the title of Best in Show for the past four years; but having seen Daisy with his own eyes, it would, in his opinion, be no less than a crime for her to be left out.

Though she is not in favour of any form of competition that might traumatise the losing entrants, Donella agrees with Georges that Daisy should be shown. Not only is the offer an honour to Daisy, it is a sign that we have become accepted in the community and that local people now recognise and accept that, despite our nationality and background, we know how to raise chickens. It will also show that her methods of treating animals like humans is not an eccentric folly. Although I see the logic of her argument, I am in two minds about the wisdom of showing Big Daisy.

On the one hand, if we enter Daisy in the show and she wins, Donella, the Jolly Boys Club and the whole of Néhou will be delighted. If we enter her and she does not win, I will feel I have let our community down, and our rivals on the other side of the crossroads will really have something to crow about.

~

We are going out on the town, and have much to celebrate. Tonight, we will be hosting a small *soirée* at the Flaming Curtains, and tomorrow I shall be visiting the Jolly Boys Club to tell them our good news. After much deliberation, I have agreed that Daisy should be entered in the Chicken Show. Much more importantly, our money troubles could soon be over.

This morning our postman finally delivered the news we have been waiting for, and we now have two major publishing houses interested in my work. The first letter came from the managing director of a company that specialises in publishing unusual travel books. He says that he had picked up the package containing my sample chapters from an editor's desk and taken them to look at while he was in the lavatory. He was, he adds, put in a spin by what he read, and compliments me on my unique style. It was, he thinks, inspirational of me to deliberately ignore the usual rules of punctuation and grammar and come up with a completely fresh and almost abstract approach to writing about a foreign culture. He is so impressed that he is considering departing from the company's normal style and presentation of travel books and setting up a division to publish what he calls offbeat work like mine. In closing, he asks me to send him the balance of the manuscript, which he will have copied and circulated to all his editors and fellow directors. If I will wait no more than a month, he believes he will be able to send me some good news.

The other letter, with a London postmark, came from a senior director of one of the largest book publishing companies in the world. He said that, of the more than four hundred unsolicited submissions his editors had been sent last month, mine was one of six that had reached his desk as having significant potential. Having read my sample, he found himself much taken with it as the stories brought back fond memories of his holidays in Lower Normandy. He would like to see the remaining chapters as soon as possible and suggests that I might call in to see him if I find myself in London in the next few weeks.

Having become to my knowledge the first local man to kiss his postman full on the lips, I raced down the track to tell Donella the news. I agreed with her that we must not count our chickens before even the eggs have been laid, but have insisted that we go out this evening to celebrate the fact that our ship has at last, if not come in, been set on an apparent course for harbour. While we danced around the sofa, I reflected that fate and coincidence can play strange games with an individual's future. It may well be that I am to become an internationally known and bestselling author just because one man chose to take his holidays in a particular area of northern France, and because another suffers from severe constipation.

~

We have arrived at the Flaming Curtains to celebrate the day's news. This afternoon, I wrote to the managing director of the travel book company to say I would send him the rest of my manuscript and promise I would not finally accept any offers (however significant) from other publishers before he made his. To the director of the other company, I said that we had already received considerable interest in my latest book from other leading publishers, but I would ask my secretary to put the balance of chapters in the post. I also said that I had to be in the Cotentin for Chicken Week, but would be visiting London shortly to appear and sign copies of my past works at a French property exhibition. My secretary would call in the next few days and arrange a suitable appointment.

Donella is worried that I may be appearing too offhand with such important people, but I told her that one thing I do know about is how to negotiate with a potential customer. If I seem too anxious to do business with them, they may suspect that I am not really confident in my book, which could devalue their judgement of its worth and how much they are prepared to invest in making it a big success. If I can make them believe they must be the ones to publish my work, they will then have to spend enough money to ensure that their decision is seen to be the right one. In any business, the ultimate level of success of a product depends as much on how well and extensively it is marketed as on how good it is. We, and many of our readers, agree that my books are at least as good as others in the same genre that have sold in their millions. As ours have not, the only reason can be that they have never been widely promoted. All I have to do now is persuade one of the publishers to spend a small fortune on bringing my work to a worldwide audience of readers and we will become rich and famous. My wife will have the security of knowing that we can spend the rest of our lives at La Puce without a single financial worry, and I will feel that my writing ability has finally been acknowledged.

Even for a weekday evening in February, the bar is surprisingly quiet, and I see that none of our friends has arrived to help us celebrate our good news. This is especially disappointing, as I spent an hour this afternoon phoning round with invitations to join us. The prospect of a free drink would normally have even our French friends turning up on time, but tonight the Flaming Curtains is devoid of all but the die-hard regulars.

At the bar, I find Coco absent-mindedly picking his teeth with a screwdriver as he works on the clutch from his ancient Land Rover. Determined that we at least will mark the occasion, I order the best champagne in the house. I start to tell him about the letters from the London publishing houses, but he says he has already heard the news from Patrick the Post, then goes back to his tinkering. When I ask again about the champagne, he shrugs and says they've run out. He does, though, have some bottles of *cidre bouché* that is at least as good as the fizzy and overrated wine from Champagne. It is also much less expensive and thus suitable for a poor author like me. Hurt at his lack of enthusiasm, I remind him that a bestselling book that features his bar so strongly would bring visitors from all over the world flocking to his doors. Without looking up, he shrugs and sucks his teeth loudly in a very French way, then remarks that the town is already the birthplace of one of France's most famous authors, but it has never brought the pub named after one of his works much in the way of tourist trade.

As he picks up the clutch assembly and takes it to his workbench in the kitchen, I suggest we go elsewhere, but Donella points out that it is after eight o'clock so the other three bars in town will be closed. Then, just as I am about to leave in a sulk, a klaxon sounds from the kitchen and at least twenty people burst into the bar. They are all wearing masks, shouting wildly and banging on an assortment of pots and pans. One of them is holding a large chamber pot, and when the lead figure rips off his mask, I see it is René Ribet. As my other Norman and British friends unmask themselves and crowd round, René slaps me on the back and thrusts the chamber pot in my direction. I look inside and see that it is filled with cider, and that a peeled and brown-stained banana is lying on the bottom. The crowd begins to chant and I realise that they are recreating the traditional ceremony once visited on newly-weds in our area. According to local lore, the rites involved the villagers breaking into the couple's house on their wedding night, rushing into the bedroom and forcing the groom to drink the contents of a chamber pot that all the visitors had helped fill. To the certain relief of young couples throughout the area, the traditional ceremony is no longer practised. It is said to have fallen out of favour in our town many years ago when the crowd broke into the wrong house and found the mayor in bed with the event organiser's wife.

I have emptied the chamber pot and eaten the banana, and we are crammed into a corner seat surrounded by an eclectic mix of locals and British settlers. Coco and René have competed to make the most moving speech of congratulations on our good news, while the Fox is now warming up for his Whirling Dervish act, which he says he intends to perform while balancing the chamber pot on his head. As he has filled the pot with contributions from all the male members of our group, I assume he will be taking much more care than usual. By the fireplace, Madame Chantal is on duty at the cauldron, distributing portions of what she says is an English curry that has been made in my honour. We are being entertained this evening by a Norman-Irish fiddle band that has come all the way from Cherbourg. Their presentation of 'Over the Hills and Far Away' in French with an attempted Irish accent makes for fascinating listening.

I start on my curried mussels and wave my spoon in encouragement at Jean-Claude, who I can see clearly in the crowd as he is wearing his professional suit of lights. The apprentice *gigolo* is making conversation at the bar with a lady of advanced years and a very severe expression. She is at least six inches taller than him, but he is standing on the bottom rungs of a bar stool to make up the difference, and they are at least seeing eye to eye from a physical viewpoint. Earlier, he told me that she is English, a widow who has come to the Cotentin to start a new life and his first official customer. They made contact through the Lonely Hearts section of the *Manche Libre*, and he says that, despite her sour expression, he thinks she has fallen for him. She speaks reasonable French and has already described him as *joli-laid*. In France, this is a way of describing someone who, like the rumpled and outrageous seventies celebrity Serge Gainsbourg, is somehow physically attractive although defi- nitely not in the conventional way. Although Jean-Claude is pleased with what he sees as a compliment, I think his com- panion may have been using the term in its literal English translation and meaning of 'pretty ugly'.

Elsewhere, our doleful folk singer André Déprimé is sitting on the corner of the stage and looking even more depressed than usual, as Coco has hidden his guitar and banned him from casting a gloom on the evening. Donella is looking a little preoccupied as she is worried that we are tempting fate by celebrating our success at this early stage, but I am awash with the certainty that we are close to a final breakthrough.

Also with us at our table are two new friends with their own reasons to celebrate a big event in their lives. Tony and Louise bought a dilapidated cottage in St Jacques last year and contacted us soon after starting restoration work to ask if I would, together with their mayor, perform at a small ceremony to mark the installation of their septic tank and bathroom. Apart from a small problem when the contractor dug the hole for the tank in the garden next door, all went smoothly in the first stages of their project, and the opening ceremony was a great success. Having invited the whole village to the *soirée*, Tony had brewed several dustbins of home-made beer, and Louise had made a finger buffet, though there was some confusion when she tried to translate the term literally on the invitation cards. At midnight, the mayor had made a short address from the top of the new staircase, then he and I simultaneously cut the ribbon across the bath-room door and, standing shoulder to shoulder, christened the toilet basin to enthusiastic applause. Tony and Louise are clearly the sort of people who know how to adapt to their new surroundings and cultural attitudes, and are so happy with their new home and village that they are moving over here to live. As they tell me, the big decision came when Tony was unexpectedly made redundant from his work as a salesman for a shop-fitting company and what would normally be a minor tragedy for a young family became the spur to take the big step across the Channel. They have sold their home in England, booked their children into the local school, and will have enough money to tide them over till they find a way of making a living by working from home. Tony is a keen gardener and intends offering his services to other British home owners in the area. Louise is to continue her part-time job as an Avon lady, only this time calling on homes and housewives in the Cotentin instead of Essex.

While there are now more British expatriates in our area offering house-sitting facilities than there are second-home owners, I think the couple will succeed in their aim to live here whatever they have to do. Often, I have observed, it is those with the character to burn their boats and take the plunge without a safety harness who make the most successful settlers. As Tony says, if all else fails, he can always try selling his body in the red-light district of Cherbourg. If he charges by the kilo, he adds thoughtfully, he should do much better than the average rent-boy.

Sitting next to the young couple is another new settler with a poignant story to tell. Gavin was a successful businessman in England whose world collapsed six months ago when he was diagnosed as having terminal cancer. A single man, he was determined to put his affairs in order, enjoy what time was left to him, and do what good he could for his friends and relatives. After giving his share of his business to his partner and selling his home in Kent, he put large sums of money in to a trust for his nephew and niece, gave his car to a neighbour and then moved over to live quietly at his holiday home in St Sauveur until the end came. Two months ago, a specialist at Cherbourg Hospital told him that, in non-scientific terms, a near-miracle had occurred, and the cancerous cells invading his body had gone into retreat. Last week, he was told that he is apparently free of the malignancy and, all being well, could expect a normal lifespan. Now, Gavin does not know whether to be delighted that he has been reprieved or desolate that he has given virtually all his worldly possessions away. He has received much encouragement in the community, and the philosophic Coco often reminds him that it was probably the stress and strains of his old life that gave him the disease and his new life in the tranquil hinterland of the Cotentin that cured it. As Coco also often reminds his customers, sometimes it is better to follow your heart than make plans for a future that may not take place.

The party is over and we are back at La Puce, having a very late nightcap by the big pond. Before we left the Flaming Curtains, Coco took me to one side, gave me a bear-hug and said he was so pleased that at last it seemed I was going to get the recognition I deserve. As a fellow artist, he believed that struggle was good for the creative process but that there was no reward, as Van Gogh would agree, in becoming fashionable and acclaimed after one is dead. He is not able to read my books, but he knows from the occasional English visitor who has translated passages for him that I write with affection and heart about this part of France and all my friends here. Some of my stories may not be true to the letter, but they are always true to life. Anyone who has been to school can write, he added, but that does not mean they have anything to say.

Except for the odd grunt, snuffle or squeak from the creatures of the night, all is quiet as we sit in companionable silence. Above us, the vast Norman sky is cloudless and the full moon dances on the dark surface of the water as a sudden buffet of wind explores the water meadow. My wife shivers and I put an arm round her shoulder. It has been a long and sometimes rocky road from our early days together in England to where fate and circumstance have brought us. Apart from the obvious material rewards that success in my chosen career would bring, I honestly believe that all I have ever wanted is to make my wife and children proud of me. If all goes well on my trip to London next month, I shall at last feel I have fulfilled my main purpose in life.

La vérité existe; on n'invente que le mensonge.
(Truth exists; only lies are invented.)
Georges Braque, French painter (1882–1963)

A Fox Among the Chickens

La Puce is emerging from its winter torpor, and tomorrow sees the culmination of Chicken Week with the grand show and competition at Cherbourg, after which I will be crossing the Channel to attend another French property exhibition in London and visit our prospective publisher.

Now that we are committed to entering Big Daisy in the show, Donella has been spending long hours at the henhouse. Apart from the daily grooming and feeding with a special high-protein diet, there are the deportment lessons so that Daisy will impress the judges with her poise and carriage. I have tried to help by teaching Daisy to obey some simple commands, but for all my efforts she seems to lack the temperament to sit or stand to my signals.

After her morning sessions with Daisy, Donella has also been trying to groom me for my encounter with the director of the publishing company in London. Comparing the relative effort and results, my wife says she finds preparing me to make a good impression much more difficult than working with Daisy, who at least has some sense of style and sophistication.

Mid-afternoon, and I have arrived at the Bar Ghislaine to report on progress with Daisy's special grooming and diet regime.

The atmosphere is unusually subdued, and I can see that my fellow members are deeply worried about how well our entrant will fare at the Chicken Show. Patrick Megère has zoomed over from St Jacques and the bar that is the head-quarters of that village's poor imitation of our club, and to his obvious delight, he brings worrying news. Although he is an honorary member of the Jolly Boys Club of Néhou because of his status as a postman and therefore the most informed purveyor of all scandal in the area, Patrick lives in St Jacques, and some of our members believe he is working as a double agent. They suspect that he has been passing information about Donella's progress with Big Daisy on to the St Jacques Fanciers Association, and he certainly seems to relish telling us just how formidable an opponent their bird will be.

According to him, the giant Rhode Island Red has been living in a secret location for the past month, and is receiving regular visits from all manner of expensive specialists. Apart from her secret diet, La Grande Rouge has been enjoying regular pedicures and massages, a mobile hair-dresser has been giving her a shampoo and blow-dry each week, and a top personal trainer from Paris is said to have been advising on exercise routines to increase the girth and tone of her drumsticks. Our postman concludes his report by saying that the turf accountant at Octeville has opened a book on entrants, and the St Jacques bird is the runaway odds-on favourite. Patrick adds that Big Daisy is seen as such an outsider that the bookie is offering ten-to-one against our champion even being placed in the event, and a staggering fifty-to-one against her winning the title outright.

His news is greeted with a deep silence, and I am so depressed that I refuse to stay for a drink. The meeting breaks up, and I am followed out of the bar by Jacques Délabré and René Ribet. As he dons his cycle clips, I ask Jacques if he thinks it too late for us to scratch Daisy from the competition. Better, I say, for us to claim that she has pulled a hamstring or is for some other reason not up to competing in the event than for her to almost certainly lose against La Grande Rouge and our club and village be subject to ridicule from St Jacques for months to come.

Our resident philosopher looks at me thoughtfully, then claps me on the shoulder and tells me not to worry. He is sure that all will turn out well whoever wins the competition, and reminds me of the truth of the Cartesian axiom that the only two certainties in life are death and taxes.

I shake hands with my friends and say it is a pity we cannot organise putting a fox among the chickens at the secret St Jacques training camp. They laugh, and as I drive away I see Jacques take off his cycle clips, put his arm round René's shoulder, and escort him back into the Bar Ghislaine.

~

Disaster has struck, Donella is inconsolable, and it is all my fault.

When we arrived at the hen-house this morning, the door was swinging open and Daisy was gone. Her mate, Barney, was sulking in the hazel tree above their coop, and Cato was sitting on the bench by the grotto looking pleased with herself. There were no loose feathers or other clues at the scene, and no damage to the door or padlock we had fitted as a security precaution when we decided to enter Big Daisy in the competition. It was hanging open from the hasp, and as I saw the chickens to their beds last night the only conclusion is that I must have left it unlocked. Our other two birds were safely in their coop, so it looks as if Daisy must have pushed the door open and gone wandering off into the night. Or perhaps, I suggest to Donella, that is what we are *supposed* to think. When we bought our hens and installed them in their luxury quarters last year, they immediately formed an escape committee and were extraordinary in their resourcefulness, but since they paired up with the two cockerels, our hens have shown no sign of wanting to wander from their luxury apartments.

It seems to me that Big Daisy has been abducted, and I don't think we need to look too far beyond the crossroads at the end of our land to find the culprits.

We have arrived at Cherbourg, but without the Néhou challenger for the Best in Show Cup. We have brought Gert and the two cocks in a cage on top of our car to take their minds off the tragedy, but still have no clues as to the likely whereabouts or fate of Big Daisy.

After spending a frantic hour searching every corner of La Puce, I raced to the Bar Ghislaine, but none of my friends were there. Ghislaine said that they would all be getting ready to put in an appearance at the show, and added that I should at least make an effort to dress for the occasion. Even René Ribet was aware of the need to look smart for the big day, and she had seen him going into the unisex hairdressers at St Sauveur yesterday afternoon.

Driving out to his home on the marshlands, I told our president the bad news and suggested that we mount a raiding party on St Jacques. He gave me a calming glass of calvados and said this would be a pointless exercise. We did not know for certain that their chicken-fancying clique had taken Daisy, or that anyone had. He said he was sure that she would turn up eventually and suggested I go home and collect Donella and take her to the competition. It was too late now to scratch our entrant, but it was important that our club shows a united front and be seen to be seen at this important occasion.

~

The annual All Cotentin Chicken Show is held in a disused warehouse on the quayside and, like all such major events, has attracted huge crowds.

It is a fine and unseasonably warm day, with only a moderate sea breeze blowing from the harbour, and there is an air of carnival about this normally deserted part of the docks. All regular markets in the area have been cancelled, and the traders have set up their stalls outside the main entrance. Many local businesses will close so their owners can attend, and few farmers in the area will do any work today. The town fire brigade band is adding to the festive air, and the temporary beer and cider stands are trading briskly. A man with a megaphone is standing on a crate and keeping the crowd informed on what is happening inside, and the bookmaker from Octeville has set up beside the men's toilet block in what, considering the amount of beer, cider and wine that will be taken this day, must be a prime position.

Through the crowd, I recognise the unusually sleek head of René Ribet. He is talking animatedly with Mr Parier the bookie or, as he likes to style himself on his board, 'The Friend of the Speculator'. In case René has not heard about the disappearance of Daisy, I shout to warn him not to place a bet. Knowing Mr Parier, I suspect that if he knows Daisy will not be appearing he will continue to take bets on her and then make some excuse for not giving the punters back their stake. René hears my call, turns and sees me waving, then thrusts a packet at the bookmaker and disappears into the crowd. I am ready to set off in pursuit when the man with the megaphone announces that the *grande finale* of the day is about to take place, and we are swept along with the crowd as it surges through the main entrance and into the show ring.

Inside, the atmosphere is electric, and I have to push my way through the crush to get us anywhere near the judging podium. Nobody seems to object, and I even get some admiring glances for my elbow technique. In my experience, when it comes to working their way through a crowd the

French are beaten only by the southern Italians, and they are the undisputed champions of Europe.

Straining to see above the heads of the taller people in the crowd and those who are standing on chairs, I see that the stage is set and the white-coated judges are about to make their final selections for the individual awards for different breeds. I ask Donella if she would like me to find a chair for her, but she says she cannot bear to see the competition won by another bird and will just listen to the commentary.

While the master of ceremonies sets up and tests his microphone, the judges walk along the ranks of cages, stopping now and then to deliberate and occasionally ask the owner to take his bird out for a closer inspection. Then, clearly playing to the audience, the judges make a great show of examining the bird minutely, and I see that each has a different technique as they prod and fondle and stroke. One of the older men makes a great performance of producing a tape and measuring the wattles of a fine-looking mottled hen, and not to be upstaged, another pries open the beak of his bird and shines a pencil torch inside as if he were at a horse show and inspecting the entrant's teeth.

Having walked the length of the cages, the three judges return to their table and go into a huddle with much elaborate arm-waving. After a satisfactory delay to build the suspense, each then takes a handful of rosettes and returns to the line of cages. Once again, every opportunity is taken to heighten the drama; rather than going straight to the winning owners they often walk past, then pantomime an agonising bout of deep thought before whirling round and slapping the rosette on the cage. Most of the owners are every bit as theatrical and some react like winners in a beauty pageant. It is quite bizarre to see sturdy countrymen clutching their breasts and putting their hands to their mouths in mock surprise and exultation; one giant with a badly broken nose and livid scar down the side of his face breaks down in tears, then appears to faint and has to be helped off the stage by three officials.

The preliminary dramas over, the stage is now set for the Best in Show judging and awards. As our compere tells us while all the cages are cleared away, each of the winners of Best in Breed will now be paraded for the judges' inspection and marking. Then last year's supreme champion, La Grande Rouge (who has of course not had to go through the elimination process), will take to the stage. There will also be a special wild-card entry, nominated by the show's organiser and president, Mr Georges Culin.

Except for the occasional cry of a baby and shout of support for a favourite, the crowd grows respectfully silent as the lights are dimmed and mood-building music issues from the loudspeakers. The compere clears his throat, takes a drink from the glass of cider on his table, lights another cigarette, then announces the first contender for the super-chicken of the year award.

The first bird is carried on to the stage and into the spotlight by its trainer. The man lowers the chicken almost reverently on to the floor, attempts to get it to stand in a striking pose, then retires as the judges approach. While the compere is telling us the name, breed, vital statistics, family tree and favourite leisure pastimes of the entrant, the members of the judging panel circle the bird, discuss its finer points, then make notes on their clipboards before returning to their table and handing their voting forms to the invigilator. He does a swift calculation, then takes a folded piece of paper to the compere, who opens it and reads out the score. This process continues until all this year's potential Best in Breeds have been assessed, judged and scored. The winner at this stage is a large and striking speckled hen entered by the Bricquebec Fancy, but everyone knows that the real star has yet to appear.

The house lights come on and are then dimmed again, and an expectant murmur runs through the crowd. Like the master of ceremonies at a world championship title boxing match, the compere now begins his build-up. As he reaches a crescendo of superlatives and shouts out the name of the reigning champion, the signature music for the St Jacques superbird thunders out and La Grande Rouge is led on to the stage.

Though I am naturally prejudiced against her, I have to admit that it is easy to see why this bird has swept the board of prizes in every competition she has entered in recent years. She is a head taller than any of the other contestants, her coat shines in the spotlight like burnished copper, and her plumage is magnificent. An old hand at these occasions, La Grande Rouge obviously loves the limelight and struts around the stage with head held high before adopting a heroic pose and staring at the judges with glittering eyes and a haughty demeanour as if daring them not to acclaim her superiority. They make hardly a pretext of examining her, and after a quick scrutiny of the voting forms, the compere announces that once again the St Jacques bird has scored a perfect ten.

It looks, says the compere, as if it is all over, but there is still the wild-card bird to be seen. Almost casually, he says that the mystery bird is known as St Georges le Noir, has been entered by the Jolly Boys Club of Néhou and replaces the bird that was withdrawn at the last minute. A wag in the crowd of St Jacques supporters shouts out that, coming from Néhou, the missing bird was probably stolen and is already in the pot, at which the crowd responds with laughter and hoots of derision. As the noise subsides, the compere asks that the bird be brought on, and then, as I strain to see our entry, all the lights go out.

As the compere calls for a technician to check the fuse box, a single spotlight high above the stage snaps on and a hush falls over the crowd. I stand on tiptoes, and through the bobbing heads get a glimpse of a large hen standing quietly in the circle of light. She is not as big or impressive as the current champion, but she is unlike any other chicken

I have seen, as her glossy coat is coal black without a single blemish.

For a long moment, there is a stunned silence, then someone, somewhere in the crowd speaks two words. They are 'Cotentin Noir'. There is a mutual gasp, then the crowd begins to chant the words and surges towards the stage like fans at a pop concert. Just as it seems there is a danger to public safety, the spotlight snaps off and we are in total darkness. When the lights come on again, the bird has disappeared.

Pandemonium breaks out, and a team of stewards have to be called in to restore order. Visibly shaken, the judges take only a moment to confer and come to their mutual verdict. As the crowd roars its approval, the title of Best in Show is unanimously awarded to the Néhou champion, the so aptly named (as the compere acknowledges) St Georges le Noir and the first genuine Cotentin Black to be seen in living memory.

~

We have gathered at a bar outside the arena to celebrate our historic victory. The cup stands on the counter, and it is good to see the name of our village engraved on its base.

Most of the spectators have sped away to spread the dramatic story of how the legendary Cotentin Black appeared out of nowhere to steal the show, and the members of the St Jacques Fancy and their supporters have slunk off to lick their wounds. We know that their president put in an official protest immediately after the awards ceremony, but he was unanimously overruled by the organising committee. Regardless of any irregularities, it is clearly in their interest that the title and winner stand. There will be enormous publicity value and prestige for an event won by a breed that was presumed extinct, and secretly believed by most people to be a total invention.

Donella is obviously pleased that our village has won

the title and glory, but also concerned that we return to La Puce and continue our search for Daisy. I agree to leave the celebrations and drive straight home.

As we reach our car, I hear Gert clucking animatedly, then realise she is having a conversation. As we draw nearer, we are astonished to see that our missing chicken is in the travelling cage with our other birds. A quick inspection shows that Big Daisy is well, and as her feathers are sleekly damp and shining, it even looks as if she is freshly groomed.

We return to tell our friends the good news and that, now Daisy is safely back with us, we are free to stay.

~

It is late, and we are about to set out on the journey back to La Puce. Gert and Daisy have joined us on a moonlight stroll along the quayside and are obviously enjoying their night out. As a sharp wind has blown up, they will travel home in style inside the car with the champion's cup beside them on the seat.

It has been a special day for us all, and we have even had a pleasant windfall. Before leaving, René Ribet shook my hand and handed me a grubby envelope. He said that he had got spectacularly good odds from Mr Parier on the Néhou bird, and had put a few euros on for me. It would make up for the worry Donella must have suffered during Daisy's temporary absence, and the money would also go a long way towards paying for our leaky roof to be properly fixed. He would, he said, be willing to take on the job himself for the right price.

I shook his hand again to confirm the arrangement, and he smiled his foxy smile and winked at me before rejoining the crowd at the bar. Although I am a foreigner and from a town, I know he knows I am not completely naïve, and I was not at all surprised when I looked at my hand and found it smeared with the raven-black hair dye that my friend the Fox buys regularly at the hairdresser's salon in St Sauveur.

Dis-moi ce que tu manges, je te dirai ce que tu es.
(Tell me what you eat and I will tell you what you are.)
Jean-Anthelme Brillat-Savarin, French jurist and gourmet
(1755–1826)

Another Night on the Town

There is a spring in my step as I walk to meet the man who may change our lives. In fact, I am limping slightly because I am wearing the purple platform-soled shoes that Didier Bouvier believes will enhance my presence at the meeting with my prospective publisher.

Although I am not known for being overly concerned with my appearance, much thought and preparation has gone into exactly how I should present myself for this vitally important encounter with a senior director of one of the biggest publishing companies in the world. Every afternoon after grooming Daisy for stardom at the Chicken Show, Donella would put me through my paces, and we would role-play with her taking the part of the publisher. While the chickens, Cato and Milly looked on, I would be made to knock on the door of my own house, wait for the summons and then go in for my mock interview. For more than an hour, my wife would ask me all sorts of awkward questions, then point out how badly I had answered them and tell me what I should have said to make the best impression.

Together with the coaching sessions, my wife gave much thought to what I should wear for the meeting. My proposal was to be as natural as possible, and so I should arrive wearing my everyday clothing. Our books are all about our life in the countryside of Lower Normandy, I argued, so what better than that I should be dressed as if I had come straight from La Puce after a day in the fields? This, said Donella, was out of the question as I would probably be refused entry into the building and risk being arrested by the police as a vagrant. In the end, we agreed that I should wear what she calls my writer's disguise, which is an old blazer and slacks together with a subtly checked shirt and fairly restrained bow tie Donella made from a half-eaten pair of curtains that a friend's goat took a fancy to when he brought her to tea.

I was also despatched to the unisex hairdresser's in St Sauveur, and have been instructed not to smoke, pick my nose, scratch myself or break wind while I am in the great man's presence. I agreed to abide by all her conditions, but have disobeyed her instructions as to footwear. She provided me with a highly polished pair of black business shoes, but I am wearing the moon boots I was given at the send-off the Jolly Boys Club organised yesterday. When I told them at a previous meeting what I would be wearing, they all agreed that there was a possibility I would appear bland and therefore unimaginative. There should also be a hint of rebellion and even danger about me, and some small symbol of my contempt for convention. As Old Pierrot said, our famous local author Jules Barbey d'Aurevilly was renowned for his eccentric appearance and was a pioneer of the Dandyism movement in France. It was also fitting that I should be wearing some small reminder of our club and all my friends at home. Finishing his address to a round of polite applause, Pierrot presented me with the shoes. When I said the four-inch soles would probably give me a nosebleed and that they looked a little dated, Didier said the added height would in fact give me more authority and presence. He also said that he knew from his trading contacts across Europe that the retro look was very fashionable in England at the moment, and most of the trendy young men I saw in London would probably be wearing very similar footwear.

I have arrived at the publisher's offices, and am impressed to see that the company occupies a whole tower block. There is even a snooty-looking attendant at the ornate doors, so perhaps Donella was right in insisting that I wore my writer's disguise. I straighten my shoulders, take a deep breath and try to walk in a straight line towards the doors.

A reassuringly familiar haze of rain and mist greets me as the ferry passes through the breakwater and into the harbour at Cherbourg. I have only been away from my adopted country for five days, but am feeling homesick. I miss my wife, my animals, my friends and La Puce. Like going to the circus, it is nice to visit London, but I would not want to live there.

The ferry begins the lethargic process of backing into its moorings, and my heart lifts as I see Donella and Milly waiting on the quayside. My wife waves, and holds up Milly's paw in welcome, and I wave back and think how lucky I am to have someone like her to come home to.

An hour later, and I am still at the customs barrier. Because of recent events, the authorities have apparently decided to make at least a show of being concerned about who is travelling through the port. As usual, they seem far more worried about who they will let into France than who is leaving the country and for what reasons. Since the closing of the Sangatte refugee camp near Calais last year, other Channel ports have become popular gathering points for illegal immigrants and some cynical observers on the other side of the Channel claim the French are doing all they can to speed the alleged asylum seekers on their way to Britain.

Donella is understandably anxious to know how my trip to England went, but I have insisted that I will only tell her after we have eaten.

We are in a bar opposite the ferry port, and one which is a classic example of everything that is good about eating out in France. Le Rendezvous des Routiers is a small and generally unprepossessing establishment on the main road leading from the ferry port and out of town, and certainly lives up to its name. The dozens of huge lorries that help turn the route into a bottleneck at this time every day probably deter many foreign motorists from calling in, but in fact the temporary roadblock is the bar's finest advertisement. Long-distance lorry drivers are the true gourmets of France, and apart from the finest quality and variety, they expect their midday meal to be served quickly, in very large portions, with a courtesy carafe of wine and all at a price that would not buy a pie and a pint in the average British pub.

Every table in the house is taken. Frustrated by the sight of so many people enjoying so much good food that we will not be able to get our hands on, I suggest we move on, but we are intercepted by a pretty young waitress hefting a soup tureen almost the size of Madame Chantal's cauldron. If we can put up with the mess, she says, we are welcome to eat in the owner's living room. The daily special is *fini*, but we are welcome to eat what the staff are having. When I ask whether Milly may join us, she says she has some leftover rabbit pieces which may be to her liking. Mentally notching up another two good reasons for living in France, I put on my most winning smile and tell her that I would listen to a Belgian comedian for an hour if it would gain me a seat at her table.

The meal has been a simple delight, and we are lingering over coffee. So far, I have resisted Donella's demands for a blow-by-blow account of my meeting, but the teasing has to end. I light a cigarette, call for another brandy and tell her my tale.

When I was ushered in to the office of the publishing director and he rose to greet me, I realised that wearing my platform shoes might have been a mistake as the head of the man I was trying to impress was on a level with my bow tie. Assuming a half-crouch to minimise the difference, I stumbled over to his desk with my hand out and wearing what I hoped was a non-threatening smile. When we sat down I launched into my carefully rehearsed opening gambit of inviting him for lunch, but he cut me short and said that he would not have the time.

He then said that he had read the remaining chapters of my book and liked them as much as the sample I had originally sent. There were one or two areas that needed attention, but apart from that, he thought it was just about right for what it was. When I asked about how enthusiastically his company would be likely to approach the publication and launch, he said he would like to think they would be very enthusiastic indeed. If they went ahead, they would not, as he put it, mess around. It would be a major publishing occasion. Of course, he added quickly, neither of us should get too excited. Although he was the publishing director, with any proposal of this size and cost he would have to put his case to, and win over, his colleagues at the monthly board meeting. That would take place in three weeks' time, and he would let me know their decision as soon as they had made it. They would all receive copies of my manuscript in the next few days, and though he could not make any promises or commitments, he could see no reason that they would not agree with him that my book should be chosen as one of their flagship titles for the coming year. With that, he rose briskly from his seat and escorted me to the lift. As the doors closed between us, I made a weak joke about me perhaps becoming the new Bill Bryson; he said he would prefer me to stay as the old George East and advised me to get started on my next book.

Finishing my story, I squeeze my wife's hand and tell her

that all we have to do now is wait, and hope that this time nothing goes wrong. Apart from our champion at the publishing company changing his mind, running off with his secretary, getting the sack or having a fatal seizure, it really seems that, after all these years of struggle and waiting, our ship of good fortune is finally appearing over the horizon.

According to most guide books, Cherbourg has more than a hundred bars and restaurants, and I have done my best to visit each of them. All have their own individual appeal depending on your mood and pocket, but there is one establishment that is certainly unique. In Paris, Madame Zizi's would be located in Montmartre; Cherbourg's own bohemian quarter is to be found very suitably on the wrong side of the tracks. Close to the docks and amidst a network of rusting freight railway lines and crumbling tenements, what was once a decidedly seedy area is now becoming trendy.

In dimly lit bars once only frequented by dockers, merchant seamen and tarts, you will now also see style-conscious solicitors and estate agents taking coffee and croissants before setting off for work. While earnest discussions on the latest *film noir* are taking place over a cappuccino in a waterside bar, there may be a fist or even knife fight taking place in the alleyway outside. This sort of interesting social brew and its accompanying *frisson* of tension has always attracted artists, writers and other creative types. When I was much younger, my ambition was to live in a garret in Paris and write great works by day and spend my evenings at a classic zinc bar in deep philosophical conversation with fellow artists and thinkers. Nowadays, whenever I am in Cherbourg and in the mood, I head for the Rive Droite and Madame Zizi's.

As we are in town, we are to look up an old friend and fellow author who lives in a former bordello located opposite the police station. This, for reasons obvious to those who understand urban Gallic culture, was a very convenient arrangement. Now, we are comfortably settled in a booth at Madame Zizi's, and Henry is telling us of his latest adventures. Despite his solid, middle-class name, my friend claims to be the son of a Polynesian chieftain, and that he was educated at a public school in New Zealand and worked for many years as a radio announcer and newsreader for the BBC. He was known for his deep yet mellifluous voice, authoritative delivery and immaculate pronunciation, and for listeners must have created an image much different from his actual appearance and character. He has, as they say in the business, a good face for radio, and is particularly, as his French friends would say, *joli-laid*. Like many artistic and thoughtful people, he is a natural rebel. But despite the Corporation's ability and inclination to absorb and convert non-conformists, he was eventually sacked for arriving late at the studio after a night out and reading the previous day's news bulletin to a bemused nation.

Since then, Henry has lived by using his talents to provide the honeyed voice-over for suitable commercial radio and television advertisements, and to present the occasional satellite programme on the history and culture of the Maori race. For these, he drops his given name and adopts the title of Kimihia Nga Rauemi, which, he says, lends much more conviction to his broadcasts.

Henry is also an author, but tells us that as a recent convert to Buddhism he is currently concentrating on not writing a book about his life. As his interpretation of the basic tenet of his religion is to live for and in the moment and make no impositions on any other living creature, he feels that, by not adding to the boundless sea of literature worthy of reading, he is keeping his faith perfectly.

Also with us is a former BBC colleague of Henry's, whom we met recently when he appeared on our doorstep and said he wished to write an article about us. Wilfred De'Ath is the author of the most popular and unpopular regular feature in *The Oldie* magazine, in which he tells stories of his travels through France, overnight stays in the *foyers* that provide beds for penniless itinerants, and his encounters with interesting and usually much younger women. Wilfred is soon to have a collection of his magazine articles published, so we have further cause for celebration this evening. I find Wilfred a complex and perversely endearing character and do not think he is as cynical, scurrilous and *louche* as he likes to appear in print. I believe he is really a sensitive man who has been hurt in the past and wishes the world were a better, gentler place. After a few drinks at our first meeting, he confided in me that he believes he has all the symptoms of genius, but not the disease. As Coco says, a cynic is usually no more than a disillusioned romantic.

There is a brief scuffle in the corner of the bar, and we watch as a small, rat-like man is helped through the doorway by the proprietor. Having seen him on his way, Madame Zizi joins us and explains that her victim is a notorious local *frotteur*. This common street expression comes from the verb 'to rub', and describes perfectly the sort of man who likes to press himself against women while in crowded locations. Adjusting her shoulder strap, our hostess explains that this would not normally cause much of a stir in her bar, but the man was so drunk he had mistakenly practised his hobby on a burly docker rather than the girl standing beside him.

Going by her stories of life in the red-light district during the last war, our hostess must be of very advanced years, but it is hard to tell Madame Zizi's age as her extravagantly bouffanted wig is sleekly black and her face plastered with a thick layer of bone-white make-up. With her deadpan features and expressive gestures, and dressed in one of the ornate and flowing evening dresses she habitually wears, she looks to me exactly like a performer in a Japanese *kabuki* play.

We spend a few moments talking about life and where we think we are all going as we journey through it, then Madame Zizi hears of our good news and decides it is time that I have my first experience of absinthe. She is surprised that someone like me has never tried the traditional drink of French writers, and believes familiarity with its effects may inspire me to produce even better work.

I make a show of resistance, but as the long glass, tall spoon, sugar cubes and secret bottle are brought to our table, I concede. It is obviously going to be a night to remember. Or perhaps not.

Early the next day, and I am feeling a little delicate. But in spite of the aftermath of my initiation to the drink of choice of some of the greatest and maddest French writers, I am in a buoyant mood. When it was clear that we were in for a long session at Madame Zizi's, Donella called a friendly neighbour and asked her to see the chickens safely to bed and we spent the night on the floor of Henry's apartment. The sleeping arrangements made a suitable finale to our bohemian evening.

Although I much prefer living in the countryside, I always enjoy walking the streets as Cherbourg wakes.

As we make our way across the Turning Bridge to where we left our car the previous evening, gulls wheel overhead and seem to be laughing harshly at some private joke as they swoop down to seek pickings in the overflowing bins outside restaurants and bars. The occasional car races by in search of an unwary cyclist or pedestrian, and small groups of dishevelled Britons look for an English-style pub that is open so they can refuel before catching the early morning ferry back to their real worlds. Although it has not been raining, the pavements gleam from the attentions of a council worker astride his ingenious water-spraying machine, and trolleys of fresh fruit, vegetables and fish are being wheeled into shops along the quayside. I breathe in the morning air and savour the heady fusion of aromas coming from the sea, freshly brewed coffee, baking bread, stale tobacco and urine, which means we could be nowhere else in the world but a French port.

Arriving in the Place du Théâtre, I am reminded that it is market day, and see that our car has metamorphosed overnight into a sausage stall. I ask the owner if he has seen a white English car in the vicinity, and he says he has seen no white cars of any nationality this morning. I remember Donella's current experiments with growing a moss culture on Victor's bodywork, and ask him if he has seen a green car with English number plates.

The man then says that, now he thinks of it, he does remember the foreign wreck that was occupying the place he and his family have been trading from every market day for the past century. I take the hint and buy a brace of large and odiferous salamis, and he tells me that the police responded to his call an hour ago and came and towed it away.

Realising what the gulls were laughing about, we start on one of the salamis as we retrace our route across the bridge. At the police station, a fat policeman eating a croissant directs us to the traffic department, where an even fatter policeman is eating a filled baguette the size of the riot baton on his desk. We tell him our problem and he suggests we try the compound behind the station.

There, we find a group of officers clustered around poor Victor, who is hanging forlornly from a tow-truck. One of them is testing the play of the front wheels with his boot and another is poking a penknife through the thinner part of the bodywork. Another whistles in amazement and almost awe as he inspects the remains of the exhaust system, and I begin to tally up the likely total of fines that could be impending, quite apart from the cost of the parking violation.

Offering the sergeant a bite of my salami, I explain that we live in the countryside near St Sauveur and I, as an author who writes solely about the Cotentin and how it is the finest area in all France, had spent the previous evening seeking inspiration at Madame Zizi's where I was introduced to and fell foul of a litre bottle of absinthe.

This is not the line one would take with a traffic officer in Britain, but we are in France. After writing down his name so I would spell it properly in my next book, Sergeant Guy Lecroix shakes my hand, wishes us a safe voyage home and orders that Victor be lowered from the back of the tow-truck and our parking ticket torn up.

I thank him for his courtesy and indulgence, and as we climb into Victor and start our journey back to the tranquillity of La Puce, I think how good it is to live in a country where the pursuit and exercise of personal liberty and creativity is often seen as much more important than observng the letter of the law.

> *It is a wise man who lives with money in the bank,*
> *and a fool who dies that way.*
> Norman proverb

Money Matters

Another week must drag by before we can expect to hear from London. The travel book company has been in touch to make us a modest offer, but despite Donella's reservations, I have replied that we are expecting a much better and bigger proposal.

At La Puce, the days grow longer as nature's yearly cycle rolls by. A single-parent wren has set up home in a hole in a wall at the ruined end of the mill cottage, and as this will be the fourth year that she has chosen to trust us and bring up her family under our protection, we feel the responsibility.

Normally at this time of year, we would be trying to enforce a Cato exclusion zone around all the nesting areas at La Puce, but our werecat appears disinterested in the prospects of torture and murder on a grand scale. In recent weeks, she seems to have grown ever more lethargic and now spends most of her time lying in the woodshed on an old pair of trousers that even I consider beyond use. Our once ferocious cat has lost weight, and her luxuriant coat is becoming increasingly drab and patchy.

Together with Cato's indisposition, my wife is also worried about the balance of relationships at the chicken run. Now that Big Daisy is the all-Cotentin superchicken, her head has been turned. Apart from a photograph and story about her on the front page of the local newspaper and her interview with a reporter from Cherbourg Radio, she is now receiving fan mail from chicken fanciers across the region – and even proposals of marriage. These are allegedly written by lovelorn cockerels, but have obviously been fabricated by owners who want to breed from our famous chicken. We are also receiving regular calls and letters from associations who want to book Daisy to make a personal appearance at their summer shows. Now, there is even talk of setting up a fan club with its own website so that enthusiasts from around the world can learn of her daily routine, favourite food, colour schemes and pop music. The most curious aspect of the whole affair is that nobody seems concerned that our hen is no longer posing as a true Cotentin Black.

When I told René Ribet about the furore and said we would be stripped of the title and have to return the cup when his trickery with the hair dye was exposed, he smiled and said that people only see what they want to see. It suited everyone to believe that Daisy was a Cotentin Black, and human nature would ensure that nobody would point out that she is actually an attractive but quite ordinary mottled hen. If singers who cannot sing, artists who cannot paint and politicians who don't care about people can become rich and famous, why not a hen who is not really what we claim she is? If I was worried about it, he said, he could arrange for a weekly colouring session to take place in the hen-house, then we could open La Puce to the public and charge people to see the famous bird. Although this seemed a good money-making scheme to me, Donella says she is having quite enough trouble with our celebrity chicken as it is. Now that our hen is acting like a film star, old problems with infidelity have resurfaced, and we suspect the torrid affair between Big Daisy and Gert's partner, Fred, has re-ignited. If Barney finds out what is going on, there is bound to be trouble between the two cocks.

~

Another big date in the Cotentin calendar has arrived, and we are off to the Tree Fair at Sourciéville. As anyone who has driven through the *bocage* region will know, Normans are fond of trees. Trees as forests mean cover for game, and one of William the Conqueror's first jobs when setting up shop in England was to plant the vast New Forest in Hampshire. Trees as firewood also spell warmth and comfort during the long Norman winter, and so trees as possessions mean added status. This is why the market square at Sourciéville will be forested with saplings of every size and variety over the weekend, and many hundreds of Cotentinese will overcome their prejudices to visit the town.

Sourciéville is said to have a dark history. The town is at the centre of the great swathe of marshlands that bisect the peninsula, and for most of the winter it is ringed and virtually isolated by what the Cotentinese call the inland sea. The same families have lived there for centuries, and outsiders, except during Tree Fair week when there is good money to be had from them, are not welcome.

Consequently, Sourciéville has acquired a reputation as being a hotbed of strange and often supernatural practices and events. There are rumours of unholy gatherings on the marshes at certain times of the year. Goats and cats are allegedly the pets of choice in the town, the local hardware store specialises in hand-made besom brooms, and it is said that chickens and virgins are always in short supply. An academic friend of mine has written and published a paper on the Cotentin, and in it he argues that all great tracts of flat and featureless marshy terrain naturally attract myths and tales of the supernatural. With its location, appearance and general ambience, Sourciéville fits within his parameters perfectly. The only abandoned church I know of in the whole region lies just outside the town, and the area seems permanently swathed in a miasma of particularly dramatic and clammy mist. Surrounded as it is by water, this is hardly surprising in winter, but there is a regional saying that the sun never shines in Sourciéville, whatever the weather elsewhere.

We have arrived, and as we look for a parking place I am especially wary when we approach any major or minor road junctions, or any passage from which a car could conceivably emerge. Most isolated towns in our region have developed their own attitude to and application of the national rules of the road, but Sourciéville is in a class of its own. Virtually all the locals observe the now extinct requirement of giving way to vehicles emerging from the right, but most choose not to conform if encountering a car driven by an enemy, visitor or foreigner. With such a major event taking place in the town, confusion naturally reigns and driving in Sourciéville today would bring the most battle-hardened Parisian taxi driver out in a sweat.

Following two near-misses and an invigorating bumper-to-bumper confrontation with an elderly lady with a squint who literally cursed me as I backed away, I manage to find a space, and we set off for the square. Although I like trees, we have several hundred at La Puce so I do not understand my wife's enthusiasm for buying and planting even more. Donella knows my views and suggests that I go off and amuse myself for a couple of hours, which is our code for my finding a bar and getting to know the locals. Making me promise not to become involved in any arguments, drinking or arm-wrestling competitions, she doles out a note of small denomination and disappears into the mêlée.

As a semi-professional in the craft of sniffing out unusual and interesting drinking haunts, I ignore the standard chromium and plate-glass-fronted bars around the square and am rewarded after ten minutes of wandering through a network of cobbled alleyways in what is obviously the oldest part of the town. People sometimes accuse me of being more interested in the bars and people who drink in and run them than the local history, industry or architecture, but they do not realise that the best way to learn about any town or city is by calling in at a local pub.

The bar I have found certainly looks as if it has been trading in strong drink and the daily life and dramas of the community for many generations. The fascia is mainly of wood that has clearly not seen a painter's brush for decades, and the satisfyingly incongruous fluted stone pillars on either side of the door are each topped with a carving of a hideously distorted face. I cannot see inside as the curtains are tightly drawn, but the bar has a promising name. Rather than a Bar Sporting, Bar Commercial or simply Bar of the Place, it is called the Bar of the Good Conversation.

Even in England, not all pubs live up to their names, and when I push my way through the old planking door I find that whatever quality and quantity of conversation had been going on has now stopped. I am clearly the focus of attention for the dozen or so men standing at the bar or seated around the smoke-filled room, and this is obviously not the sort of premises where the owner claims a warm welcome will always be found. Though I am not usually deterred from entering any bar by the appearance or manner of its users, I pause at the doorway and think about leaving. From the Gorbals in Glasgow to the docks area of Marseille, rarely have I been in a pub where the air of hostility is so tangible and the customers so clearly not pleased to see me, but as I turn away, someone calls my name and I see a familiar face. It is our village's own international entrepreneur, Didier Bouvier.

He beckons me over and calls to the barman as I try to walk nonchalantly past a table of men who look as if they are waiting to audition for a re-make of *Night of the Zombies*. We shake hands, and I notice that Didier does not introduce me to his companion, who makes the rest of the clientele look almost effete. He is a tall, strongly built man with greasily slicked-back dark hair, and was either born with a prognathous jaw or the whole top half of his face has at some time been pushed back beyond its original alignment. During what must have been an interesting life of encounters, his nose has suffered even more collateral damage than mine, a livid scar stretches from beneath one eye to his upper lip, and the puckering of the surrounding skin gives him a permanent but most unfriendly smile. The overall impression of a man you would not wish to meet in even a well-lit alley is enhanced by the selection of crudely-made tattoos on his neck, arms and knuckles. After a cursory inspection, the man pointedly turns his back on me, bangs his glass on the counter and the barman scurries obediently over with a bottle of vodka.

As we wait for our drinks, Didier asks how Donella is getting on with her scrub-burner, then says he has a proposition that could earn me some nice pocket money. This should set warning bells ringing immediately, as Didier's proposals always seem to make money for him and lose money for his partner. But, as usual, I tell myself it will do no harm to at least listen to what he has to say. As someone who uses words for a sort of living, it is a beguiling pleasure to listen to a real master at work. As usual, Didier's proposal is persuasive and, as ever, there does not seem to be any catch. In fact, he claims that his idea involves absolutely no investment from me and I will receive a guaranteed and generous cash payment each week for just two hours of my time.

Didier is to set up a language school. There are hundreds of English people buying homes and moving into our area every year, and all will have regular need of the services of local tradesmen and other service and goods' providers. Hardly any of the local people speak a second language except patois, and their potential English customers are virtually all free of any knowledge of French. Didier knows that I hold informal classes in French for English newcomers at the Flaming Curtains, and proposes that I now turn my attention to helping local people communicate better with their potential customers. He has been to see a variety of craftsmen and shop owners in the area; a surprising number of them have signed up for a year's course even after hearing that I would be their teacher. Most people who have met me are aware of my severe limitations in French, Didier says, but this will actually be an asset to the scheme. As well as learning basic English, the students will be getting hands-on experience in communicating with any foreign customers who insist on trying to speak their language. If I am in agreement, the first lesson will take place at the Flaming Curtains early next week and, if I wish, he will actually pay me in advance.

Although, as I reply, we shall have no money problems when we have made a deal with our new publisher, it would be an interesting project to help the local business community make the most of the influx of English home-buyers and settlers. I would also be very pleased to give something back to an area that has given me and my wife so much. But, I add swiftly, I will accept payment just to put our arrangement on a business footing.

When Didier and I shake hands on the deal and I have made my usual pleasantry of pretending to count my fingers to see if they are all still there, I empty my glass and try to catch the eye of the barman. He is engaged, and I see that he is methodically recharging his cigarette stations. Technically, smoking in bars has been prohibited throughout France for almost a decade, but as nobody agrees with the diktat it has gone completely unobserved. Nearly all French barmen I have done business with could smoke for their country and, in some busy bars, staff will light a cigarette in an ashtray at each end of the counter so they will not be caught short as they shuttle back and forth with orders. This man, like a polar explorer on the outward leg of his expedition, is carefully leaving supply stations at regular intervals along his route. Together with the emergency rations, the man obviously likes to have back-up facilities in other areas of his life, and is on clearly intimate terms with two women who are standing alone at either end of the bar. One is short and blonde with a low-cut blouse that exposes a pink chasm of a cleavage, and the other dark, tall and willowy. As the barman reaches either end of the bar and completes an order, he will lean across the counter and murmur a few endearments before returning to the neutral zone. My admiration of him only increases when the bead curtain to one side of the bar rattles, and a sharp-faced woman of middle years emerges to pick up a packet of cigarettes from the back of the bar. By the way she talks at him then looks scathingly at each of the women, it is obvious she is his wife. When he finally serves me, I ask the man how many cars he owns, but he misses the joke and looks blankly at me before returning to stare with fond affection into the bright eyes and swooping *décolletage* of his blonde friend.

I pay my bill and Didier walks me to the door. Outside, I follow him round a corner to his pick-up van. As he takes a large holdall bag from the cab I ask about his friend, and Didier casually explains that the man who looks as if he enjoys rat *fricassée* for breakfast is actually the professor of Humanities at a university in the former Yugoslavia. He is visiting Lower Normandy to investigate the possibilities of a twinning arrangement between Cherbourg and Sarajevo, and Didier is using his wide circle of contacts with the *beau monde* of the town to help smooth progress.

We shake hands again, and I watch as he re-enters the bar with the holdall. Hearing the bolts shoot, I walk over to the door, gently try the handle, then put my eye to a gap between the warped planking. I see that Didier is at the bar busily pulling cardboard cartons from the holdall. Most of the customers have formed a ragged queue, and money is changing hands. As the barman rips open one of the boxes, I realise that I am witnessing the bizarre spectacle of contra-band tobacco being sold in a French bar to French smokers. In many British pubs, this would be a common sight, but until recently, tax on tobacco was so low that smokers were prepared to pay the over-the-counter price. But France is many billions of euros in the red, and so the duty on ciga-rettes has risen dramatically in the past year. As in Britain, the government is trying to take the moral high ground by pretending they are only cranking up the tax to dissuade people from killing themselves, but the inevitable result will be that more and more smokers will buy stolen and thus totally duty-free supplies. It is even being forecast that the French government's next cash-cow target will be wines and spirits. If this happens without a revolution and tax levels eventually overtake those in Britain, a complete reversal of the normal situation could take place. In the future, we could become used to millions of French people crossing the Channel to eagerly stock up on what they see as cheap tobacco and drink, and there would inevitably be teams of bootleggers making daily runs from Calais to Dover in the French equivalent of an unmarked white Transit van.

~

My wife is happily planting the last of the dozen expensive saplings she bought at Sourciéville. I am in the caravan, considering whether bank managers are attracted to the profession because of their nature. I also wonder if they go on special training courses in how to upset their customers. If there is such a course, I suspect that our local branch at Argenteville is the regional training camp and was probably chosen because we do business there. Seven managers have moved in and out of our lives in recent times, and all have acted as if they were practising their customer-alienating techniques on us.

Reaching the end of his latest letter, I realise that our new tormentor is not making a bad joke when he talks of his bank not being an arts foundation with special grants for struggling writers. We have, says Mr Connarde, come to the end of the road. The temporary overdraft we arranged with one of his predecessors three years ago now seems to have become a permanent lease loan, and as we are not registered as a developing country, it must be repaid within the next three months. If not, the necessary action will be taken to recover the full sum owing. I think for a moment about calling the bank and asking how Mr Connarde proposes recovering money we do not have, and explaining that this is actually the reason we have and need an overdraft. He could, I would say, send a snatch squad to take goods to the sum of our debt, but I doubt if the combined worth of our twenty-year-old Volvo, our scrub-burner, livestock and all our furniture and other possessions would make much of a dent in the sum we owe.

After thinking up other similarly tart responses, I actually compose and write a grovelling letter explaining that we are going through a temporary cash-flow crisis but are expecting to receive a significant offer from a major publishing house within the next week. Then, we will be in a position to repay the overdraft in full and have a comfortable sum in our account. I cannot resist adding a subtle sting in the tail by saying how I may even dedicate the new book to him in recognition of all that he has done to keep us afloat till we made our breakthrough. He can be sure that, when the book is an international bestseller, the world will know exactly how he and his bank have treated us.

Feeling a little better, I make coffee and go to see how Donella is getting on with her reforestation of the roadside copse. I shall not spoil her day by telling her about the letter from Mr Connarde. Though I usually leave all official correspondence for Donella's attention, our relations with the new manager at Argenteville have become so strained that I have been dealing directly with him. For some reason, this hands-on approach, rather than smoothing things over, seems to have made the situation worse.

Although I don't like to think about it, our debt is secured by La Puce, and it is not uncommon for banks to repossess a property and sell it off to the highest bidder. Technically, there is a stringent process and code of conduct to ensure that a fair price for a repossessed property is achieved and that there will be money left over for the owners when the bank has received its dues, but this does not always seem to happen. Sometimes an archaic 'candle sale' auction will be advertised and take place at the property that is to be sold off, with interested parties putting in their bids till the flame dies. Then, details of the highest bid will be placed in local newspapers to see if anyone wishes to top it. Though it may not be true, I have heard that quite often the notices do not appear either before or after the candle sale, and that some properties are sold for a fraction more than the debt that has been secured against them. Often, the buyer will also be someone who is known to the person responsible for organising the sale. Whatever the facts, I know of Britons who have invested all their money, dreams and countless hours of hard work in buying and restoring a home in France, then lost everything when money troubles have arrived. It must be devastating to watch a stranger wander round the home you have devoted so much time and effort to, then see him take it from you with a casually raised finger. This is an experience I could not bear to see my wife endure, and I would do almost anything to stop it happening.

I arrive at the copse and Milly comes streaking through the trees to greet me. Donella is sitting on a tree stump, and I pass her a mug of coffee, put my arm round her shoulder and ask her if she is happy with the planting. She nods contentedly, rests her hand on mine and says it is very satisfying to know that the result of her morning's work will be that our grandchildren's children may one day be climbing the sturdy trees these small saplings will become.

Vivre est une chute horizontale.
(Life is a horizontal fall.)
Jean Cocteau, French artist and writer (1889–1963)

French Lessons

I am at the Flaming Curtains to give my first English lesson to members of our local business community. It is nice to know that, for the first time in our long association, I shall be leaving the bar with more money than when I arrived.

As I wait for Didier and my students to arrive, I am sitting at the British Embassy table thinking of how best to structure the course and individual lessons. While I make some hasty notes, Milly is playing football with some local children and Morton the pub dog lies at my feet pretending not to be watching her every move.

English breeds are popular in France, and Morton is a very large and unkempt example of a pedigree Airedale. In some aspects of his character, he is almost as eccentric as his owner, our host at the Flaming Curtains. Although born and raised in this country, there is something of an old-fashioned English gentleman about the way Morton likes to go about his daily routine, and at rest he has the air of a retired army officer taking a post-prandial nap at his club. But Morton's Norman upbringing is evident in his attitude to what he sees as his property and those who trespass on it. Morton views not only the Flaming Curtains as his personal terrain, but also the square and pavement outside. Although he affects a Gallic indifference to what is going on around him, he has very strict rules about who he considers welcome to pass through and on to his territory. All male dogs are permanently excluded, and they and their owners obliged to cross the high street if they wish safe passage while passing the Rideau Cramoisi. Customers with bitches are welcome, and Morton, like his owner, is regularly surrounded by an admiring audience of females. Unlike his owner, he tends to treat his fan club with an air of indifference and often casual disdain. If in the mood, he will acknowledge his favourites, and there is always keen competition to win the favour of a cursory sniff beneath the tail or a passing nod of recognition. But since Milly has become a regular at the Flaming Curtains, things have changed. Morton is obviously smitten with our pretty collie, and she delights in leading him on.

At whatever time I arrive in the square, a giant woolly head will appear at a window or doorway and Morton will bound over to the car and wait to escort Milly inside. As is often the way with relationships between the sexes, the more he pursues and woos her, the more she enjoys keeping him at a distance. The tables have been turned, and now Morton knows the pangs of unrequited love. When Milly is elsewhere, I have often advised him that he should begin to show an overt interest in the vivacious spaniel who arrives with her owner most evenings. In my experience of the curious nature of sexual politics, I say, the more attention he pays to the spaniel, the more chance he will have of gaining Milly's interest.

~

I have taken my first English-language class and, all things considered, it seemed to go well. Some of the local traders were clearly more interested in numeracy than literacy. The craftsmen were particularly interested in how best to say to their English clients that the work would take much longer than anticipated and would therefore cost considerably more. They were also surprised to learn that their traditional sharp intake of breath and shake of their heads when surveying a proposed job is as common in Britain as it is in France.

Peculiarly, among the local students were a handful of strangers who seemed to be as unfamiliar with their own language as they were with mine. When I asked Didier about them, he said that they were country people from the Basque region and not used to speaking proper French. They were planning to move to this area and find work, and so would benefit from the classes by getting to know the local people while learning English and reminding themselves of how the rest of France communicates. I have never met any Basques and did not realise how different and guttural their language sounds, but can understand the problems and frustrations of not being able to speak properly with people from even your own country.

After handing over my fee, Didier said that although he knew I did not need the money, there was another job I might like to do for him. Now that the English courses were established, he would like to move on to the next phase of the project, which was to organise educational and leisure visits to Britain for some of his clients. This application of the system of French students spending some time with a typical English family and learning about their home life and culture would be invaluable to some members of our class, he said. Another bonus would be that the craftsmen would be able to study the favoured building techniques in England, and by eating with the family, might even develop a tolerance for English food and cooking that would stand them in good stead if invited to dinner by their clients in Lower Normandy. He knew that I would have the names and addresses of many readers who had written to say how much they had enjoyed my books, and he would pay me a good price for every one I contacted and introduced to the scheme as a host family. They too would gain much from the experience as they would get to know the real people who actually live in our area of France. I said it seemed a good idea, and would put it to some of my readers. I like the thought of them meeting some of the characters I write about, but have insisted that the name of René Ribet will not appear on the list of Didier's proposed foreign placement students.

~

The end of a pleasant night by the fire. I have given what is left of my tuition fee to Donella after the cost of the round or two of drinks I stood in the bar, and the bouquet of flowers I bought at St Sauveur. In return for the unexpected contribution to the housekeeping budget and the even more unexpected gift, my wife let me win the nightly round of killer dominoes and opened a bottle of our special reserve sparkling nettle wine. Not only does last autumn's brewing have a pleasant flavour, but it is particularly satisfying to gain revenge on an old enemy by first boiling him alive and then drinking his juices.

And so we sit in the comfort of our home and all seems well in our small world. Our old applewood clock sporadically chimes to mark the passing hours, the rain drums on the window in frustration, and the dancing flames from the wood-burning stove cast flickering shadows across the undulating whitewashed walls. Donella is working on a tapestry for the hen-house, Milly is curled at my feet, and we are making plans for the future. When our offer from the publisher comes through, we will have enough money to pay off our overdraft and to finally restore the ruined end of the mill cottage. I have also thought of a refinement to Didier's student placement scheme. Earlier this evening, I phoned or sent e-mail messages to several British readers and three have already said they would be interested in accommodating one or more of my students. When the system is up and running and the extra rooms have been built here, I propose that we offer our hosts and perhaps all our readers what I shall call the Mill of the Flea Experience. For much less than the price of renting an anonymous *gîte*, they will be able to stay with us and discover what it is like to live here. We can take them on guided tours of the area and meet the people who feature in my books. As I have said so many times before, money makes money and it is easy to action good ideas when you have some.

Donella looks at me over the top of her glasses and reminds me that I have had this idea before. As she said then, it has several drawbacks. The first consideration is that I do not like having visitors, and it would not be fair on them to see me parading around the cottage at all hours in my underwear. Also, finding out what life is really like at the Mill of the Flea may not be the sort of experience for which most people would wish to pay...

~

Milly and I are taking a late-night stroll around our land. I need to walk off the effects of the nettle champagne, and my mind is full of thoughts of how the events of the next few days could change our lives. The publishing company's board meeting takes place tomorrow, and it will be hard to resist phoning the director and asking him how his proposal was received. I know I should wait for his letter, but perhaps I will ask Donella to call his secretary and ask if she knows what happened at the meeting.

As I think about the way our lives are shaped by other people and by events over which we seem to have little control, Milly stops in her tracks and lifts her head to scent the air. It is a quiet night and we have not seen or heard anything unusual, but Milly has detected something happening by the chicken coop. I signal for her to stay, then get to my knees and crawl towards the enclosure. Perhaps it is only a prowling fox, or perhaps the visitor with an interest in our celebrity chicken has two legs. As I draw nearer, I hear the sound of rustling and muted squawking, so pick up a fallen branch and launch myself round the corner of the compound.

Instead of intruders, I see that I have caught our unfaithful hen in the act of betraying her partner. Daisy and Fred have slipped away from their marital beds to make the two-backed beast behind the manure pile. They are so engrossed in each other that they do not notice me, and feeling uncomfortably like a voyeur I sneak away.

~

The day of the board meeting in England, and I have already gathered enough wood to see us through until autumn, taken an early breakfast at the big pond with Hen the duck and fed the chickens. When I topped up their food dispensers and cleaned their quarters out, Fred avoided eye contact and Daisy brazenly stared me out, so perhaps they know I was a witness to their late-night coupling. There was also a strained atmosphere in both their apartments, so I think their partners must suspect what is going on.

To keep myself occupied until it is a respectable time for Donella to call the publishing house, I intend working off my nervous energy on our land. After setting fire to one of the tool sheds while I was practising with the new scrub-burner, I am not allowed to use it without supervision so am going to employ more traditional methods to attack the bramble patch by the big pond. In fact, the bramble patch by the big pond is now mostly *in* the big pond. From what I have read about *Rubus fruticosus*, it cannot survive under water, but our variety has obviously not read the same book. Although it is supposed to be a strictly vegetarian plant, I think it may have developed a taste for protein from our bloody encounters and has now decided to try fishing for additional nourishment.

An hour has passed when I sense a presence and look up from my work to see our nosey neighbour Mr Trefle regarding me with his usual expression of pained incredulity. He asks me why I am attacking my pond, and when I explain that I am lopping off the tentacles of a fish-eating bramble patch, he nods, looks warily at my sickle and takes a step back. I ask him what he wants, and he says my wife called to tell him that one of his steers has escaped and is loose on our land.

I have heard people who live in urban areas say that nothing much happens in the countryside, and that they would be bored just watching grass grow. They do not realise how much time is taken up dealing with apparently trivial events and their consequences in a rural setting.

For the past three hours, we have been chasing Mr Trefle's steer around La Puce. Together with breaking three flower pots, several panes of glass in the greenhouse and doing serious damage to the vegetable garden, the frightened animal has also left its mark on the terrace and all along the track up to the road. Ironically, the only place it did not deposit any of the contents of its stomach was on the vegetable garden, where at least it would have done some good. I also sprained my wrist badly when attempting to wrestle the creature to the ground by its horns. The technique works well in movies about the Old West, but is not as easy in practice as it appears on film.

To add insult to all the physical injury, I have had a stand-up row with Mr Trefle. Rather than apologising for the damage caused by his steer, he blamed our lack of skills in helping capture it and even threatened to sue me if the beast has suffered any physical hurt or mental trauma. He says that our clumsy attempts to catch it caused his valuable and sensitive animal to panic, and it was anyway our fault it got out of his field. He claimed that under Norman law, I had a duty to help maintain the rotten fence running alongside the boundary with his field and it was my side that gave way when the steer charged it. Although I have seen how Mr Trefle treats his animals and his claims are patent nonsense,

I have had enough experience of how the law is applied in any dispute between a local landowner and a foreigner to think twice about taking him on in court. As if all these distractions on such an important day were not enough, when the steer was finally back in its paddock and I had repaired the broken fence, Mr Trefle's old car would not start. He is now sulking in the mill cottage until his son arrives with the family tractor and a tow-rope, and we are marooned as his car is blocking the track. My only consolation is that he has been helping himself to our nettle champagne while he waits, and I know how he will feel when he sobers up.

~

Now that a sort of peace has descended on La Puce, I have retreated to the caravan to wait for news from London. During our dramas with the steer, Donella called the publishing director's secretary every hour and we know that the board meeting that will decide our future is still in session. The secretary says that there are several manuscripts being proposed for major publication this autumn, and there has been disagreement on which ones to choose. She has promised to call us with any news as soon as she hears it, and if her boss asks her to send us a letter, she will let us know what it says before she posts it. While Donella entertains Mr Trefle and waits for any call, I pull the curtains, switch on my portable computer and prepare to go online.

Although I am by nature and age opposed to those advances in technology that require us to spend time and money doing things we don't really need to do, I have found the electronic superhighway of communications a generally useful and interesting road to travel. I like the feeling of being able to talk with and travel the rest of the planet while sitting in a leaky caravan in a field in Lower Normandy. It is said that the telephone killed off the practice and art of letter writing, but it seems to me that electronic mail has revived it, and this can only be for the good.

The screen glows, the connections are made, and a series of messages appear on the screen. Looking at the addresses of the senders, I see I have news from friends and readers in California, South Africa and Pudsey. There is also a handful of unfamiliar names and call signs, which will introduce new Friends of the Flea wanting to share with me their plans and dreams and schemes for buying a home in France and perhaps one day moving over the Channel to start a new life.

It has been an absorbing hour. Apart from news from regular correspondents, I have made several new friends and been able to give some practical advice. Although we are still strangers, most of the people who contact me on this subject end by asking whether I think they will be happy and successful if they take the big step across the Channel. It is flattering that they should ask my opinion, but I am always non-committal. I usually say that it seems to me to be impossible to define the sort of character best suited to living in a foreign land. I have, however, noticed that British expatriates seem to fall into three broad categories.

One is made up of those types who become curiously more British the longer they stay in another country. They develop a nostalgic longing for things they often took for granted at home, and can become quite obsessive about reminders of what they left behind. In our area, I know of one couple who regularly drive to the ferry port at Cherbourg to watch cars with British number plates coming out of the gates.

The second category contains the Britons who wish to become totally absorbed into the culture of the country in which they have chosen to live. In extreme cases, they go native and go to great lengths to break any links with their heritage and past. They will actively avoid any British visitors or fellow settlers, and if approached by them will often pretend to be French and unable to speak a word of English.

The third general category includes those who have no wish to disassociate themselves from their upbringing and culture, but who are able and willing to adapt to their new circumstances and surroundings. They will always be foreigners, and will strive to understand and accept that, like the past, where they have chosen to make their home is a foreign country and things are often done differently there. Of those broad groups, people within this category seem to be the most content with their new lives in France, and I like to think my wife and I fit, however awkwardly, into it.

Sometimes though, even the most adaptable types can encounter problems in whichever country they wish to settle. A classic if extreme example among my e-messages today was from an American reader who said she was inspired by my books to buy a holiday and retirement home in Brittany, and she was particularly enthused because she thought even she could not possibly make as many errors of judgement as me.

With her second home a little over seven thousand miles from her front door in California and scant knowledge of Breton-French, the lady found and commissioned a British builder to conduct or oversee every stage of the restoration of her impressive but dilapidated nineteenth-century townhouse. After setting up a bank account in Brittany and giving him access to it, she arrived a month later to find no work done on the house and her account empty. The rogue builder had obviously gone off in search of his next victim. Determined not to make the same mistake again, the lady decided to employ a local builder. To be doubly sure, she also appointed a local businesswoman to manage the project and keep a watchful eye on the builder. Hearing nothing from and unable to contact the woman after the initial progress reports, she took another unplanned flight to France. Arriving at the village, she learned that the prolonged and intimate contact between her builder and his minder had flowered into romance, and the couple had run off and left their families to start a new life elsewhere.

Now, said my correspondent, she has decided to take a hands-on approach and is staying in France until her future home is totally restored.

~

My electronic letters answered, I draw the curtains and wave encouragingly to Hen the duck, who is helping with my pond-clearing efforts by launching a series of underwater attacks on the bramble tentacles. As I turn to switch it off, the computer emits an urgent bleep, and a new message flashes up on the screen. I put on my glasses, and see from the sender's address that it comes from the London offices of the publishing company. I walk around the caravan, roll and light two cigarettes, run my hand through my hair, sit down and stand up several times, cross and uncross my fingers and legs, then reach out and tentatively touch the button to reveal the message that may change our lives.

C'est le commencement de la fin.
(It is the beginning of the end.)
Charles Maurice de Talleyrand, French statesman (1754–1838),
to Napoleon after the battle of Leipzig

Under Offer

The swallows have returned to La Puce, so summer is on the wing. Of all species, I think I like and admire these tenacious and energetic little birds the most. When I am low, it lifts my heart to sit and watch them swooping and wheeling joyously above the pond and making the most of their time with us. It is said they spend every moment of their short lives in the air, and sometimes I wish that I could join them and be as free from concern as they seem. Like us though, I am sure they have their own worries.

It is early morning and I have slept badly. The black dog of depression is a rare visitor to our home, but he has been my constant companion for more than a week. When I had not appeared at the cottage by dusk on the day we heard from the publishing company, Donella came to look for me. She found me sitting beside the Hobbit Tree, and when she asked me what was wrong I told her about the message. It was apologetic, but short and to the point, saying that the board had decided not to make a major investment in publishing and promoting my new book. In a curious application of logic, the publishing director said that he thought that my book was too good to be published in a small way, so they would not be making me an offer to publish it in *any* way.

Because she is who she is, my wife refused to let me wallow in self-pity, and became angry when I said we should stop struggling against fate and give up trying to make a living from my writing. When I said I was going to burn all copies of the manuscript for our new book and write off the last thirty years and look for a proper job, she said I should stop acting like a spoilt child. She could name a hundred writers and artists who struggled all their lives, experienced dreadful poverty and did not become well known until long after they died. Besides, who did I think was going to give me a real job? The only person I had worked for in the past twenty years was myself, and that was rarely a smooth working relationship. She then reminded me that the reason I became self-employed all those years ago was because I am basically unemployable. What else did I think I could or would do rather than write?

I replied that I knew – or hoped – that she was trying to cheer me up, but that I would much rather have greater recognition and the consequent rewards while I was still around to enjoy them, and being unrecognised does not mean that I am a great or even a good writer. It could just be that I have been fooling myself all these years, and nobody wants to hear what I have to say.

Also, we might not be living in poverty, but I was sure she did not realise just how serious our money problems were. When I began to tell her about the latest letter from Mr Connarde, she said she knew all about it and had been corresponding with him for weeks without my knowledge as managing money was far too important a subject to be left to me. She had spoken to our bank manager earlier that day, and he had agreed to extend the deadline for settling our overdraft by another month. I refused to be optimistic, and said that if we had another year of grace we would not be able to raise such a large sum. Without telling her, I had already talked to the other major banks in the region to see if they would lend us the money to pay off Mr Connarde, but all had turned me down. We are, I said, in a classic Catch-22 situation. The advance royalties on the new book would have solved all our money problems, but now we have no publisher. We cannot bring the new book out ourselves as we do not have the money that we would have had if someone else had published it.

I have also shut our last remaining escape hatch from the wrong side. Immediately after getting the message from London, I had called the director of the travel book company and said we had changed our minds about his offer and we would accept any level of publication and promotion of my new work. He was sympathetic, but said I was too late. When he learned I was not interested, his company had looked elsewhere for a new author to take on and had now allocated their publishing budget for the year.

With no income to come from the new book, I said, we had finally reached the end of a dead-end road. In three months the bank would repossess La Puce, and we could lose nearly everything. With the boom in property prices in Britain, we would not be able to afford even a one-bedroom flat there, and would probably end up living in a council house if we were lucky.

I have read about people snorting in derision, but before our exchange I had not heard anyone making that specific noise. After giving a good impression of a horse with a novice and very stupid rider on its back, my wife told me to pull myself together and said that I had no excuse for being so morbid and histrionic, especially as I had not been drinking. There was an obvious solution to our financial problems, and one which we had discussed before when times had been especially tight.

We should put our home on the market and get the best price for it. Although not on a level with Britain, property prices have been steadily rising in Lower Normandy. If we were to sell La Puce, we would easily be able to settle all our debts and still have enough money to buy a new home.

It would not be anything like La Puce, but as long as there was enough room for us and our animals, we could make it a home. If we were to set ourselves a budget and find a real bargain, we would also have enough money to publish my new book in a big way. Then, when my work was at the top of the bestseller lists, we would have enough money to buy a bigger, better place to live. We could even buy back La Puce. Most importantly, my new book would be published, and I would be able to keep on writing. She knew that there was nothing else I wanted to do with my life, and whatever it cost, we must follow my heart. To stop now would be a waste of half a lifetime of struggle. Even if success did not come until after my death, she would hopefully still be around to enjoy the benefits.

~

Donella is cooking our evening meal, and I am sitting by the cascade. I went into the cottage earlier and saw that she had been crying. When I said I hated myself for what was happening and for making her so unhappy, she told me not to be stupid and that she was crying because she had been peeling an onion. It was not a good excuse as I know we are having egg and chips for supper, but I loved her even more for it.

~

I have agreed that we will go through the motions of putting La Puce on the market, but I really cannot imagine us actually leaving our home. I have also told Mr Connarde what is happening and he sounded quite unhappy. I think he regrets being the cause of us selling our home, but Donella thinks he is just annoyed that his bank will not be able to sell it to someone they know at a knock-down price.

We have been in tight corners before and something has always turned up, and since Donella helped me chase the black dog away I am in a very positive mood. Yesterday, I bought twenty tickets in the National Lottery and I have been investigating all sorts of money-making schemes advertised on the Internet. According to some of the claims, it is possible to make thousands of pounds a week in return for a few moments' work and a very small investment. I do not think I am particularly credulous, and know that the only people making money out of most of the proposals are the individuals and companies who are making them. But there may be some genuine business opportunities among the junk mail, and I shall be very selective before taking any risks with money we do not have.

Although we need such a large amount to pay off Mr Connarde, I must also be sure not to neglect any opportunities to bring in less spectacular sums, and I think my partnership with Didier in the foreign exchange scheme could be quite rewarding. Before this evening's lesson, he told me that my Basque students had been so pleased with my tuition and the foreign placement scheme that they had asked to continue their studies by going to stay with a family in Britain. I would now be due a commission fee for providing the introduction to the hosts. Even better news was that the Basque contingent had told their friends at home how pleased they were with the scheme, and another six students from a village near the border with Spain would be joining us for the evening's lesson.

After our session in the upstairs room, I invited the students to join me in the bar and tried to give them a practical demonstration of the rules of engagement in a typical British public house. I think they enjoyed the session, but, like nearly all my French friends, had real difficulty in understanding the idea of taking it in turns to buy rounds and paying with the order rather than at the end of the evening.

It is good to have real friends.

Before he closed the bar, Coco invited me to stay on for a nightcap, and when the last customer had left we settled down at the bar with a bottle of his good wine and the distributor head from his Land Rover. After we had adjusted the gap and smoked and drunk and talked about nothing, he said he had heard that I was thinking of selling La Puce. As I had only talked about the sale with Mr Connarde and our English agent, this was more evidence that our area's communications system is at least as efficient as the Internet. When I said it was true that we were considering moving on to somewhere smaller and more manageable, Coco remarked that, as the local expression has it, one should never try to blow smoke up a bull's backside. He knew that we had money problems, and this was nothing to be ashamed of. I was an artist, and he would somehow think less of me if I had learned the trick of popularising and making real money from my work. He did not wish to embarrass me or spoil our friendship, but he and Chantal had a small amount they were saving for retirement. If it would help, I would be welcome to the money and could pay him back when things got better. I looked at my friend and wondered how many local people he has quietly helped over the years, then thanked him for his offer and refused it. After he had opened another bottle and we had talked some more, he came up with a compromise. From now on, I would pay for all my drinks at the Flaming Curtains with copies of my books, valued at the cover price. He would sell them to English visitors at an advantageous conversion rate into euros, and we would both make a profit from the arrangement. As he said, it was unlikely that the savings on my weekly bar bill would be enough to pay off our overdraft within the next three months, but given my rate of consumption it would surely make a healthy dent in it.

～

We are visiting a friend's home to talk about the sale of La Puce and start the search for a new home in Lower Normandy.

At the Château Epinguet, we find the owner looking bemusedly at a small mountain of septic tanks on his driveway. To visitors, the collection of large plastic boxes might seem at odds with the imposing façade of the great house and its landscaped gardens. To us and those who know Mark Berridge, the serried ranks of waste-disposal units are just a sign that it is business as usual.

Although he occasionally seems to be living in another dimension, Mark is one of the most decent and genuine men I know. Being also adaptable, durable and more than a little what some people might call eccentric, he is ideally suited to living in Lower Normandy and helping other people find property here. Having moved to the Cotentin to set up as a property agent fifteen years ago, Mark is a veteran at dealing with his British customers and the owners of the property they wish to buy. He has also become adept at dealing with the regulations and authorities whose job it is to make property transfer as awkward and time-consuming as possible. It was Mark who helped us find and buy La Puce, and it seems fitting that it is to him we come to talk about the possibility of selling our home and finding a new one.

With his wife, Fiona, Mark runs what is almost a one-stop-shopping service from their home. Those in search of property in the area can stay at the château, be taken on tours of available properties in their price range and then nursed through the buying process. They can also take advantage of Mark's experience and contacts throughout the region after they have bought their home in the Cotentin, which explains the mountain of septic tanks.

Having negotiated the *fosse septique* chicane, we are invited into the private quarters and take a seat under the boar's head that is mounted on the wall and for some reason has been named George. When we explain our situation, Mark appears crestfallen. He knows how happy we have been at La Puce, but understands our reasons for having to put the cottage, farmhouse and grounds on the market. He is sure he can find us a buyer for La Puce. It is, he says politely, a most unusual property, but over the years he has found that there is always a customer for every house, wherever it is and whatever condition it is in.

When we have agreed on what seems a fair price for La Puce, we climb over the pile of septic tanks, and while Donella goes to speak to Fiona, I confess to Mark that I may be wasting his time. I have only agreed that we should sell La Puce because I know my wife is concerned about our overdraft and is also determined that my new book be published. I know that, whatever she says, it would break her heart to have to leave our home and I intend to do everything I can to stop that happening.

Mark says he understands and that he would probably feel the same. He will do his best to find us a buyer and another property at a bargain price, and if it will help he will forego his commission on the sale. But knowing how much we love La Puce, he will be more than happy if his efforts to sell it are wasted.

Before we get into the car, Donella turns to Mark and says in a small voice that he must, of course, accept an offer from anyone who comes up with the asking price, but it would be nice if they were the sort of people who he thinks would love and look after our old home and be as happy there as we have been. Our friend nods and kisses her cheek, and as we drive off I see that he has taken out a handkerchief and is pretending to blow his nose. It is good to know that despite their reputation, some estate agents, unlike most bank managers, have a soul.

~

As if my poor wife did not have enough to worry about, my fears that Cato is fighting his last fight may be well founded. Without telling Donella, I took our cat to the vet at La Haye-du-Puits this morning, and he says that Cato has stomach cancer. He said there was a very expensive course of treatment, but all he thought it could do was delay the inevitable. I paid for the box of powder anyway, and promised him I would not let Cato suffer by avoiding our duty when the time came to give her her final freedom from pain. I will add the medicine to Cato's food when Donella is not there to see me, and not tell her the result of the tests. I am sure she knows what is happening to her beloved cat, but it must be best for her to live in hope for a little longer.

Du sublime au ridicule il n'y a qu'un pas.
(It is but a small step from the sublime to the ridiculous.)
Napoleon Bonaparte (1769–1821)

On the Road Again

It has been a long and disappointing day.

In spite of my determination that we shall not have to sell La Puce, I had been looking forward to our first viewing trip. Though we have had no reason to consider buying another property in France for more than a decade, I still find it almost impossible to pass an estate agency without looking. As some women are drawn to clothing, shoe or cake shops, I cannot resist pressing my nose against any window through which I can see property details.

When we began looking for a home in Normandy, the region appeared to be overflowing with characterful old properties just waiting for their potential to be unlocked. Every visit to an isolated hamlet, village or town was a journey of anticipation, and what lay hidden at the end of a pot-holed track was often a treasure. During our journeying around the peninsula, we saw once grand *manoirs*, decaying yet enchanting cottages and deserted farmhouses still alive with the echoes of their past. All were waiting patiently for someone to arrive and bring them to life again, and some of the prices made it seem that we had travelled back in time as well as across the English Channel. But today has shown us much evidence of how times change.

During our journey, we looked at derelict and unappetising

cottages with little or no land for sale at twice the value we would have placed upon them. We also saw empty properties that had obviously been commercially restored and dressed for sale, even down to a pile of artistically arranged logs next to the unused stove. For the first time since moving to Lower Normandy, we were seeing homes that had obviously been bought and renovated and converted for no other purpose than to sell at a profit. With what the French have started to call *l'invasion* of buyers from other parts of Europe, this should not be an unexpected development, but it was somehow sad to see the evidence that property speculation will inevitably play a large part in the economic future of our region. However unlikely it may have seemed a few years ago, it is possible that the French will now become as obsessed as the British with the value of their homes. Until recently, people in our towns and villages mostly looked on a house as somewhere to live and raise the family. When they died, the family home would be passed on to the next generation. Lives and futures were not governed by how much you had paid for your house and how much it might be worth now. From what we have seen today, it seems that this traditional attitude may change dramatically. Homes will inevitably become valuable commodities, and the character of the rural landscape and the sort of people who live there will change, just as it has in Britain.

When we stopped at a bar and I voiced my fears to Donella, she said that I should not condemn other foreigners for wanting to do what we did, or local people and places to stay unchanged just to suit my romantic notions. And if I was looking for someone to blame, she reminded me, I must bear a tiny fraction of the responsibility as I have spent the last ten years telling people how wonderful life can be in the French countryside.

My wife is probably right, but I still feel saddened to think that, by their desire to be part of all that has been so unchanging about rural France, the very people who so admire it will be those who help to destroy it. On a practical note, what we have seen today could mean that our chances of finding an interesting old property at a good price are, to say the least, remote.

~

More tales of the unexpected in the mail today, and our postman had a decidedly different look about him. As he rolled down the track, I saw that Patrick was sporting a new uniform and trendy high-heeled boots, and had neglected to wear his official crash-helmet. He was smoking a long cheroot rather than his perennial roll-up, and his normally lank and mousy hair was standing to attention in rigid black tufts. When I asked him if he had forgotten his helmet and if his hair was standing on end because one of his customers had asked for a loan, he gave me a condescending look and said it was obvious that I was completely out of touch with modern fashion. His hairstyle was all the rage in Paris, and he was not going to spoil it by wearing an ugly non-designer helmet. Besides, helmets were for women and sissies. Life was for living, and a whiff of danger added to a man's appeal. Coming from someone who wears a surgical mask to deliver his letters to our doctor's surgery, this new attitude to risk-taking was as much of a surprise as his sudden attack of fashion-consciousness. He said that his recent trip to Paris had opened his eyes to a whole new world, and to the fact that life was not a rehearsal. He added that he also had Didier Bouvier to thank for his transformation, and took out and showed me a small bottle of what looked like cough medicine. It was, he said, a very expensive vitality tonic, but worth every euro. Since he had started taking it, he had become a new man and was now determined to make up for lost time. The most amazing thing about the potion was how well it worked below the belt. Such was his potency now that even his wife had begun to complain of headaches at bedtime, and was talking about moving in to the spare room. With that, he winked broadly and said he would not be staying for breakfast as he had a large package to give to the Widow of Négreville and knew she was anxious to get it. After attempting a wheelie on his moped in our turning circle, he shouted out that I should try a bottle of Didier's elixir, as with all the beer I drank I would otherwise soon be needing a pair of splints to perform my marital duties.

After I watched our dramatically revitalised postman gunning his *mobylette* up the track and straight out on to the road to a chorus of squealing brakes and lorry horns, I opened the day's post and learned I may be able to help avoid a serious international diplomatic incident.

Among the bulky envelopes of property details, there was a letter containing a plea from a reader who lives in the picturesque and normally tranquil Dorset village of Corfe Castle. My correspondent explained that, some years ago, his village received a visit from the then mayor of our nearest town. The purpose was to discuss the twinning of Corfe with St Sauveur-le-Vicomte. The idea was mooted because both places boast a ruined castle. After several days of earnest discussion and civic junketing, the mayor of St Sauveur was presented with a souvenir in the form of a cannon ball that may or may not have been fired in anger at or from Corfe Castle. As is the way of these things in France, time slipped by after the mayor of St Sauveur returned to his day job as an ironmonger and nothing more was heard of the twinning idea. Now, I read, the Corfe sub-committee set up to administer the project wants its ball back.

Knowing about my connections with St Sauveur, my correspondent proposes I try to locate the cannon ball and reclaim it for its original owners. My reward, if successful, will be a large bottle of champagne. The committee will also be happy to pay the postage on the missile, which they realise may be costly because of its weight. There is even talk of granting me the freedom of the village if I bring their ball back in person.

I shall write and say that I am honoured to be offered this opportunity to prevent a possible rift in the *entente-cordiale* between the two locations. I shall add that I will visit the castle at St Sauveur on my way to the Flaming Curtains today, but if it is there I will clearly have a problem in identifying the English ball among the dozens on show at the castle and, given the occupation of the former mayor, there is always the chance he may have absent-mindedly had it melted down for its scrap value.

~

Another day of driving around the peninsula looking at unsuitable properties. The deadline for repaying our overdraft approaches inexorably, and I have not been able to come up with a scheme to save us from having to sell La Puce. I am now becoming almost resigned to moving to a smaller, cheaper property so that we will be able to settle our debts and pay for the publication of my new book, and if we are to find an interesting new home at a reasonable price, it looks as if we are going to have to move to the inner reaches of the marshlands.

Today, we have been exploring the villages and hamlets around Sourciéville and calling in at bars and shops to ask local people if they know of any houses for sale. While Mark is doing his best to find somewhere suitable and at a good price in the north of the Cotentin, we have been doing our own investigating further south. This will widen our choice of properties at an affordable price, and if we find somewhere by using local knowledge, we may be able to pick up a real bargain.

Although I had thought that we had passed by, if not through, every commune in the Cotentin, it has been a revelation to travel deep into the interior and discover places we had not known existed. We have found hamlets and even whole villages that do not appear on the most detailed of maps, and some which appear not to have been visited by outsiders for generations. We have also found and looked at some properties that appear not to have been lived in for generations, if at all. The good news is that prices are markedly lower in this isolated and often brooding area of the peninsula; the bad news is that we have seen nothing which caused even a flicker of interest. But we have seen some remarkable buildings masquerading as homes.

Dusk is falling, and as we reach the end of our viewing list we find ourselves outside a property at the bottom of the longest and most poorly maintained track I have encountered in all my years in Lower Normandy. While I am trying to close a broken gate outside what appears to be a derelict and therefore uninhabited cottage, Donella calls a warning and I look round to see an ancient Renault trundling down the track. It is heading straight for me and has no driver. I immediately take cover behind the stone wall in front of the cottage, and hear and feel the car arrive. Climbing over the bonnet, I look inside and see an elderly man slumped in the passenger seat. Obviously revived by the collision, he stirs and grunts, then kicks open the door and staggers out. Ignoring us, he makes a half-hearted attempt to open the gate, then gives up and simply throws himself over the wall. Crawling up the garden path, he disappears inside his home. After closing the door of the battered Renault, I call a polite good evening to its owner and we set off to navigate the long and treacherous track back to civilisation.

~

We have solved the mystery of the driverless car. I have also added to my list of interesting rural bars and their often unusual toilet facilities and arrangements.

A mile or so from where the track to the cottage joined the main road, we arrived at a small village. Alongside the church was a bar and grocery shop, run by a small, bird-like woman with a big and nervous-looking dog, which seemed to be named after a chain of convenience stores. When we had settled down with a drink and had passed the time of day, I told Madame about our experience. After aiming a stream of invective at the dog when it tried to approach Milly, Madame explained that what we had seen was a quite normal occurrence. The man was a retired farmer, and liked to visit his old friends at the market at Sourciéville every Monday. After selling his farm, he had missed the camaraderie and hard bargaining, the general atmosphere and, most of all, the prodigious drinking sessions when business was done.

To begin with, he would drive his car to and from the market, but after several expensive encounters with other drivers and the local policeman, the old farmer realised he would have to make other travel arrangements. He had many offers of a lift to and from the town, but could find nobody who would risk their suspension by venturing from the road and down the long and spectacularly unkempt track to his home. So he had devised a system that would suit everyone. On the morning of a market day, he would drive to the top of the track, turn his old car around in the road and leave it pointing downhill. He would then wait for the market bus to pick him up and take him to town. After the traditional session in the farmers' favourite bar, his friends would escort him to the bus for the return journey. At the top of the track, the driver and one or two passengers would help him to his car. If he were capable, he would then start the engine and negotiate the bumpy half-mile of track down to his home. If he were not feeling up to driving, he would simply unlock the handbrake and let gravity take its course. If he was beyond even that simple task, the bus driver would do the honours and send him on his way like a fallen Viking warrior laid out in his longboat and sailing towards the setting sun with nobody at the rudder. The track was fairly straight, said Madame, and generally the car made the journey to the house. The old farmer had even devised an ingenious arrangement of baling twine, which could be lashed around the steering wheel to keep the car on course. If it did not complete its journey, the farmer would stay there till he sobered up enough to reach his home on foot. It was, she concluded, a very practical and logical solution to the problem. The man was helped by his friends at a time of need and, most importantly, he had kept his independence.

Having agreed that it seemed a very satisfactory arrangement, I ordered another round, and when Donella asked for directions to the toilet, Madame explained that there were no facilities in the bar. In the traditional manner, men abused the wall of the alleyway alongside the shop; the occasional woman visitor in need of relief was always welcome to use Madame's private toilet. The shop and bar were rented from the people who lived above the premises, but Madame's home was just across the street. It was the small house with the green door, which my wife would naturally find unlocked.

While I waited for Donella, I asked the proprietor the origin of her dog's unusual name. She explained that, since a chain of grocery stores moved into the area some years ago, her business had been on a downward spiral. At about the same time, the dog had turned up on her doorstep. She had tried to discourage it, but it would not go away. Like the rival store in the next village, the dog was costing her money and was a blight on her life, so she had naturally called it Proxi. It was a badly behaved dog, she added, so she was constantly required to chastise it. Although she could do nothing to halt the decline of her business or get rid of the dog or the nearby grocery franchise, she found it gave her a little satisfaction to have the opportunity and excuse to curse the very name of the company that had given her such unhappiness.

As the lady came to the end of her story and shook her fist in mock-anger at the dog, my wife returned. When Donella said she had closed the door safely and had enjoyed meeting her family, Madame said that she had no family and lived alone. Further enquiries revealed that my wife had gone through the wrong green door. She had, she said, found the toilet at the top of the stairs, then returned to have a brief chat with the family who were eating dinner in the front room. They had seemed friendly if a little bemused when my wife had explained that she was just passing through, and had even wished her a safe onward journey.

As she waved us on our way, Madame said that my wife should not be embarrassed by the mistake. It was, in a way, poetic justice that she had made a convenience of the family's home as they now did all their shopping at the rival grocery store in the next village.

~~~

The deadline draws ever closer, yet we have not found a new home or received any offers on La Puce. Our agent arrived with several potential buyers this week, but none seemed interested. One couple said they had not realised there would be so much water at a water mill. Another fleeting visitor explained she was an artist and looking for an atmospheric and peaceful setting to inspire her, but was disappointed that the mill cottage had no view. She had hoped it would have been on a hilltop with a striking pano-rama, not buried in a valley and surrounded by trees that stole the light. I explained that because rivers tend to run downhill, water mills were generally built at a lower level than the surrounding landscape, but my attempt at sarcasm was obviously wasted.

At other times of financial crisis, we have put La Puce on the market to stall our creditors, but have never before made a real effort to sell. Last year, my wife spent much of her time putting potential buyers off by pointing out severe and sometimes even imaginary defects in the fabric and structure of all the buildings at La Puce. Now we are in des-perate straits and will probably have to sell, it is frustrating that nobody seems interested in an unusual property that is known to many thousands of people around the world.

Yesterday, I called Didier Bouvier and asked about expanding our language school and student placement scheme, but the news was bad. He said that most of the local people had told him they were giving up trying to learn such a complicated and illogical tongue. There had also been certain problems with the placement scheme that he would explain when we next met. He did offer me a case of his vitality tonic at wholesale price, but refused credit and would not tell me the recipe or if it really worked. Whatever is in the tonic, it is certainly effective as Patrick the Post is fast becoming a living legend in the area. Not only has he registered with Jean-Claude's escort agency, but his moped has also been seen outside the houses of a number of young women while their husbands are out at work. As at least two of the ladies are not on his round, it appears it is not only letters he has been delivering.

～～～

It has been a sad end to a bad month. Donella needs to be alone, so I have come to talk to my old friend Lucky at the Hobbit Tree. Earlier today, we took Cato to the veterinary surgery at La Haye-du-Puits and have returned without her.

She had grown steadily weaker since the vet diagnosed her cancer, and Donella spent every moment of her last days with her. After we had said our goodbyes and the vet had slipped the needle into Cato's leg, she gave a soft sigh and then lay completely still. When I reached out my hand to give her a farewell pat, her eyes opened and focused on me. The old feral gleam flashed momentarily, and before I could react she struck out and drew her claws down the back of my hand. Then, as if she had used up her last spark of energy, her eyes clouded over and her head fell back on the table.

When the vet had cleaned and put a plaster over my scratch, he closed the surgery and took us over the road for a drink. There were customers in the waiting room, but none complained when they knew where he was going and why. For half an hour, we sat and told him about the adventures we had had with Cato, and he listened without embarrassment as we laughed and cried. Before he went back to work he said that the wound on my hand will probably not scar, but I hope it does. It will be good to carry a permanent and suitable reminder of such a special animal.

~

It has happened.

Donella was sitting with Milly at the grotto when Mark Berridge called to say that we have had an offer on La Puce. He had arrived with a couple while we were at La Haye-du-Puits, and they spent no more than an hour looking around before saying they would like to buy our home. They have returned to London and left their offer with us, and Mark believes, if we really intend to sell, we should think seriously about accepting it. This couple seem genuine, but can withdraw their offer at any time without obligation until they sign the first stage of the contract. Sometimes when people return to Britain after seeing a property they are sure they want to buy, their enchantment fades and they begin to have second thoughts. If we do want to go ahead, Mark recommends that we sign our side of the *compromis de vente* as soon as possible so he can post the contract to them.

As if I am listening to someone else speaking, I tell Mark that I will talk to Donella in the morning. Until now, I had never really believed that we would be selling La Puce, or that his call would come. I know that he needs an answer, but I must speak to my wife before giving it, and she has other things on her mind at this moment.

Je me presse de rire de tout, de peur d'être obligé d'en pleurer.
(I make myself laugh at everything
for fear of having to weep at it.)
Pierre-Augustin Caron de Beaumarchais, playwright (1732–99)

Taxing Times

A perfect summer's day, and to me La Puce has never seemed more beautiful.

Our hedgerows have been transformed by an explosion of snow-white elderflower, and the water meadow is a field of gold. The land itself seems bursting with promise and vitality, and I wish I could paint well enough to capture this moment and keep it for ever.

My wife and I spent most of the morning discussing the offer to buy La Puce. I spent the first hour trying to persuade her that we should take our time before signing the contract, as something might happen to give us a last-minute reprieve. We might hear from one of the dozens of minor publishing houses to whom I sent the manuscript of the new book, or Mr Connarde might have a change of heart on calling in our overdraft. We might even come up with the right numbers to win the National Lottery. Having heard my arguments, my wife said that our neighbour's pigs might also start practising aerial manoeuvres above the water meadow. We both know what has to be done, and must get on with it. We have to sell La Puce. There is no realistic choice, so we must bite the bullet and sign.

I know she is right, though I still find it hard to believe we are about to sign away our home of thirteen years. I had convinced myself that something would turn up and solve our financial nightmare. Now I can see that we are going to lose La Puce.

~

Life goes on, and I am in the caravan dealing with a torrent of e-mail messages. I spoke to Mr Connarde earlier and, when I told him that we had been made an offer for La Puce, he sounded quite disappointed and said I should not count my chickens before they are hatched. I said I was a little tired of hearing that expression lately, and that our buyers were paying a small fortune for the property. He replied that he had heard English people would pay crazy amounts for any old ruin in the French countryside, but had not realised some of them were that naïve. When I asked him if the good news meant that he would defer the date by which we had to pay back our overdraft, he said that he would give me an answer when he had seen the contract. And he would want to see it signed by our alleged customers and attested by our *notaire*. To lighten the tension between us, I told him the old joke about a verbal contract not being worth the paper it is written on, but he completely missed the point.

I have dealt with all my correspondence, including some worrying e-mails from the readers who I chose as hosts for Didier Bouvier's foreign placement scheme. Eight of them have sent a message to say that their guests have disappeared. In each case, the student arrived, stayed for a day, then packed up and left with no explanation after receiving a call from the organiser of the scheme. All the hosts say they have received no money from Didier, and one said that the family car went missing at the same time as his guest. A reader from Ealing says that he is very angry about an incident featuring my student, his daughter and a loofah in the bathroom, and another said that he does not believe that his fleeting guest was French. He said that he had spent some time working in Eastern Europe, and the language he heard his lodger using during his telephone conversation with a mystery caller sounded much more Albanian than Basque.

～

We are at the Château Epinguet, ready to sign the contract to sell La Puce. Fiona is up a ladder trimming the two tall palm trees guarding the entrance to her stately B&B enterprise, and the mountain of septic tanks in the driveway has been replaced by a huge pile of ancient radiators that Mark says he bought as a job lot from a demolition contractor in Essex. The winters here can be long and cold, and Mark says he will be able to let his clients have the radiators at a good price. They are of an early manufacture, impressively massive and made of cast iron, and I agree with him that they will look more suitable in older buildings than the modern and bland designs.

Sitting at the table under the disinterested gaze of George the boar, we have been going through the first-stage contract and at the same time catching up on the current state of the laws governing the exchange of property in France. It is a long time since we bought La Puce, and it seems many of the rules of engagement have been amended. Predictably, it seems that rather than being simplified, the process has become even more complicated, especially with respect to foreign buyers. Mark has also told us that there are some small complications with the proposed arrangements between the buyers and ourselves.

As he explains, when we have signed the contract he will post it immediately to London. After our customers have added their signatures and the date, they will return the document to Mark, and he will physically put it in the hands of our local *notaire*. Mr Remuen will then take over and prepare everything for the *Acte Finale*. This is the official completion of the sale, which will take place in his office at a time and date convenient to all parties. Although there are two separate stages to the transaction, Mark reminds us, the initial contract is virtually as binding as the final document. Our customers will be agreeing to buy La Puce at the price stated and in the condition in which it is found on the day they take it over. We will be agreeing to sell it to them at that price and on the agreed date, and there can be severe financial penalties if we withdraw. However, as long as the notary agrees, any number of reasonable (and sometimes completely unreasonable) suspensive clauses may be written into the contract to avoid penalties in the case of withdrawal. The most common get-out clause relates to the buyers not being able to secure a mortgage on the property, but our customers will not be seeking a loan. I ask if it is possible to insert a clause that we can withdraw from the sale if we win the lottery, or otherwise find the money to pay off our overdraft before completion date; Mark says that Mr Remuen, though a helpful and understanding man, is not likely to agree to this proviso.

As to the most suitable date for the *Acte Finale*, Mark says that our buyers are anxious to complete in the near future; they have asked to move in to La Puce no later than two months from today. He realises that we have not yet found a new home, but advises that we agree lest they lose interest and look elsewhere. He also knows that we need to settle our debt with the bank by that date. My wife and I look at each other, then nod agreement.

As our agent indicates where we must make our signatures on the contract, he says the buyers wish to make a rather unusual condition. They do not have a French bank account, and for some reason do not wish to pay for La Puce in euros. If we agree, they will arrive on the day of completion with a banker's draft made out in pounds sterling.

Mark says this is the first time he has heard of buyers making this condition. Perhaps they are worried about a sudden downturn in the exchange rate at the time of the sale, or perhaps they are just not comfortable dealing in a foreign currency. For whatever reason, our buyers are insistent. But, as we will know, a bank draft is as good as cash, and any change in the rate may equally well be to our advantage. The euro has been strong against the pound in recent times, but all the forecasts are that what goes up must come down. If that happens, we would receive a considerable bonus. Most importantly, Mr Remuen has agreed to the arrangement. Finally, says Mark, he hopes we realise there may be some capital gains to pay on the profit we will, at least on paper, be making by selling La Puce.

I laugh without humour, and say that this is the last thing we need to worry about. Although the sum we are receiving for La Puce is more than ten times what the property cost us, we shall actually be losing money on the deal. We bought the two completely ruined buildings thirteen years ago, and in real terms have spent much more on the property than the selling price. Apart from the cost of completely restoring the mill cottage and farmhouse, we have spent tens of thousands of pounds on the grounds over the years, to say nothing of the many thousands of hours of unpaid labour we have invested. I am sure that we will make no gains – capital or otherwise – on selling La Puce.

In spite of my confidence, Mark looks concerned, then gives an almost Gallic shrug and says he thinks we will need to talk quite urgently to Mr Remuen about the situation. After a moment of silence broken only by the ticking of the long-case clock in the corner, he clears his throat and asks us if we are ready to sign.

I look into my wife's eyes for the third time in half an hour, then reach for my pen.

~

We have been on a sentimental journey and have stopped for a drink at our first local in Lower Normandy. On the way home and feeling low, we crossed the Route Nationale at Brix and took the back roads to Valognes and on to the hamlet of Yvetot Bocage. It is the way we drove with Mark Berridge nearly fourteen years ago to see what would become our first home in France. We had a very limited budget and even less idea of what we were seeking, but Mark came up trumps when he showed us the Little Jewel. As it turned out, we were to sell Le Petit Bijou quite literally before the new paint on the living room walls had dried. The little cottage with its sharply pitched roof is still in the same caring hands in which we left it, and looks somehow contented. As we sat outside and recalled the small adventures we had there, I said it was strange to think how different our lives would have been had we stayed a little longer. If nothing else, we would probably not be deeply in debt and having to sell our home. Donella reminded me that I had persuaded her to sell the Jewel, but also that if we had not moved on we may never have found La Puce or met and made all our friends at Néhou.

Perhaps because our lives are about to change, I find it reassuring to be in the Café de Paris bar where we would come to relax after a long day of working on the Little Jewel. Outside, the same people are still going about their business in what is said to be the largest square in Normandy. The boys who would race their mopeds up and down the cobbled pathways all those years ago have married the girls they were trying to impress as they performed their tricks, but a new generation of acrobatic suitors has taken their place.

Inside the bar, things seem to have changed little. Although a little greyer in the hair and even more florid in the face, Freddo the patron is still on duty behind the bar and the customers are still betting on when the ever lengthening ash on his cigarette will fall into the glass he is filling. His wife, Collette, is still waiting tables and showing genuine interest in and concern for her customers and their lives. Most reassuringly of all, Collette's aged mother is still wielding her broom and sharing a joke or a few sharp words with those she thinks deserve them. In her time she has dealt with drunken German occupiers and marauding English hooligans, and I suddenly realise that I have never asked her who she found most difficult to control.

I signal for another bottle of Normandy champagne, and ask Collette if there is still room on my slate. She says that it is a very accommodating slate, and leaves us to talk about the immediate future. I say to Donella that now we have signed the contract, I have accepted that we are to leave La Puce and I realise what lies ahead. Together with negotiating all the complexities of selling our home, we have to find a new one in less than two months. With no credit facilities at the bank, we shall probably have to move out of La Puce and in to our new home on the same day, with a lengthy session in the notary's office in between. And this will not be like any other move.

We shall have to clear out and transport all our furniture, furnishings and possessions from the two buildings at La Puce, as well as everything that must be moved from the ten acres outside. This will include the contents of the outbuildings and my tool sheds, my stores of building materials, and perhaps even the caravan by the big pond. As I start to make a rough list on the back of a beer mat, my wife says that I have forgotten to mention our animals and her special things. Apart from Milly, there are the chickens, Ermintrude the balletic goose and Hen the duck, and we must take at least a selection of our crayfish, frogs and goldfish. Then there is everything in her potting shed and greenhouse, and cuttings from her favourite plants.

Without thinking to engage my brain before opening my mouth, I say that we have more important things to consider than a few cuttings, and it will be hard enough work shipping our chickens across the peninsula without worrying about whether a dustbin of goldfish are suffering from travel or homesickness. It is almost a relief that we will not have the problem of capturing and caging Cato for the journey. Donella falls silent and I realise what I have said. I start to apologise, and for the first time since I have known her, my wife begins to cry in public. Reaching out towards her, I say that I will ring Mark now and tell him to tear up the contract. I would rather rob a bank and go to jail than be responsible for taking her away from La Puce.

My wife smiles a resigned smile, wipes her eyes and says that, all things considered, that has been the best suggestion I have made for thirty-four years.

~

Six weeks and five days to go before the *Acte Finale* is to be signed. We are sitting outside Mr Remuen's office, waiting for our first meeting to discuss the sale.

As we wait, I flick idly through a magazine of properties on sale in the area. Yesterday, we took our tenth expedition into the Cotentin interior in as many days, but have yet to see a single house that could become a home.

The door to the office eventually opens and an elderly couple emerge, followed by Mr Remuen. He is as tall and spare as they are short and wide, and he leans down towards them as they shake hands and exchange farewells. The man is wearing a green bib-and-brace overall and brown Wellington boots, and his face records at least sixty years of exposure to summer sun and all-year-round wind and rain. He has obviously kept his peaked cap on throughout the meeting, and now doffs it briefly as he turns to leave. The woman has obviously made an effort to dress up for the occasion, and despite the warmth of the day has chosen her church-going black coat, which is buttoned severely up to the neck. On her head she wears a smart bonnet that must have seen as many weddings and funerals as her husband's face has seen seasons of the year.

Mr Remuen is in his shirtsleeves, and boasting a silk tie that would give a chameleon a nervous breakdown. On his wrist is an elegant designer watch, and on his feet an equally expensive pair of casual shoes. I know from their parting conversation and the slightly dazed expressions on the faces of the elderly couple that Mr Remuen is arranging the sale of their house to an English buyer. They will soon have more money in their savings account than the man has probably earned in half a lifetime of hard work.

After seeing the couple off the premises and glancing at his watch, our notary hurries over to apologise and usher us towards his office. As we settle down and talk about the weather, I have a sudden premonition that we will be spending a lot of time in this office over the coming months. I don't know why I am feeling so nervous, as we should by now be familiar with what lies ahead, but, of all people, I *know* that it is a general rule of buying or selling a house in France that something will go wrong. Sometimes I think that it is written into the constitution that people wishing to buy or sell a property must be made to suffer. Sometimes I think these problems arise or are manufactured simply because of the French love of theatre. I also believe they like creating so many regulations and laws just so they can bend, break or ignore them. While sitting in a chair like this one, I have also observed that the average notary seems to work hard at finding a stumbling block that he will only dismantle when you are just about to fall over it.

In spite of my foreboding, I cannot see that we should have too many heart-stopping moments with Mr Remuen. It was he who oversaw our purchase of La Puce, and he knows in what condition it was in when we bought it and how much we must have spent on restoring it. He has driven past our home every day for the past thirteen years, and has seen how it has changed. I also know that Mr Remuen is a good and honest man and that, if there are any problems, he will do his best to make them go away. After, of course, he has built a suitably high stumbling block. I know that this is not because he wants to put us through torment, but just because that is the way the game is played here.

Our meeting begins, and Mr Remuen opens his bulky file on La Puce with the air of a surgeon making the first decisive incision. In the folder will be every scrap of paper relating to legal entanglements to which our home and its surrounding land have been subject over the past century and beyond. There will be hand-drawn plans of the once constantly changing jigsaw of individual plots within the boundaries, and letters to and from their long-dead owners. The folder will also hold the deeds of the property and the contracts we signed in this office thirteen years ago. Although those years have sped by, I can still recall the exact moment when Mr Remuen put the key to La Puce in my hands and how I felt as I passed it to Donella. So much has happened since then, and our home has been the witness to so many moments of joy, frustration, occasional sadness and not infrequent farce.

~

As I begin a countdown to my estimate of when he will first use the p-word, he congratulates us on our sale and for achieving such a good price on the property. Our buyers have signed and returned the contract, and he anticipates no real difficulties with the transfer. There may, of course, be some small *problèmes* to overcome. As I congratulate myself on the accuracy of my forecast, Mr Remuen says he has yet to receive the passport photographs and other proof that our customers are who they say they are. Also, their condition that they will only pay with a banker's draft is most unusual. After giving the matter much thought, speaking to our agent and talking with several colleagues in the region, he is prepared to proceed if we are satisfied with the method of payment. I nod agreement, and Mr Remuen continues. We will be aware, of course, that because of the difference between the price we paid for La Puce and the price at which we are selling it, the question of capital gains tax will arise.

I reach for the metaphorical ace up my sleeve while he lists all the allowances that can be set against our alleged profit on the sale. Firstly, there is the 5% discount from tax liability for every year we have owned La Puce. Had we stayed at our home for another seven years, he says with a wry smile, the bill would have been wiped clean. Because we bought at the end of one year and are selling in the middle of this year, two of the years will not be admissible, but that still means a discount of 60% from any liability. Then there will be the adjustments for inflation over the years, and the interest we paid on the loan we took out to help pay for La Puce. He has been making his initial rough calculations, and has arrived at the remaining sum on which we will owe capital gains tax. This, of course, is before any deductions for the improvements we have carried out on the premises. With another grade of smile, he says that he knows just how much work we have undertaken at La Puce. He passes me the piece of paper and I look at it, sigh theatrically with relief and hand him my envelope.

Inside is an invoice from the builder who carried out most of the restoration of La Puce. Although we used local labour and did much of the unskilled work ourselves, the amount on the invoice and receipt in the envelope comfortably exceeds our theoretical profit on the sale.

My moment of smugness evaporates as Mr Remuen puts his winning card on the table. After unfolding the receipt and examining it, he smiles sadly, shakes his head and returns it. Unfortunately, he says, the document is not valid. If it were from a French builder, all would be well. Even if it were from a British builder who had paid his taxes in France, it would have been valid. As it is, it is from a British builder who pays his taxes in Britain and is therefore inadmissible, so it looks as if we shall have to pay the substantial duty on the profit he knows we have not made.

As usual when big problems arrive, we have come to the pub. We are alone in the back room of the Flaming Curtains, and Coco is at the bar continuing work on degreasing the back axle of his Land Rover. He is a sensitive man, and can see that my wife and I will not appreciate company at this time.

I am still in shock from Mr Remuen's estimate of our capital gains bill, and can now see no way that we can go ahead with the sale of La Puce. As my wife points out, there is also no way we can withdraw from the sale. The cooling-off period after we signed the contract has expired, and we are committed to selling. We have no choice. We know that we shall not be making a profit, and so does our *notaire*. But the Republic demands proof of all the money we spent in restoring La Puce, and have changed the rules about what constitutes that proof.

As Mr Remuen explained, the law invalidating British builders' invoices only came into force this year. It was obviously brought in to encourage foreign home owners to employ French builders, and incredibly, even for France, the new law is retrospective in that it applies to the time before it was invented.

Now we are really in trouble. If our notary can find no way round the problem, we will owe the French government almost twenty thousand pounds in capital gains tax. If we have to pay the duty, there will be barely enough left to pay off our overdraft and buy a very modest home. And my new book will have to remain unpublished.

~

It looks as if we are to be given a reprieve, and it may be possible to leap nimbly over our giant stumbling block.

Mr Remuen called today to say there is a way to make our *problème* go away. He knows that we employed a number of local craftsmen on the restoration of La Puce, and that they and our British builder will have bought their materials in the area. If he pretends that he has not seen our invoice and we can produce the evidence of what we have spent on building materials in the past thirteen years, he will be able to estimate what we will have paid in fees to our real and imaginary French craftsmen. He realises that I will not be able to produce any invoices from the local people who did or did not work on La Puce, but that will not be a problem. The permitted formula in these situations of trebling the cost of the materials used should arrive at a total that will just about defray our tax liabilities. What he is proposing is quite legal, providing he ignores the document I showed him yesterday. I told him that I had already forgotten what was on that piece of paper, and that I shall dedicate my new book to him.

~~~

Our reprieve is on hold.

We spent an increasingly frantic hour in the loft of the mill cottage after Mr Remuen's call, but have found no more than a handful of receipts for the tons of building materials we bought over the years. Donella and I are not enthusiastic keepers of accounts, and anyway, I could have no idea that our British builder's invoice would one day prove useless. Virtually all the tens of thousands of pounds worth of receipts have long been discarded or turned into bedding for the family of mice who live in our loft.

But I think there is a way out of our problem. Nearly all the materials used on La Puce were bought from a family-run building supply company in the area, and they are sure to have a record of them. In France, householders are required to keep telephone bills for a year, water bills for two years, and TV licence receipts for three. Serious documents like electricity and gas bills must be held for five years, and bank cheque stubs and statements for a decade. The laws on keeping business records are even more draconian, so

Mr Branluer must have details of every penny we have spent at his yard.

~

Another stumbling block has been erected. During our time in Lower Normandy, we have met some exceptionally helpful people, but Mr Branluer does not feature on that list. He and his family have been happy enough to sell us many thousands of pounds worth of building materials, but I do not think they like us.

When I called to ask for copies of the receipts for all the materials we had bought from him over the years, Mr Branluer laughed as if I were making a joke. When I explained our situation and said that Mr Remuen would accept a signed attestation from him of the approximate total, he said he was horrified that I should suggest a collusion to rob the government of its dues. In any case, what I asked was not possible as he had recently sold his business and was now acting merely as a consultant to the new owners. All his records were locked away for safe keeping in a vault at his bank, and his secretary had retired when the new firm took over. If he were to help me, he would have to ask her to come back from her daughter's home in the south and go through all the books. For her to examine every transaction over thirteen years to find our entries would take a long time, and he would have to pay her a special fee as well as all her expenses. He would also have to make a small charge for all the work and time it would take him. I thought about my options for a moment, then agreed. Before hanging up, I asked him to be sure that his secretary checked the true version of the two sets of business records that I knew he kept, but he pretended not to understand what I meant.

Exactitude is not truth.
Henri Matisse (1869–1954)

Encounters With the Count

We are on the road again, and completely lost. Our search for a new home has led us deep into the heart of the Cotentinese *marais*, and we have seen no signs of civilisation for more than an hour. Our journey has taken us on a winding route through vast stretches of the central marshlands, and signposts are as rare as other vehicles. In rural Normandy, a lack of signposting is unusual, so it seems that in this particular area the authorities do not want travellers to know exactly where they are. Perhaps, my wife suggested, it is the people who live here who do not want to advertise their presence. If I am going to rob a bank to get us out of our financial problems, she said, this would be an ideal area in which to hole up.

To add to the problem, we are now becalmed in a most unseasonable mist, which appeared suddenly like a shimmering grey wall across the road ahead. Our headlights can do no more than dent the swirling wraiths, and I have left the car to see what lies beyond the wall. The blanket of mist has also insulated us from any distant sounds of water or wildlife, and I am accompanied only by the sound of my own breathing. Just as I am about to turn and grope my way back to the car, a giant figure appears above me. When my knees start working again and I realise that the figure is not moving, I investigate and see that it is a life-size portrayal of the Crucifixion made from local stone. Roadside shrines are common in rural France, but this one is a monster.

Fortunately, I know that shrines are always sited near habitations. As I move closer and the fog lifts momentarily, I see that this shrine does not as usual mark a crossroads. The figure on the giant cross has his back turned to a single lane which leads from the highway. There is no other clue that we may find life at the end of it, but we must take every avenue in our search for a new home.

～

The fog has lifted, but we have still seen no evidence of civilisation. Curiously and although the sun has returned, it feels noticeably colder than when we left the highway. As I shiver and wind up the window, I see a car in the wing mirror, and Donella wrenches at the wheel as it races by. It is travelling at a tremendous pace and I cannot see the driver, but I tell my wife to hang on to its tail as it must be going somewhere where there is at least one house, whether or not it is for sale.

～

We have lost the car but found a village. After a mile of tyre-squealing pursuit, we rounded a sharp bend and the road ahead was clear. There were no houses or tracks leading off the route, and even the yawning ditches on either side of the road could not have swallowed a car whole, so where it went is a mystery. The name of the village is also a mystery, as we have yet to see a sign announcing its presence. Apart from this, the habitation looks much like any other small Norman commune. A handful of dilapidated houses are perched alongside the road on the outskirts, and we have seen an apparently uninhabited water mill, which looks quite promising. Although it is very close to the verge, there should be little noise from passing traffic as we have not seen another car since the mystery vehicle disappeared. The mill cottage has become worn and dishevelled by time and the elements, but is in a basically sound condition by Norman standards for old and unoccupied buildings. There is a bonus in that it still retains what looks like the original wheel. This is most unusual, and adds to the air of promise. A large ånd currently dry field, which would have been the reservoir, lies directly behind the cottage, and alongside runs a pretty stream that disappears beneath the ancient stone bridge that spans the road. We can see no *A VENDRE* sign, but this may not matter if we can locate the owner and make him or her an attractive offer.

In spite of the drop in temperature my spirits are up, and I feel destiny might have led us to our new home in the Cotentin.

As we turn into the village square, I see other promising signs. In front of the church is a parking area occupied by a tractor, a mobile grocery van and an interesting old Citroën. With its marking and blacked-out windows, it is obviously a former police vehicle. As we pull up, I see that the van is standing in front of an equally interesting *pissoir*. Compared with the rather basic facility at Néhou it is quite a sophisticated affair, and has a roof as well as walls. In spite of these embellishments it has no door, and so falls reassuringly short of appearing pretentious. I also note that it is very convenient to the bar and grocery store opposite. Adding to the general appeal of the village centre is the shop next door to the bar and *épicerie*, which appears to specialise in the restoration and sale of clocks. Well, at least one clock, judging by the window display. The square is deserted, but as we cross the street I sense someone is looking at me and turn towards the graveyard alongside the church. Before its owner ducks below the low wall, I get a glimpse of what seems to be a very odd face. I blink, look again, then call a greeting to put him at his ease before we walk on.

Inside, the empty bar is unremarkable except for two

curiosities. It is the only bar I have visited in France that does not have the walls festooned with mirrors advertising brands of beer, soft drinks and cigarettes. The premises also contain a rare treasure in the shape of an original zinc covering to the bartop. Once, this type of metal surface was a common feature, and in Paris *le zinc* became an affectionate slang expression for any favoured local. Nowadays, nearly all of those once characterful haunts have been turned into trendy bistros, and the ultimate irony is that many of them have replaced their old metal bartop with a fashionable but very pale imitation of the original.

Apart from these two anomalies, what could become my new local looks much like any other rural bar. I ring the imp-faced hand-bell on the bartop and, as Donella goes off to investigate the grocery department, a man appears through the curtain-covered doorway connecting the two premises. He is an open-faced and pleasant-looking individual, despite a nose that has been even more spectacularly broken than that of Didier's new business partner I encountered at Sourciéville. I can also tell from the set of his shoulders and how he moves that he is probably a premier-division shrugger. The patron gives me his hand and a cheery welcome and introduces himself as Bernard. As he pours my beer, I say that we are looking for a home in the area and notice that his hand jerks slightly and causes the rim of the glass to glance against the side of the pump. He puts the glass on the counter, wipes the spilled foam away, then says that there are certainly many empty properties in and around the village, though few are officially for sale. The population of this part of the *marais* is dwindling, and not many people seem to want to live here nowadays. I ask why this is, and he gives an exploratory non-committal shrug and says he cannot say. He is a comparative newcomer himself, and has only been running the bar and grocery store for a few weeks. He used to be an executive with a national chain of food retailers, but always wanted to be his own boss. He bought the business for a very good price, and did not realise why he had got such a bargain until he and his wife and children moved in. When I ask him what the local people are like, he looks at the door before saying that, as in any small and isolated community, they can be insular and sometimes even odd to the eyes of an outsider. If one keeps on the right side of them, however, they are not a danger. The word for danger is the same in both our languages, and seems a curious one to apply to the population of a village. As I begin to ask him if I have misunderstood its use in this context, he asks if I would like a drink on the house. I thank him, and ask if he knows who owns the old mill on the road into the village. Bernard gives his answer with a subtle negative twitch of the collarbone, then says some of the regulars will be in later and one of them is sure to know.

As we talk, I tell him about the car that overtook us and then vanished, and his hand trembles again as he lifts his glass to his mouth. After gulping a mouthful of beer, he says that he does not recognise my description of the car, so it could not have been a local driver. I pretend not to notice his agitation, then am distracted by a movement in the street outside. A face has appeared at the window, but is gone before I can register anything more than a fleeting impression. I ask Bernard who it was, but he says he saw nothing, then offers me another drink on the house.

A little later, and my wife appears through the curtained doorway. She is laden with a selection of small packages, all artfully tied with variously coloured ribbons. I ask if she has found a rich admirer and solved our money problems, and she explains that she has unfortunately only been shopping at the cold counter. The choice was so great and everything looked so tempting that she could not make up her mind what to buy. A compromise was reached at the suggestion of Bernard's wife, so she has bought a small amount from every dish. It will not be wasted, as what we cannot eat will be a treat for the animals. I explain quickly to Bernard that this is not an insult to the quality of his food, and that it is quite normal for my wife's pets to dine on *haute cuisine*. I turn down his suggestion of a bottle of fine wine to help the members of our extended family wash down their meal, and then begin to investigate the contents of the packages.

Opening each one like an impatient child on Christmas morning, I see there is another good reason that we should try to find a home in this vicinity. Before us are the parts of animals that many people would not want to even think about eating, now transformed by their creator into classic Norman dishes. There is tripe in the mode of Caen, pig pudding, tongue of cow and tail of ox, sweetbreads in jelly and a rabbit terrine so strong and obviously fresh that I half expect it to bound from the bar in a bid for escape. To follow, we have rice pudding and slices of apple tart and a pot of what looks like, if such a concentration were possible, quadruple clotted cream.

As Donella begins to rewrap the packages, she says that the sign above the display cabinet said all the dishes were home-made, and asks if Bernard was the maker. He looks at her as if she had asked if he did the odd spot of brain surgery in his spare time, then says they were indeed all made at home, but not his. The food comes from the kitchen of the butcher in the next village, but the finer points of the French Trades Description Act have not as yet infected this part of Lower Normandy. I say they will taste none the worse for their journey, but our kitchen table is many miles away. I am not sure that I or the food will be able to last the long trek. Bernard takes my hint and says he will go and fetch some plates. He will also bring the bottle of wine he recommended for our pets so that we can see if it will prove suitable to accompany their supper. As he makes for his kitchen, I ask if he might also be able to provide a morsel of crusty bread, some *demi-sel* butter, perhaps a few gherkins, a dab of full-grain mustard and a sprinkling of garlic salt. He stops in mid-stride and I see his hand twitch again as he lifts it in an apologetic gesture. All the other things he can provide, he says, but he keeps no garlic salt in his kitchen or shop.

While we set about reopening the paper parcels, Donella mentions that the shop stocks no garlic in its natural form. I agree that this is curious, but remind her that the people of the *marais* are said to be a race apart from the rest of Normandy, and probably all France.

We have had our first picnic on an original zinc bar, and the day is drawing to a close. Donella is now concerned that we will not be able to find our way home. I say that we need to wait for the regulars to arrive so I can ask about the ownership of the old mill. Donella observes that it is getting very late, and the regulars seem to keep strange hours in this area. I see some dark clouds gathering above the spire of the church opposite and think to myself that a summer storm may be on the way, which would make our journey back to La Puce even more difficult. I propose that we wait to meet the regulars, and then I will treat her to a night in a nearby hotel. If it is good news about the mill, we will have something to celebrate. If not, we can continue our search in the morning. It is very unlikely that we would reach La Puce before dark even if we knew the way, so all she has to do is phone our neighbour and ask her to see the chickens to bed.

I am probably clutching at straws, but this is the first time since we started our search that I have seen a property and a place where we could possibly find contentment.

A regular customer has arrived, and he has a familiar and most unusual face.

The door opened to admit a flurry of wind, rain and a very strange figure. The man was exceptionally tall and his angular body was enveloped in a sheet of plastic tied at the waist with baling twine. Above this bizarre parcel was an electrifying shock of red hair and a curiously asymmetrical face of the colour and texture of an overcooked pizza. I also noted he had the yellowest teeth I have seen in the mouth of a living person, and the lenses of his rain-spotted spectacles were as thick as the bottom of a cider bottle. It was the memorable face that I had glimpsed at the cemetery wall and through the window of the bar, and I could now see why he might wish to introduce it to strangers in stages.

The newcomer was introduced to me as Christian, and when I offered him a drink and asked his *métier* and if he had lived in the area for long, Bernard spoke for him. Christian, he said, was born in the area and does valuable work around the village. He is employed by the commune to keep the streets clean, tend the cemetery and maintain the *pissoir*. He does not say much, but takes his job seriously.

Shortly after he had settled in a seat near the window, I was to see that Christian takes his job very seriously indeed. After staring fixedly at the nearest table, he began to inch his hand towards an ashtray where a fly was taking its ease on the rim. The village's *agent de nettoyage* continued his stealthy approach, then pounced. His long fingers closed on their victim and he held his clenched fist aloft in triumph like a golfer who has just holed a tricky putt. Then he began to move his hand towards his mouth. As I watched in fascination, Bernard coughed sharply and Christian looked quickly towards him, hesitated, then dropped the dead fly in the ashtray like a dog reluctantly surrendering its bone.

Although I think this area may suit us well as a location in which to set up a new home, I am now beginning to realise why the heart of the *marais* has a reputation for being a strange place, and the properties here consequently so much of a bargain.

Summer storms are not uncommon in the Cotentin, but this one seems to have the energy and malignancy of a full-blown *tempête*.

Rain is streaming down the window of the bar, and the squalling wind is doing its best to join us inside. The occasional flash of lightning illuminates the deserted square, and long rolls of thunder echo along the street. It is now highly unlikely that any more customers will arrive, and it seems we are in for an interesting night of camping in the car. Bernard says that there are no hotels in the area, and the idea of providing *chambre d'hôte* facilities for tourists has apparently not occurred to the people of this part of the marshlands. Our host is unable to offer us any proper accommodation, but says we are welcome to sleep on the sofa in the adjoining room. I can think of worse places to spend the night than a bar, but my wife says she will be uncomfortable with this arrangement.

As I say that she is likely to be more uncomfortable in the car, a sudden gust of wind throws the door open. I walk over to close it, then step back as a dark shape appears in the doorway. As if on cue, a searing flash of lightning is followed by an ear-splitting crack, and the figure steps through the door, looks round and bids us good evening in an educated, softly measured and modulated voice. Considering the appearance of the last person to enter the bar, I should be immune to further surprise, but our latest guest makes Christian look almost normal.

The man is tall and thin to the point of emaciation, and wears his silver hair pulled back in a tight ponytail, which reveals a sharp widow's peak. His features are gaunt and almost deathly white, and there is a neatly trimmed moustache and goatee beard beneath his aquiline nose. While trying not to stare, I notice that his deep-set eyes are darkly rimmed and the eyeballs veined bloodily like the network of cracks on an old oil painting. His mouth is closed, so I am unable to see what condition his teeth are in, or how pointed and sharp the canines look. He is wearing what at first I take to be a billowing cape, then realise is a black overall draped across his shoulders, which the buffeting wind is causing to flap like the wings of a great, menacing bird.

As he moves with an elegant glide into the room and approaches me, I smile nervously and cannot help but wonder if he is the reason that the bar has no mirrors on its walls, and the grocery shop next door is probably the only *épicerie* in all France that does not stock garlic.

~

The sun is shining and we are safely on our way home. As my wife said when we went to bed last night, my overactive imagination has been in overdrive. As I replied, a lively imagination is a valuable asset to any writer, even if I sometimes see things that are not really there.

Despite my misgivings of yesterday evening, it seems that Nulléplace is no more than a typical Norman village with the quite usual mix of diverse if sometimes unusual residents. The absence of signs on the road is because the authorities are replacing them with new ones in time for the tourist season. There was no garlic on sale at the *épicerie* because, as Bernard's wife had actually said to Donella, there had been a heavy demand and the shop had temporarily sold out. The bar had no mirrors on the wall simply because its owner does not like to advertise products he does not sell. I suspect that, because Bernard is a sensitive man, he also does not want to remind some of his customers what they look like. Most reassuring and interesting of all was the discovery that our red-eyed visitor is not one of the Legion of the Undead and, although aristocratic blood does run through his veins, he has no interest in that which belongs to other people.

Henri Chartier is actually the owner of the clock-repairing business next door to the bar. He is a Parisian by birth but has ancient roots in the area, most of which his ancestors seemed to own before the Revolution and *les sans culottes* removed the noble family's properties and heads at a stroke. Because the last surviving descendant of the Chartiers has to work for a living, he spends his week in the shop and travels to the capital at weekends to return the clocks he has restored. His face is so pale and his eyes so red because he sits in a darkened room looking through a magnifying glass during daylight hours. Due to his resulting sensitivity to strong light, he rarely leaves his home during the week until after nightfall, and then usually only to call in next door for a drink. When we had established his true identity and shared a drink, I confessed my earlier impressions and he was most amused. When he learned that we were faced with a night in the car, he insisted that we take advantage of his spare room, and promised he would not look in on us as we slept.

I now have another good reason for searching for a new home in this area, as Henri is a cultured and charming man. The walls of the room behind his shop are lined with books on every subject from architecture and anthropology to zoology and Zen Buddhism, and we sat long into the night talking of the ways of the world and the conceits and curiosities of humanity.

Unfortunately, we will not be able to make an offer on the abandoned water mill, as Henri knows the owner and is aware that he dislikes Britain and the British even more than other would-be newcomers to the area. However, Henri knows of a small but impressive *manoir* once owned by his forebears, which sits at the bottom of a narrow dead-end lane and looks out across around twenty thousand hectares of the central Cotentin marshlands. The location, he feels, would suit an *auteur* like me perfectly. Unlike in his ancestors' days, all the enchanting and fertile terrain it commands does not go with the house, but there are more than enough acres for sale with the property to keep even my wife happy. The *manoir* is not officially for sale, but he knows the owners wish to move to a smaller house in the nearest town, which is seven miles away. If we are prepared to put up with the isolation, the sometimes dramatic weather and, of course, having the Count of Nulléplace as a near-neighbour, it might suit us very well. In fact, we might even get to like being the lord and lady of this bijou *manoir*.

As we reach the oversized shrine that guards the lane leading to what could be our new village, I say to my wife that life has a funny way of leading us on to new adventures and experiences. Although I am sad at the thought of leaving La Puce, there may now be something to look forward to. As well as having a very fertile imagination, any writer needs constant stimulation and new experiences and situations to invigorate his powers of creation.

Donella agrees, though says that we of all people should know not to count our chickens before they are hatched. If the manor house has not been sold yet and is within our budget, it may be what we are looking for. If it is big enough, we will be able to offer bed and breakfast accommodation to help keep us from falling in to debt again. But that, of course, depends upon the little matters of our avoiding the swingeing capital gains tax on the sale of La Puce, and the sale actually going through without any further and terminal stumbling blocks.

As we turn on to the main road, I tell Donella that I have a feeling that our minor tragedy may be turned into a triumph, and point out the spray of unfamiliar flowers someone has placed at the foot of the outsize shrine. When I ask her if she knows what they are, my wife smiles and says that perhaps my imagination is not, after all, that vivid. The surprisingly delicate and sophisticated blooms, she believes, are those of the *Allium sativum liliaceae*, or the common garlic bulb.

La vie est ce que notre caractère veut qu'elle soit.
Nous la façonnons, comme un escargot sa coquille.
(Life is what our character wants it to be.
We fashion it, like a snail fashions its shell.)
Jules Renard, Norman author (1864–1910)

Moving Times

Smoke rises lazily and hangs stubbornly in the breathless air. Like us, it is reluctant to leave La Puce. We have begun the great clear-out of all the things we will not be taking with us when we leave our home of thirteen years, and I have been making a bonfire of some of my vanities.

I am in the water meadow watching the flames devour dozens of boxes containing old manuscripts that will now never appear in book form or on any stage or screen. It is hard to see so many of my rejected literary efforts go up in smoke. The burning boxes represent not only my contribution to our agreement to travel as lightly as possible when we move, but also my determination to start afresh. At breakfast this morning, my wife and I made a pact, and my smoke signals are making a sharp point about keeping my side of the bargain no matter how great the apparent sacrifice. In fact, I have kept copies of most of the burning scripts but wanted to make a dramatic gesture.

Less than a month before we must leave La Puce, still so much to do, and still nowhere to live after the sale. The thirteenth day of August falls on a Friday this year, and I don't know if Mr Remuen chose this date for completion at random or was displaying an unsuspected penchant for black humour. I shall have to ask my colleagues in the JBC if the date has the same gloomy significance in France. As the official name for fear of Friday the thirteenth is the grimly impressive paraskevidekatriaphobia, I am sure that Patrick the Post and Michel le Scabeuse will want to add it to their vocabulary of ailments from which they allegedly suffer.

Tomorrow, we are going to look at the *manoir* in the marshlands, but before that I have two important meetings. Later today, we are seeing Mr Remuen to find out if the building material invoices will defray any capital gains demand, but first that I have to tell my friends in the Jolly Boys Club of Néhou about our move.

As I should have known after living in this small community for so long, my shock announcement came as no surprise to a single member of the Jolly Boys Club. In fact, some of my colleagues seem to know even more about what has been happening in our lives than I do.

When I arrived at what is usually a poorly attended weekday meeting, I found it difficult to park outside the Bar Ghislaine. Inside, it was standing room only, though I noted that a path was immediately cleared to the bar as I came through the door. It appeared that every past, present and still-surviving member had made the effort to turn up and mark the occasion and listen to me tell them what they already knew. Noticeable by their absences, however, were our rogue trader and the postman who now styles himself as the Stud of St Jacques. The official excuses were that both were away on business, but Didier Bouvier has been avoiding me since the problems with our student placement scheme arose, while Patrick is doubtless doing his business with one of the members of what he calls his female fan club.

After I made my carefully prepared speech about our need to move on to a new home and area in my constant search for new people and places and situations to write about, there was a polite round of applause followed by a predictable rush for the bar as I invited all my friends and fellow members to toast my health. While Madame Ghislaine struggled to cope with the demand, I was invited to join my special friends at the table reserved for committee members.

Our president then conducted a simple but moving ceremony by saying how sorry he and the other members were to hear that we were leaving the area. Unlike the rest of the membership, the committee knew I had money problems and would otherwise never have considered leaving La Puce and all my friends. They initially believed that I had invented my story about the reason for our departure as most of the rank-and-file members were convinced that by being English, keeping farm animals as pets and spending such a fortune on attempting to make a proper home out of an old water mill, my wife and I must be eccentric millionaires. The committee had realised just how serious my financial problems were when it heard that my wife and I were looking for a new home in the depths of the *marais*.

Old Pierrot then presented me with a framed photograph, taken at last summer's village *fête*. It showed Donella and me sitting at a table, with all our closest friends gathered around and raising their glasses to the camera. As our chairman said, if I were to hang it on the wall in our new house it would remind us of the good times and good friends we had made in our time at Néhou and the Mill of the Flea. While I cleared my throat, wiped my face and sniffed and complained of a summer cold, our president and official philosopher Jacques Délabré gave me a rolled sheet of thin cardboard torn from a beer pack and tied with a red ribbon. On the reverse side was a certificate made out in his best hand and confirming me as a lifelong member of the Jolly Boys Club of Néhou. In an attempt to distract my friends from my moist-eyed condition, I said he had forgotten I was only an overseas member and would have to buy another carton of beer and redo the job. He smiled and said the committee had decided that, wherever the accident of fate had caused me to be born, as far as they were concerned I had proved myself to be a true member of their community and always would be, wherever in the world I travelled.

~

We are outside the office of our local *notaire* again, and are becoming such regular visitors that I am now on first-name terms with his receptionist.

When he has escorted another couple of dazed Norman house vendors from the premises, Mr Remuen ushers us in and we repeat our ritual of sitting on the still-warm seats and talking about nothing as he opens our case file. After studying the contents for a moment, he shakes his head and passes three sheets of paper across the desk. The first is a letter from our one-time building materials supplier. In it, Mr Branluer says that he and his former secretary have spent virtually every moment of the last week working together on his business records for the past thirteen years, sifting through the tens of thousands of business transactions noted in his ledgers, and he takes great relief and pleasure in enclosing an attestation to the sum total of the value of the materials purchased in my name from his business in the specified time period. He also takes pleasure in enclosing for my attention an invoice to cover the time spent on the project, and his former assistant's travelling, hotel and subsistence expenses.

I look briefly at the sheaf of receipts and see that Mr Branluer's long-rumoured close friend as well as secretary has expensive eating habits and what must obviously be a very big car. I also note that in spite of her being a small woman, she booked a room with a double bed for her stay at the best hotel in Bricquebec. I then turn to what I at first think is the attestation by the large total at the foot of the sheet, but quickly realise it is only Mr Branluer's invoice. Moving on to the next sheet I scan it, blink, then read it again. According to Mr Branluer, in thirteen years of buying tons of timber, shingle, sand and cement, countless packets of nails and screws, miles of copper and plastic piping and electrical wiring, dozens of doors and windows and their frames, hundreds of tools and other small items, to say nothing of veritable oceans of paint and wood stain, he vows that our total spending at his premises amounts to less than three hundred euros.

I look up at Mr Remuen. He gives a shrug that somehow conveys a mixture of sympathy, resignation and embarrassment, then adds another version of his sad smile. He says that he understands how much more I must have really spent at Mr Branluer's yard over the years. Clearly, Mr Branluer does not keep very accurate records, or not all of his transactions find their way into his business accounts.

After allowing us to absorb the full impact of the blow for a minute, our *notaire* purses his lips and then adopts the air of a magician about to pull a rabbit from his hat and says that, although the continuing lack of building receipts constitutes a serious *problème*, there may be a way to solve it. In cases like these, he says, there is what one might call a final court of appeal. When, for one reason or another, there are no receipts and invoices for work that has obviously been carried out, the owner may call in the services of an approved estimator. This specialist surveyor can be employed to visit the property, use his skills and training to assess all the materials used in any renovated part of the building, then calculate how much had been spent on them. He can also estimate the length of time each job would have taken, and allow an additional sum for labour charges. Mr Remuen informs us that the estimator's bill for his services is likely to exceed a thousand euros, but that that amount will also be deductible from the alleged profit on the sale. With my permission, our notary will contact a highly recommended and approved estimator he has worked with in past and similar cases.

Even though I am wondering why Mr Remuen did not simply tell us about this avenue of escape in the first place, I get up to make a celebratory jog around the desk. At last it seems we will be able to clear the capital gains tax hurdle with ease. Before I set off on my victory lap, Mr Remuen smiles his wryest of smiles, and says there is another quite significant *problème* which has arisen since we last met.

I slump back into my seat. Steepling his fingers, Mr Remuen says that he had a call from Mark Berridge this morning and is much concerned about a change of plan by our buyers. Rather than arriving with a certified banker's draft on the day of the sale, they now intend bringing a building society cheque. While our *notaire* knows that a British bank draft is unlikely to bounce, he is not familiar with cheques from what we call building societies, or how well they are underwritten. I do a passable imitation of a very bemused goldfish, then say that, at worse and if the cheque were to bounce, the sale would surely be declared null and void. Mr Remuen shakes his head and says I am mistaken. Once the *Acte Finale* has been signed in his presence, the transaction will have taken place and La Puce will belong to our buyers. If their cheque should not be honoured, I will have in effect and in law sold them our home for a piece of paper, regardless of its worth. The deposit they have already paid would be taken up with the fees due to Mark, Mr Remuen and France. Ironically, says our *notaire*, I will have given away La Puce for less than nothing, as I would still owe all our side of the fees and charges on the transfer, the cost of the estimator's services ... and, of course, any residual capital gains tax due on the profit we would not be making on the sale of La Puce.

After having a lie-down in a darkened room for a while, I called Mark Berridge and then spoke at length to the manager of our buyers' building society. She said, quite sniffily, that as far as she could see we had nothing to worry about. Our buyers had already made arrangements for the building society to issue a special cheque drawn on their account. I would not be receiving a personal cheque from the buyers, but from the building society itself. Unless her company carelessly frittered away several billion pounds worth of assets between the time I accepted the cheque and when it was honoured, there would be no problem. As I thanked her and prepared to hang up, she did a fair impression of our *notaire* and said there could be a problem for us if the cheque were lost or stolen after the handover. Providing whoever stole or found it was able to cash or put it in their account, of course. She had never heard of that happening in England, but as we were talking about a foreign country …

I thanked her for her reassurances, made some enquiries of our banks in Normandy and Hampshire, then went to warn my wife to pack her sewing kit. If all goes to plan, we will get our hands on the cheque late on Friday afternoon. Although our local bank will still be open, it has no facility to accept a building society cheque. If Mr Connarde were to make a special arrangement to do so, there would be a substantial charge and the bank's rate of exchange from pounds to euros would be punitive. Our best plan now seems to be to deposit the cheque in our English account, then have enough of the money transferred electronically back to France so that we can pay off our debts to the bank and buy our new home. The amount remaining in England will pay for the publication of my new book. The real problem is that we cannot risk posting the cheque to England, so will have to physically take it back to where it came from in the first place. This means that, as well as moving out of La Puce and into our new home on the same day, we shall have to cross the Channel that weekend and wait for the banks to open on Monday morning. The current owners of the house we have as yet to find will have to agree to wait for their money until it has crossed the Channel for the third time, and we will have to baby-sit a flimsy piece of paper worth more than a hundred thousand pounds for a whole weekend. After discussing the best security options with my wife, I propose that we toss a coin to decide whether the secret pocket and the cheque it will contain should be stitched for safe keeping into my underpants or her brassiere. Donella refuses to gamble, and says that as a perfectly innocent man or woman at our bank counter in Hampshire will have to handle the cheque, she insists that in the interests of safety and hygiene she should be the bearer.

~

Now it seems we have cleared all the major obstacles to the sale of our home, we must turn our attention very urgently to the finding of a new one. I must also make arrangements for the moving of all our goods, chattels and livestock. We are to visit the *petit manoir* on the marshes tomorrow afternoon and, knowing what I know, I think it may prove easier to find a house for us to live in than an easy and economical way of moving the things that will go in and around it.

A standard-sized removal pantechnicon would completely block off the main road passing the farmhouse for hours on moving day, and to avoid chaos and possible carnage, I would have to go through the authorities and pay them to organise a suitable diversion, lots of official warning signs and at least two policemen to share arm-waving duties. Much more complicated will be the access to and loading of the contents of the mill cottage, the various outbuildings and all materials and livestock from the fields. The cottage lies at the bottom of a narrow and winding track that was more than roomy enough for the biggest eighteenth-century grain cart, but will be far too narrow for the most modest removal van. I suspect I would also have difficulty in persuading the average removal company that four chickens, a duck, a large goose that thinks it is a duck, ten breeding pairs of frogs and other amphibians, at least a dozen dustbins full of assorted crayfish, goldfish and aquatic plants, together with several hundredweight of small trees, shrubs and immature vegetables are standard items for carriage. And that is to say nothing of an embedded caravan, two chicken coops and a former cement-mixer now masquerading as a floral display. Even if I could find a professional company willing to take on the job, they would obviously charge a small fortune. But as I have learned during my time in Lower Normandy, there is always a way to achieve your objective at the right price if you go about it in the proper manner.

A bottle of my best home-brew calvados and a few euros slipped to a friendly off-duty motorcycle policeman should ensure his apparently official attendance to manage the traffic. I can ask René Ribet to acquire a handful of suitable road-under-repair, diversion and even unexploded bomb signs to add to the general air of official business taking place. I also have many friends with small lorries, large vans, versatile tractors and even earth-moving machines. With a few phone calls and the promise of free drinks and food after the event, I should easily be able to summon a flotilla of vehicles and their drivers. The only major problem that I can foresee is the sale of La Puce falling through just as we complete the evacuation, and my friends having to move everything back again.

~

We are on our way to view the *petit manoir* near Nulléplace, and in spite of all her concerns I think my wife is quite looking forward to seeing what could become our new home.

On route to the marshlands, we will be stopping off so that I can do my duty at today's Grand Festival of the Carrot, and while Donella is ironing my costume I am sitting by the grotto reading my overseas copy of the *Daily Telegraph*. In the first of two otherwise unrelated articles that could explain the growing exodus from Britain to France, I read that England now sustains three hundred and eighty three people to the square kilometre. This is double the ratio to be found in Germany, and four times that of France. The article goes on to say that more than half the Britons questioned in a recent survey said that, given the chance, they would prefer to live elsewhere, and the most popular destination was France.

On the facing page is an article claiming that people who live in rural areas of Britain are more than five times as likely to smile as those who live in cities or towns. The statistical evidence was garnered by researchers who stood on corners, smiling invitingly at passers-by and noting down their responses. Given what life seems to be like on some of the streets in the major urban centres of Great Britain, I hope the researchers were on danger money.

~

I have learned another important lesson in life. When dressed as a carrot, driving a car is even more difficult than playing the spoons. After a few false starts and a collision with the woodshed, I have handed over the controls to Donella and am vegetating in the passenger seat. I dislike being a passenger unless I have been drinking, and having my arms trapped in the costume means I am unable to indicate the correct route and any passing points of interest, oncoming cars or other possible hazards. I am also extremely uncomfortable as it is a hot day, and the height of the carrot suit means I have to kneel on the seat with almost half my body out of the window. There is some pleasure in nodding gravely at drivers and seeing their reactions as we pass, but I am relieved when we park on the outskirts of the venue for the *fête de la carotte*. This year, it seems the weekend celebrations have attracted an even bigger crowd than usual, and we have to walk at least a mile to the centre of town.

Créances is a small town on the west coast of the Cotentin peninsula, and is known throughout the region for its carrots.

Normans are not particularly enthusiastic about vegetables, but are fiercely proud of any regional claims to singularity. In the Cotentin we claim the highest cliffs in Europe, arguably the worst weather in the country and inarguably the biggest, reddest and most succulent carrots in all France. The fine and sandy soil of the miles of flat coastline on this side of the peninsula is an ideal breeding ground for root vegetables, and Créances is proud to be the carrot capital of the Cotentin. Other towns in our region compete to have the finest floral arrangements marking their boundaries, but on the roundabout outside this town, pride of place goes to an ornate carrot mosaic.

Now, this particular weekend brings the commune's major opportunity of the year to show off their claim to fame. The early crop has just been pulled, and for the next two days Créances will abandon itself to a near orgy of celebration and self-congratulation. During the festival, tens of thousands of people will throng the streets and marvel at the wealth and variety of uses for the town's signature vegetable. At dozens of stalls lining the square, visitors will be able to sample and buy carrot-flavoured cake, bread, terrine, soup, wine and calvados. At some stalls, they will even be able to buy carrots in their natural state.

Many artists and craftsmen will have taken on the challenge of working with the most common local material, and there will be intricately carved miniature sculptures of birds, animals and buildings, and minutely detailed representations of historical characters and events. Last year, the visitors marvelled at a complete representation of the storming of the Bastille crafted entirely from carrots. At other times I have seen chess sets and small items of jewellery fashioned from the town's premier product. One year there was even an attempt to hold a fashion parade of *haute couture* clothing made entirely from carrot peelings, but it was not a success.

We have reached the market square, and I have become almost anonymous. It is a tradition that all the traders at the fair mark the occasion by wearing carrot colours or favours, and orangey-red hats, scarves, rosettes and complete ensembles are common. But I am pleased to note that nobody else seems to have copied my carrot suit as I battle my way through the crowd to report for duty.

At the *épicerie anglaise* stall, I find our friends Sally and Alan Offord struggling to cope with the demand for their carrot fudge. Retreating from the fray, Sally tells me that our appointment with Captain Vasco is in an hour and hands me my sandwich board. Officially I am in Créances to help advertise the presence of the English grocery stall, but I have also arranged a meeting with a locally renowned removals specialist. When I made the mistake of broaching the subject of a DIY moving operation to Donella, she was adamant that we employ a team of skilled professionals, so I have made a compromise. Although I know of no furniture removal companies in our area, I have been told of a man who makes a living from shifting unusual and challenging objects from one place to another. Captain Vasco is said to have inherited his talent from his father, who is alleged to have been a key figure in the evacuation at Dunkirk and his great-grandfather was allegedly responsible for shipping the Statue of Liberty to America.

When I called, his wife said he was working in Créances today, and will be supervising the movements of the most ambitious float the festival organisers have attempted. I am now sure that he is the man for our job. Anyone who can manoeuvre a fifty-foot carrot through the crowded and narrow streets of Créances today will think little of the challenge offered by our situation and, if the stories are true, he has the special abilities in his blood.

An hour later and I have returned the sandwich board and we are sitting outside a bar while we enjoy the carnival procession. It is very impressive, and also the first time that I have seen a boat run aground in the middle of a town. In a perfect demonstration of the French creative-thinking process, the committee had obviously decided to embody the two main characteristics of Créances in the design of this year's float. Together with its vegetable enterprises, the town is a fishing port and the float takes the form of a fair-sized trawler which has been disguised as a carrot. Unfortunately, it is obvious that practicality has been sacrificed in the pursuit of creativity. The only access to the square from the slipway is a narrow lane between two bars, and while the tractor towing it has passed through the gap with ease, the boat has become stuck fast.

Predictably, rather than inviting ridicule or irritation at the delay as it might in Britain, the incident has actually added to the enjoyment of the crowd. As the tractor driver attempts to free the boat, the crowd has surged forward to help with offers of advice on what he should be doing. The owners of the two bars have also seen an increased business opportunity, and are busily setting up chairs and tables around the beleaguered vessel. Before long, waiters are ferrying dishes of *moules aux carottes* to the spectators who have decided to make a meal of the event.

However, I now realise I may not have found the right man to handle our removals. It appears that Captain Vasco has more alcohol in his blood than inherited transportation skills. After watching the bearded and nautical-looking driver of the tractor empty the bottle in his hand, then fall from his vehicle and become involved in a heated exchange with a baton-waving policeman, I suggested we finish our drinks and continue our journey to view the manor house on the marshes. Captain Vasco may be a *spécialiste* in his occupation, but I do not think he will be up to getting out of all the tight corners at the Mill of the Flea.

We are lost in the heart of the *marais* again, and for once I cannot blame the navigator.

I am still an enforced passenger as Donella has, she claims, forgotten to bring a change of clothing from my carrot suit and we have seen the same cow three times in the last hour. We have found Sousville, the nearest village to the mini manor house, but one country lane looks much like another in this area of the marshlands, and so far we have seen nothing that looks remotely like a *petit manoir*. When I say that the Count's directions seem faulty, my wife suggests dryly that they were meant to be followed after dark and perhaps even as the bat flies.

Having given up our latest attempt, we return to the village and wait for evidence of human life. It is an old joke in other regions of France that whole towns in Normandy close for the winter, but I know of some small communes where you could spend an entire day without seeing another human being. Curiously, the French word for nobody is the same as the word for somebody, and you can see how this may have come about. We have been sitting in the square for nearly an hour, and have yet to see a single *personne*.

Eventually, I hear a noise in the churchyard and heave myself out of the car. Turning a heavily buttressed corner of the square tower, I find myself standing over an open grave and looking down at the man digging it. He is busy at his work, and when I ask him if he knows of a *petit manoir* in the locality he shakes his head without looking up. I say that I believe the house was the property of the Chartier family in the old times, and that the present Henri Chartier is a personal friend of mine. At this, the man's full attention is gained. Standing up, he takes off his cap and looks up and begins giving directions before his voice trails off. I ask him to continue, then repeat his words carefully before thanking him and making my way back towards the car. Continuing to memorise his directions, I reach the corner of the church before remembering that I am still wearing my special outfit. Looking back, I see the man stumbling between the gravestones towards a gate in the far wall. I think it would be interesting to be in his local bar this evening and hear what he has to say about his encounter with a giant carrot who asked directions and claimed to be on close personal terms with the Count of Nulléplace.

Chaque personne est une armoire pleine d'histoires,
il suffit d'ouvrir les tiroirs.
(Every person is like a cupboard full of stories,
you only have to open the drawers.)
Tahar Ben Jelloun, French-Morrocan writer and poet

Local Knowledge

I think we have found our new home.

Of all the truisms regarding the buying of property in France, perhaps the truest is that Britons rarely buy the type of home they set out to find. The miniature manor house is everything we have never wanted, or rather did not think we did. The asking price is also almost twice what we can afford. I have often mocked Britons who arrive in France with plans to buy a modest home and are then wooed by the seductive evidence of just how much property so little money can buy on this side of the Channel. But, having accepted all that, the aptly named Le Marais is really special and I think it could even pay its own way. It is a gem. Apart from anything else, the property combines the practicality and homespun attractions of a farm with the history, grace and quirky appeal of a miniature stately home. As we both agree after our long search around the peninsula, it is pretty near perfect.

At the end of a narrow but well-metalled lane, the impressive stone house sits along one side of a gravelled yard, which is also bounded by a stable block and a barn at least as big and well maintained as our mill cottage. Facing the stables and stretching beyond the barn is an acre of beautifully landscaped garden. Dotted around the immaculate lawn are ornamental and fruit trees, and a central rockery of granite boulders dressed with a profusion of alpine plants and spreading juniper. At the end of the stable block is a chicken run and coop that makes our accommodations at La Puce look like slum housing. And around the corner there is more. Much, much more.

The stone balcony to the back of house overlooks at least two acres of neatly trimmed grass surrounding a large pond and another rockery of giant stones down which a cascade of spring water bubbles. A line of tall pine trees marks the boundaries on either side of the property, and beyond a white post-and-rail fence lies the *marais*. At this time of year, the great plain is not in flood, and appears as a seemingly limitless expanse of lush green veined with dozens of meandering tributaries and straight, narrow canals. Drawing on them as it makes the final stage of its journey across the plain and to the coast beyond is the majestic River Douve. At least three miles from where we stand, the roofs and windows of the nearest town sparkle in the afternoon sun, and a distant train speeds silently on its journey to Paris. Along the canals, tiny punts bob at their moorings and a vast army of tall and slender reeds moves gently in the breeze. High above, ducks and egrets and seagulls swoop and wheel, and a dozen horses make their desultory way to investigate the promise of a pick-up truck bouncing towards their feeding troughs. It is so quiet that I can hear my wife breathing and, like me, she is breathing quickly with sheer excitement at the beauty of the panorama.

Inside, the big house is almost as breathtaking as its surroundings. Used as we are to the cramped quarters of the mill cottage, it seems that the current owners of Le Marais have had to think hard about how to put to use so many rooms, and been almost cavalier with the huge amount of space. Between the stable block and the house is a window-walled room that serves no other purpose than to take in the sun and the spectacular view across the marshlands. Beyond that is a spacious area which we first take to be the kitchen, but discover is merely a pantry. This leads on to a high-ceilinged and tiled-floor dining room with an oaken staircase in one corner, and beyond that lies the huge kitchen. The gleaming ultra-modern cooker, dishwasher, cabinets and work surfaces make a striking contrast to the biggest fireplace I have seen in anything less than a castle, and the blackened back wall and rows of traditional cooking implements hanging from the mantle show it is not just for show. A door from the kitchen opens on to a small lobby and another staircase leading to what must once have been the servants' quarters. From the lobby, other doors lead to a cloakroom and toilet, a utility room and a downstairs bedroom which is almost as big as the ground floor of the mill cottage at La Puce. Just when I think we have seen all the ground floor has to offer, Donella discovers a wallpaper-panelled door which leads to a shower room, complete with bidet and even a twin set of wash basins.

The upper reaches of the building give us even more reason to catch our breath. At the top of the winding staircase from the lobby are three more bedrooms and a bathroom with a set of stairs leading up to a loft which could hold at least four more. Finally, beyond the bedrooms, through a panelled door and down two steps is the *pièce de résistance*. With so much space in which to let their imaginations roam, the owners have sacrificed at least three of the upper rooms to make one. All the ceilings and the attic flooring in this part of the house have been removed to reveal the rough-hewn roof supports, and the space above our heads ends only with the giant ridge beam. At one end of the huge room is a raised dining area, and at the other a fireplace even bigger than the one below. Alongside the fireplace, a door leads on to the balcony and its endless views of the marshlands beyond.

I think we may have made a big mistake just by looking at

what we cannot afford. After more than ten years of writing books warning of the pitfalls on the road to finding a home in France, it seems I have fallen headlong into the most common of them all.

~

We come to the end of our tour and are recovering our breath back in the sun room. Our guides have brewed a pot of English tea in our honour, but the apple pastries are very definitely Norman. After several false starts, I manage to do them full justice by tearing armholes in the now badly wilting carrot suit, which I note the vendors have been too polite to mention.

As I should have suspected from what has been done at Le Marais, Georges tells me he is a designer, and has spent ten years restoring the ancient house. His wife, he says, is Mad. I consider making a joke about her being crazy to even think about leaving such a place, but decide it will not translate well. It also seems a little presumptuous to question someone else's sanity while you are dressed as a carrot.

As we talk, it is clear that Georges is not as anxious as his wife is to leave the home he has just finished painstakingly restoring. Apart from all his family roots and connections binding him to this area, Georges says he is a keen *chasseur* and there is no finer hunting ground than the *marais*. But Madeleine wishes to live closer to her relatives and the town. She loves the house, but finds the sometimes brooding vastness of the marshlands oppressive. If we buy Le Marais, Georges says as he walks us to the gate, he would like to keep the several hectares and the lakes and orchards he owns on the other side of the lane. That way, he feels he will not have lost his connections with the area completely. If we can come to an arrangement on this piece of land, he will be able to visit and tend it at weekends, and use the old hut there as a base for his hunting expeditions while Mad remains in the townhouse she wishes them to buy. We would, of course, be welcome to use the lakes and land at any time, and he could perhaps help me with work around the house and its gardens.

I shake his hand and say that if we were to buy their home, I would be more than pleased for him to keep the extra land. I would also be honoured if he would be my guide to the area and its special places and people. As it is, I have to be honest and say that his enchanting home is far too rich for our blood. Georges gives the classic Gallic shift of the shoulders, which signifies polite rebuttal, and says that there are always ways around these things if someone wants something badly enough.

I agree, and as we wave goodbye and I take up my position half in and half out of the car, I think of what he has said and suggest to my wife that we find the nearest bar so I may ply her with drinks and come up with all the good reasons we should make Le Marais our new home.

~

We have found another minor but persuasive reason for finding some way to raise the money to buy Le Marais. It is little more than a mile from the house to an absolute gem of a rural bar.

Hidden behind the church at Sousville, the business is disguised as a house. The building has no plate-glass window showing provisions on sale, nor any name sign or advertising hoarding. There is not even the most basic *pissoir* for the male clientele. In virtually all other remaining examples of the rural *bar-épicerie* in our area, the owner lives above the shop; at Sousville, the owner clearly prefers to be in even closer contact with her business. On one side of the central door is the grocery department, which is also the living room to the house. A few shelves of basic provisions line the walls, but the sideboard, dining table and chairs take pride of place. At the other end of the building is the proprietor's front room, in which customers are obviously allowed to take their ease and drinks. Through the window I see that the floor is carpeted rather than tiled, and the neat row of Wellington boots outside the entry door signals what must be a basic rule of the house. Shrugging off our boots, we enter and find we have travelled in time. The bar at Sousville is a perfect replica of the best room in millions of small houses in France more than three decades ago. In fact, I realise, this is not a replica, but the real thing. Times have changed even in rural Normandy, but not in Madame's front room. In one corner, there are two plump armchairs dressed with crisp lace antimacassars and arm covers, and a faux-bamboo table stands before them. Alongside is a sugar-twist standard lamp in applewood topped with a large, tasselled shade. A highly polished upright piano stands against one wall, and its lace-bedecked top bears a dozen framed family photographs. On the wall above the piano is a shelf with ornamental brackets, and on that is a model of the Eiffel Tower in cast iron and an aged Bakelite radio. The far wall is dominated by a large portrait of General de Gaulle at his haughtiest, and the sides are draped with black crêpe. This is obviously not a house in which to acclaim the benefits of a left-wing socialist government.

I become aware of three men sitting on a bench in front of a low table and beneath a serving-hatch through which pleasantries, orders and drinks are presumably exchanged with the proprietor. Having seen through the hatchway that Madame is engaged at the stove in the kitchen beyond, I incline my head as best I may, and they return the courtesy in sombre and exact unison. One of the men is the grave-digger I encountered a few hours earlier, which explains why his friends seem unsurprised by my choice of dress. They return to their business of staring reflectively at the portrait of the General, and I order our drinks after apologising to Madame for disturbing her at her work. Though consider-ably older, she is not unlike our own Madame Ghislaine in stature. She is also possibly of similar temperament, as she replies quite sharply that serving drinks is her work while the cooking is for pleasure. The aroma is delicious, and when I ask her what she is having for dinner, she asks me if we would like some. It is only a simple *cassoulet*, but there is plenty to go round if we have not yet eaten. I thank her and return to the armchairs and the task of persuading my wife that we have found our new home.

The bean stew has come and gone and was as rich and satisfying as the bouquet promised, and we are on our second bottle of wine. While we have been eating and before moving on to the subject of Le Marais, I have become absorbed by the mutual mannerisms of our fellow customers.

Each member of the trio seems to be of approximately the same pre-war vintage, but each is markedly different in size and appearance. The man at one end of the bench is large and heavily built and wears an old three-piece suit, with the remaining buttons on his waistcoat straining to restrict his giant paunch. On his massive head, he wears a small and decidedly incongruous pork-pie hat. Like his friends, he is shoeless, and sports a much-darned pair of rainbow-hued socks. In the middle of the trio is my grave-digging acquaintance, who is dressed in his workaday outfit of mud-stained brown overalls. He is slight in build, sockless and his headgear is the ubiquitous artisan's cloth cap. I notice his toenails are the colour of Normandy butter and long and sharply curved like the talons of an elderly buzzard. The third member of the group is tall and thin with a long, scrawny neck. He is wearing a beret and a collarless and faded black shirt, with his grey trousers held up by broad braces. I notice that one skinny toe pokes through a hole in his off-white socks.

Despite their dissimilar appearances, the three companions have obviously spent so much time in the bar together that they have become creatures of habitude. Lined up on the low table in front of them is a tumbler of *pastis*, a glass of wine and a mug of beer. In the ashtray in the exact centre of the table lay three smouldering cigarettes. As I pretend not to stare and at no given signal I can detect, the three men lean forward, pick up their cigarettes, take a draw, then put them back in the ashtray. After a moment's pause as they exhale almost identical spirals of smoke, the three lean forward again, pick up their respective glasses and take a drink. Then they lean forward and replace the glasses in exactly the same spot and at exactly the same time. I see that the man with the *pastis* has drunk slightly less from his glass than the man drinking the wine. He in turn has taken less of a draught than the man with the beer glass, so I conclude that they are even co-ordinating their consumption rate so that each glass will become empty at the same time.

I drag my attention away from the synchronised drinking and smoking team of Sousville, and turn to the task of convincing Donella of the virtues of the house and grounds we have just inspected. But before I launch into my carefully rehearsed sales pitch, my wife says she knows exactly what I am going to say. Before I say it, she would like to remind me that, although Le Marais could never replace La Puce in her heart, it is a wonderful place and she thinks that she could be very happy there.

I begin to say we will be able to use the spare rooms to make money, but she interrupts to say that she was thinking of the accommodation for our chickens. The pond with its running water supply would also be a perfect home for our frogs, cray and goldfish; and Hen would obviously be able to make friends with the wild ducks we saw flying above the *marais*. Milly would enjoy the freedom to roam the grounds, and in the summertime have unrestricted access to the thousands of acres beyond with no danger from traffic. In time, we would find a new cat, and she could think of no finer hunting ground for it than the marshlands. As well as thinking about the benefits to our animals, she has given some thought to what could be done at Le Marais to make it pay its way.

For relatively little cost, the small barn could be converted into a very attractive two-bedroomed *gîte*. To remind us of the home we have left behind, it could be called the Little Flea. Part of the stable block could be converted into a bathroom and four bedrooms, each with a French window leading out on to the grounds facing the *marais*. If the sun room became a lounge and the utility room next to it were equipped as a kitchen, this would make another complete *gîte*. Naturally, its name would be the Big Flea. This would leave us the whole of the main house for ourselves. Until we converted the loft into further bedrooms, I could use it as a study. In the summer, we could let out all three of the upstairs bedrooms to visiting cyclists, ramblers and other tourists exploring the marshlands. If we became really busy, we could sleep in the loft and let out the master bedroom. This left the great room overlooking the *marais*. In summer, it could be used by our bed and breakfast visitors, and through the winter it would be ideal as a study and discussion room for guests on activity and hobby holidays. We could set up and stage courses for amateur painters and those interested in learning more about colloquial French. I could host a course for anyone interested in not making money from creative writing, and we could adapt my idea of inviting our readers to come and stay with us as paying guests. I might not like being the centre of their attention for weeks on end, but would have to put up with it if I wanted to live at the big house, which would of course be renamed the Marsh Flea.

As I open my mouth to comment, Donella holds up her hand for silence and continues. As I will already have calculated, the asking price of Le Marais is more than the total we shall be getting for the sale of La Puce even if we have to pay no capital gains tax. Then there is the cost of publishing the new book and paying off our old overdraft.

There would also be the considerable expense of converting the barn and stable block to self-catering accommodation. She had done some rough mental calculations while I had been staring at the three men on the bench, and worked out what we would need to borrow from the bank if we were to achieve all our objectives. The sum might sound daunting, but if we approached the bank with a proper business plan and offer them Le Marais as security, she believes they will lend us the extra money. If they are amenable and we go ahead with the purchase of Le Marais, it will mean some hard work in the future. But we shall have a new home, and one that we can afford to live in. One day, my writing will be recognised and we will not have to worry about letting rooms to make a living, but until I become well known it would be nice to be able to pay our way through life.

After opening and closing my mouth and looking blankly at her for a moment, I hug my wife as best I can given the strictures of the carrot suit, ask the Sousville synchronised drinking team if they would care to bend their elbows in time with ours, and call for another bottle of wine. Sometimes I think I do not give my wife enough credit for her business acumen and imagination, and perhaps I should think about asking her to do more of the conceptualising and planning and even execution of my money-making schemes.

Plus ça change, plus c'est la même chose.
(The more it changes, the more it stays the same.)
Jean Baptiste Karr, French novelist (1808–90)

New Horizons

Although we are in high summer, it seemed there had been an overnight frost as I arrived in the water meadow this morning. When I drew closer, it was as if a monstrous spider had been at work. Long skeins of gossamer thread stretched across the grass to the oaks at the far end of the meadow, and the droplets of dew sparkled like perfectly cut and polished gemstones in the morning sun.

The stunning tableau soon evaporated, as has my enthusiasm for Donella's plan to borrow a huge amount of money so that we can buy and convert the house at Sousville. Although I like to affect a sometimes casual attitude to money, the thought of increasing our debts rather than settling them has kept me awake at night for the last week. In our long years together, my wife and I have always managed to survive and turned our hands to anything that would keep us afloat until my writing began to pay off. We have pickled and sold onions, repaired old clothing, and sat up into the small hours stuffing, licking and sealing tens of thousands of envelopes at a penny a time. I have always been a dreamer rather than a doer, and never had the courage to risk all and take on a significant challenge. I know in my heart that what she has proposed makes sense, but I am still afraid. We have an appointment to see our bank manager tomorrow, and I am almost hoping he will turn our proposal down.

TUESDAY 3RD

Mr Remuen called this morning to say that there is a new law he had forgotten to tell us about. Although he will calculate the final tally of what we owe to the government, his figures must be checked and confirmed by a department in Paris that has been set up for this purpose. For their services, we will have to pay a fee of three-quarters of 1% of the selling price of La Puce. When I ask the question, Mr Remuen gives a dry laugh and the predictable answer that the fee will not be refunded if his sums are proved to be right; nor is it likely that they will decide his reckoning is too high and that we have been charged too much. Our real *problème* will be if the estimator's assessment of how much we have spent in restoring La Puce does not arrive in time for Mr Remuen to send it off to Paris with the rest of the paperwork. In that case, we shall be liable for the full capital gains tax without any allowances for all the money we have spent over the years. He has persuaded the estimator to find time to visit La Puce at the end of next week.

As we make our goodbyes, I ask Mr Remuen if he thinks there are any other new laws regarding property exchange in the pipeline. He laughs again and says he is not aware of any, but reminds me that in the Russia of Peter the Great's time there was a special tax on beards. If he hears any rumours that this is likely to be applied to property sellers in France, he will call in good time for me to have a very close shave before the completion date. He also advises me not to eat any English baked beans before coming to his office on the big day, as I will know about the rumour that there will soon be a tax on farting. After hanging up, I reflect bitterly on the French government's creative approach to maximising revenue, and how much its executors seem to enjoy a joke when it is at other people's expense.

We are sitting in front of our not-so-friendly bank manager, Mr Connarde, as he goes through our business plan for buying and converting Le Marais into a home with income. Actually, he is going through Donella's business plan, as she refused to let me make any contribution to the project. For the past hour, my wife has done all the talking as she outlined our proposals and I have done little more than nod in agreement and smile encouragingly.

As he reads he gives the occasional grunt, which sounds to me like a combination of bemusement and incredulity. Eventually, he looks up and smiles like a hanging judge with a busy day ahead. He is a very thin middle-aged man with pointed ears and sharp features, and has the overall appearance of someone who takes little pleasure in anything that life has to offer except the opportunity to pass on bad news. He carefully shuts the folder and hands it pointedly back to my wife. After a long period of inspecting a single fingernail, he puts his head to one side and regards Donella as if she were a horse he was considering backing.

Finally, he snaps his head back upright and nods. He is, he says, broadly in favour of our proposal. In principle, the bank will lend us the extra money we will need to buy Le Marais and make the conversion. The loan will of course depend on our selling La Puce and receiving the full amount so that the overdraft can be cleared, while leaving sufficient funds to pay our share towards the purchase price of Le Marais. The rate of interest and repayment schedule will need to be discussed and determined, and the bank will obviously require the deeds of our new home to keep in their safe possession. He will set things in motion, and we shall meet again next week to sign the necessary documents. Then the money will be credited to our account. But only, of course, after La Puce has been sold.

I do not know whether to be jubilant or downcast. My

wife has pulled it off, and if all goes well in the next fort-
night, we shall become the new owners of Le Marais. We
shall also be in hock to the bank for approximately three
times the amount we owed them before starting to look for
a new home.

WEDNESDAY 4TH

We have returned to the marshlands, and I am much
more enthusiastic about the prospect of us making a go of
Donella's plans. On the way to tell Georges and Mad our
news, we have been talking about our meeting at the bank
and why we each think Mr Connarde agreed to the loan.
I said it is all very suspicious, as the man who has been
dunning us for our overdraft for months is now willing to
lend us a much greater amount. He obviously feels thwarted
because we stopped him repossessing the Mill of the Flea
by selling it, and now wants to see us fail with the Marsh
Flea. Now that we are even more entangled in his web, he
can pounce like a spider at his leisure.

My wife gave another of the intolerant snorts of which
she is becoming increasingly fond, and accused me of over-
dramatising the situation as usual. We had to look at it from
our bank's point of view. Before, we had an overdraft that
was growing steadily with no sign of us redeeming it. Now
we would have an official loan. If our plans work, the bank
will get hefty interest on the money for at least the next ten
years. If we fail, they have the house as security. Donella
does not think that even Mr Connarde really wants us to
fail, but if we do, he will be in the clear. If we succeed, he
will get the credit for making a good business decision.

It is now up to us to show Mr Connarde and his bank
that we are not a pair of woolly-minded dreamers with no
business sense or ability. Or at least, that one of us knows
that two and two make four.

While I think about what my wife has said and what it
implies about her view of me, a fox breaks cover and streaks

across the road ahead. A large tortoiseshell cat is close on its heels. As Donella brakes sharply, my heart lurches. It is not just the shock of the sudden stop, but that the cat looks so like Cato. We look at each other and smile at our unspoken thoughts and memories, then continue our journey.

We have arrived at Le Marais and find the house apparently under siege. At least a dozen cars are lined up on the verge outside the gate, and double that number of men are crouching behind the wall or milling about in the lane. All appear armed to the teeth, and some seem to be aiming their guns at each other. We have happened on a hunting party in full hue and cry. The men pointing their shotguns at each other are arguing about which way the quarry went, and the men crouching by the wall are the sensible ones who want to keep out of the line of fire.

I advise Donella to stay in the car, then open the passenger door and roll out on to the verge and throw myself over the low wall and into the courtyard. Though my wife may accuse me of being overly dramatic, I know that the number of innocent bystanders killed or maimed by hunters in France each year is only marginally exceeded by casualties among the shootists. I crawl painfully across the gravelled yard and arrive at the door to the kitchen, which opens to reveal Georges. He too is armed for battle and, as I get to my feet, ushers me in by pointing the gun barrel first at my chest and then at the doorway, and I gingerly squeeze by. Inside, Mad is making coffee and sandwiches and adds to my feelings of vulnerability by cheerily waving a large carving knife as a greeting. Georges explains that a fox has been spotted in the cornfield along the lane. I explain that we have seen it, and it is now long gone. I add that it was being chased by a cat, and he gives me the look that country people reserve for those who have lived most of their lives in an urban environment. While obviously struggling not to sound scornful, he says that this is impossible as a fox would never be in fear of a cat. Indeed, they regularly kill and eat them. I nod appreciatively and raise my eyebrows as if I have learned something new. I also resist the temptation to tell him that, while I may be a relative newcomer to the Norman countryside, I know a thing or two about the ferocity levels of feral cats and have the scars to prove it.

The Sousville Hunting Club meeting has disbanded, and it is safe to walk the streets again. I have given Donella the all-clear, and Georges is taking us on a tour of inspection of his property on the other side of the lane alongside Le Marais. Before they left, the members of the club were introduced to me as the possible new owner of Georges's house. They seemed friendly enough in spite of their obvious frustration, and I think we will be accepted into the community as long as I pretend to be interested in blood sports and Donella can be persuaded not to broadcast her feelings. That will be difficult as this part of the peninsula manages to sustain more wildlife than the population can kill, so hunting is even more popular here than in other more barren areas. According to Georges, there are just under two hundred residents in the commune, and more than one hundred and fifty of them are active members in the local association. With the normal ratio of genders and ages this means that as well as every male adult, most of the wives, daughters, grandparents and even toddlers must be enthusiastic bearers of arms. Before we leave, Georges shows us a photograph of a recent club outing, and I glare at Donella to make sure she does not alienate the person whose home we are hoping to buy. The picture is of our host and three friends sitting proudly among the carcasses of six wild boar, which are dangling by their back hooves from a horizontal pole. The animals understandably look as glum as the men are triumphant, and the picture captures the primeval relationship between hunter and hunted that still thrives in our civilised world. To be fair and although I find the photograph somehow depressing, there is nothing that I like better than the crackling from the cheek of a young and wild pig. As Jacques Délabré says, if you want to eat a fellow creature, you must accept that it has to be killed even if you do not want to do the dirty work yourself. I do not mind the dirty work being done, but am saddened when I see human beings enjoying it.

Our visit to Georges's private pastures is complete, and I can see exactly why he wants to keep them to himself. Through a rickety gate and alongside a track stands a giant corrugated-iron shed, which is obviously his retreat from the world. Inside is a collection of tools, artefacts and weapons that would make a collector of rustic memorabilia go weak at the knees. Standing in a corner is a vintage punt gun, the muzzle of which nearly reaches the high roof, and alongside it a jumble of animal traps of various designs and savage capabilities, and a rack of traditional bamboo fishing poles is fixed to a glass-fronted cabinet containing all the accessories needed to entice and catch every sort of fish that could possibly frequent the local waters. In another cabinet is an array of shotguns, ranging in gauge and period from a beautifully engraved and double-hammered fowling piece to a shiny new pump-action model. Neatly arranged on the wall above the workbench are rows of craftsman's tools, some of which are clearly from the same era as the house across the lane.

After showing us around what he modestly calls his *petite hutte*, Georges took us to a parcel of land to which he has obviously devoted much time and work. There are a series of artificial ponds fed by a passing canal, a virtual plantation of apple and other fruit trees, and what seemed like miles of shrubs and plants in various stages of development planted in regimental rows. At the end of our circular tour, he invited us to inspect what looked like a small cottage sitting comfortably at the top of a giant oak tree. Climbing the rope ladder, we found a well-appointed hide looking out over the *marais*, complete with a brace of comfortable armchairs, a dining table and chairs and a gas cooker. In one corner was another glazed cabinet, containing books on wildlife, philosophy, biographies of France's most famous sons and a complete range of *cordon bleu* cookery recipes.

By now, I had realised that as well as an accomplished designer and restorer of old property, Georges is also a knowledgeable and enthusiastic horticulturist, gourmet, collector, hunter and breeder. If we do buy his home, I shall be more than happy for him to keep his feet on the ground across the lane. I think that I can learn much from this man of so many parts.

There is even more to Georges and his marshland domain.

After returning to the house, he suggested that his wife took my wife on an inspection tour of the workings of the kitchen equipment, boiler, central-heating system, water pumps, fuse box and all the other things that women understand and maintain. We men, if I was interested, would take a drive out to see his *gabion*. Without knowing whether this was local patois for a friend from a former colony of France or a euphemism for his mistress, I agreed, and moments later we were driving deep into the heart of the *marais*.

As we bumped across a plain that will be under a metre of water when the rainy season returns, Georges warned me not to try to navigate the marshlands on my own at any time of year. He and the local people were familiar with the ancient pack and wagon trails that zigzag through the marshes, but to go off the track in even the dryest months was to risk disaster. Quicksand was bad enough, but many apparently innocent patches of reed-grass disguised bottomless pits of ooze from which there was no escape for man or beast. Every year at least one cow would defy the electrically charged wire boundaries of its grazing area and disappear beneath the *marais*. One of the villagers had vanished inexplicably just last month, and some local people were convinced that he and his car are now sitting for all eternity below the great plain. But Georges does not think this is true as the man knew the dangerous areas as well as he knew the sharp end of his wife's tongue. Besides, the butcher's widow went missing at the same time, so it is more likely that they are together in quite a different place and circumstance.

Eventually, we arrived at a lake a mile or more from the house and beside which stood a clearly man-made, grass-covered hump. On the surface of the lake at least a hundred birds bobbed serenely, and seemed curiously undisturbed by our arrival. When I explained the English expression and observed that shooting such sitting ducks would not be much sport, Georges laughed and said it would also be a pointless and wasteful exercise as they were all wooden decoys. When I had parked the car carefully, he led the way up the slope of the hump before pulling aside a square of turf and introducing me to his *gabion*.

If my new friend's tree hide was comfortable, his mostly underground bunker was little short of luxurious. Along one wall was a pair of bunk beds, and against another was a cooker, sink and provisions cupboard. In the centre of the room stood a well-scrubbed pine table and two chairs, and on top of yet another glass-fronted cabinet filled with books was a portable television. From the tiled floor, a short series of steps led to a padded bench facing a narrow opening looking out on to the lake.

Inviting me to take a seat at the table, Georges produced a bottle of home-brew apple brandy and two glasses. Placing them between us, he sat opposite me and said we could now get down to business. When he had important things to think about, it was to his *gabion* he came. I was one of the handful of people who had visited it or even knew where it was. In the shooting season, he and a close friend would often spend days on end here, recording the passage of all varieties of birds and only shooting enough ducks to fill the pot at home. Often he would come here alone, just to sit and look out across the *marais* and think about life and why it took us where it did. Although we had only recently met, he believed that I too liked to think about these things. I would also obviously be thinking why any man would want to sell a house with which he is so clearly content. As he had said when we first met, his wife now wants to live in town, but that is not the full story. Madeleine suffers from depression because of a tragedy in her past, and it has become worse. She has taken against living at Le Marais and on the marshlands, and so they must leave. It will give him great sadness to go, but it is his duty. She is his wife, and more important to him than what is, after all, just a house. But it is also important to him that the right person buys their home. He would like to think that the new owners will appreciate what they are getting and where they will live. He has already had an offer on Le Marais, but the couple were from Paris. They told him that they would only be using his home as what they called a holiday cottage and that they were cash buyers, but he did not really want to take their money. If I and my wife want to become the new owners and are content that he keeps the land across the lane, he would be happy to help us.

I explain that, like him, my wife and I are also sad to be leaving our home. But for our own reasons we too must go, and can think of nowhere better than here to start our new lives. We have been to see our bank manager, and he has agreed to lend us the money we need. To pay it back, we shall have to let other people share our new home, but I think it will be good for them to see what this part of Normandy has to offer, and why people like him are so happy to live here. Instinctively, we stand up to formally shake hands and then sit down again. Georges lifts his glass and holds it towards me. As far as he is concerned, he says, the deal is done. We touch glasses and empty them, and as he picks up the bottle he tells me of his plans for the future.

When he and Madeleine have found and settled in their new home, he intends to start work on his shed across the lane from Le Marais. If I have no objection, he means to turn it into a clubhouse for his fellow hunters. He will put in an upper floor and windows with views across the marshes, and is thinking about building a proper bar in the clubroom. He has heard from Henri Chartier that I enjoy drinking and talking about the things that matter in life, and he would like to invite me to become a member of the club. When I am not writing my books we could spend some time together, with him showing me more of the marshlands and the secrets they hold. If I like the idea, we can even give the clubhouse and bar a name to mark our meeting and, hopefully, friendship.

He fills our glasses again, and I reply that I am honoured by his invitation and suggestions. I am a member of another very special club at Néhou, and we could perhaps arrange exchange visits from time to time. I have also always wanted to live near a good bar, and can think of no better location for it than a few steps from my new front door. With his permission, I would like to make my first move as a club member of the Sousville Social Club. In the circumstances, I think a very apt name for the bar would be Les Deux Georges.

THURSDAY 5TH

A busy day ahead. We will occupy the rest of this morning packing, and the afternoon moving Hen and Ermintrude to their new home on the marshlands.

Since I struck the deal with Georges yesterday, our situation has moved on at a pace. We have agreed a price and the notary responsible for the Sousville area has already been charged with drawing up the initial contract. Because of the special circumstances, no completion date will be set until La Puce has been sold and the money from the sale has made its way across and back over the Channel, our overdraft settled and the loan released by the bank. Other potential *problèmes* have also been solved. If Georges and Mad had not come to the rescue, the open-ended arrangement for completion on Le Marais would have left us with nowhere to live immediately after the sale of La Puce. More problematical would have been where to store all our possessions, livestock and plants.

Georges has offered us the use of the stable block to store all our furniture, and invited us to stay with him and Mad until they move out and we officially take over at Le Marais. He has also suggested we move the chickens to his coop, and house Hen and Ermintrude in an enclosure by one of his ponds so they can become acclimatised to their new surroundings. He has even said that we can transfer the cray and goldfish and frogs to the pond at Le Marais at the same time. I know that the only regular residents of the pond are some large and very voracious roach, and am hoping they will be able to survive their sudden encounter with our psychotic goldfish tribe. Georges says that Donella is also welcome to ferry all her shrubs and saplings from La Puce and plant them where she wishes. She is even welcome to dig a vegetable patch in the landscaped garden and attempt to transplant her vegetable crop, though he seems as doubtful of their chances of survival as I am fearful for the life expectancy of the current residents of his pond.

Now that we know where all our possessions are going, I can go ahead with my plans for the great move and in tribute to the complexity and success of the D-Day landings and because our convoy will be travelling across the Cotentin rather than the English Channel, I have called our great enterprise Operation Overland. I know that taking a few loads of household and garden goods from one place on the peninsula to another hardly compares with the biggest coastal invasion and logistics exercise in history, but I hope my small *hommage* will help bring us fair weather, luck and as much success as Operation Overlord.

～

I have seen many examples of what is called animal instinct over our years at La Puce, but none more striking than what happened at the big pond this afternoon. Even if they could understand English, both Hen and Ermintrude have been well out of earshot when we have discussed the move and their part in it. They may have guessed that something was going on when they saw Donella digging up one of the giant gunnera plants that line one side of the pond. Perhaps they realised that the move was on when they watched me netting dozens of goldfish and tempting the crays to the surface with a piece of mature Camembert tied to a string. Whatever tipped them off, they have both refused to come out of the water and into the carrying case that Donella had hidden behind the caravan. After almost an hour of frustration, I stripped off, dived in and tried to wade and then swim after them. Although I am the holder of the Cottage Grove primary school record for the fastest length of the local swimming pool in 1949, they easily outdistanced me and all I achieved was a nasty gash to the knee from a submerged and broken cider bottle.

As dusk fell on the big pond, we decided to try again tomorrow and went back to our packing in the mill cottage.

FRIDAY 6TH

No luck with my plan for trapping Hen and Ermintrude, but I have other things to worry about. Mr Remuen's official estimator arrives today to take his measurements and assess every scrap of work we have done in restoring La Puce. He will then go away and make his calculations and come up with a figure that will hopefully cancel our alleged capital gains debt to France. If his estimation of what we have spent in terms of time and materials does not agree with mine, the purchase of and move to Le Marais will be off, and we will be out on the streets from next Friday afternoon.

~

Almost overnight, the French government has thought up another excuse to punish house sellers. Mr Remuen has called to say that, before the sale can go ahead, we must be in possession of a certificate declaring that La Puce is free of any traces of asbestos. Our notary has arranged for the specially trained investigator to call next Monday. He will examine all our buildings for any signs of the dreaded substance, and his search may involve pulling up floorboards, removing roof tiles and even stripping plaster from the walls. My part of the arrangement will be to make good the damage and pay his fee.

Mr Pédan has been and gone, and we have been well and truly estimated. A small man with a large clipboard, a row of coloured pens in the breast pocket of his jacket and a tape measure the size of a cart wheel, he refused all offers of coffee or a drink and set immediately to work. He also refused my offer of a complete list of all the materials we have bought over the years that I had made to save him the trouble of doing his job, and would not even allow me to hold the end of his tape in case I cheated. For more than four hours he went over every inch of the farmhouse and mill cottage, poking and probing and measuring and making notes on his clipboard.

Afterwards, he spent another hour asking me questions and challenging some of my more extreme claims as to the amount of hours and money we had spent on various jobs. He is obviously no fool, and could not be persuaded that I had personally deconstructed and rebuilt the eighteenth-century stone bridge on the mill track. Although he was not taken in by this attempt to emulate René Ribet's wheeze with his alleged re-tiling of the cottage roof, Mr Pédan did concede that we had obviously devoted much time and money to the restoration of La Puce. But he still turned down my offer of a set of my books about our life at La Puce as evidence of all the work we had done over the years.

As he left, I casually mentioned the figure that would cancel out our potential capital gains tax but he affected not to hear, so we will have to wait until virtually the last moment to know if we will be moving to Le Marais or be truly homeless by this time next week.

Tirez le rideau, la farce est jouée.
(Let the curtain fall, the farce is over.)
François Rabelais, French Renaissance writer (1494–1555)

Moving On

MONDAY 9TH

We have spent the weekend continuing our preparations for the move, and I can now imagine what it must have been like for the bomb-disposal teams who had to clear up after the D-Day landings. I intend taking my entire collection of sparkling wines to our new home, and it has been a very tense, delicate and dangerous operation just moving the hundreds of wire-topped bottles from the loft of the mill cottage to the terrace outside. A bottle of ten-year-old nettle champagne exploded at the start of the operation, and had it not been for my protective clothing of a sofa cushion strapped to my chest, a reinforced balaclava helmet, wicket-keeping gloves and a pair of swimming goggles, I think I could have been severely injured. As it is, the Mouse family who live in the loft have lost most of their possessions and also, tragically, a young member of the family. I put his remains in a matchbox and conducted a simple ceremony as I hid it under the floorboards, and shall not tell Donella about the first casualty of Operation Overland.

~

The asbestos man has made his inspection, and was as apparently casual in his assessment as Mr Pédan was thorough. When I asked if I could provide a ladder and torch, he said he would have no use for them and suggested we open and inspect one of my attempts to create wine from weeds. He said that his real passion in life was not locating dangerous building materials but the study and appreciation of fine alcoholic beverages.

For the next hour we sat in the mill cottage as he examined and sampled a selection of my best efforts, and he finally said he was most impressed that some of them were almost drinkable. After I reminded him why he had come to La Puce, he excused himself and went on a wander around the grounds. Looking out of the window, I saw him look briefly at the roof before relieving his bladder on the compost heap by the hen-houses. On his return, he pronounced himself satisfied that La Puce was free of all contamination and we shook hands and exchanged the all-clear certificate for a cheque together with a bottle of the blackberry and marrow wine he had particularly liked.

TUESDAY 10TH

Another call from Mr Remuen.

Today's *petits problèmes* concern the mortgage we took out to help buy La Puce. The final payment was made several years ago, but the interest we paid over the ten-year period is allowable against tax on our alleged capital gains. Mr Remuen called to say that, although he accepts we no longer have a mortgage, under French law it will still exist somewhere in hyperspace. Accordingly, the former mortgage must be officially declared dead, which will mean a payment of several hundred euros for the work involved in laying it to rest. The other problem is that this process cannot happen until the original existence of the mortgage can be proved. Neither can he make an allowance for the interest we paid until our bank provides the details. He has been in touch with our local branch and they have been in contact with head office at St Lô. At neither place is there any record of a mortgage having been issued on a Mill of the Flea. Unless they can find it before Thursday evening, he will not be able to make the necessary allowances; the good news, however, is that we will then at least not have to pay to have the phantom loan exorcised.

The fifth call of the day from our notaire, who began by making a joke that his invoice to me for telephone charges could soon mount up to rival our likely tax bill. Although there is still no news from our estimator, Mr Remuen said he had heard some good news from our bank manager. After an afternoon searching through the records, his staff have found the details of our mystery mortgage. The cause of the trouble, Mr Remuen says Mr Connarde said, was my abysmal pronunciation of French words when we arranged the loan. After an unsuccessful trawl through all the documents filed under '*Puce*' as in flea, the mortgage papers and record were finally found under '*Pouce*' as in thumb.

WEDNESDAY 11TH, 8 P.M.

Operation Overland has taken place and was, all things considered, a success. We have lost several breakable items in transit, and more than a few other more robust pieces when Coco's Land Rover hit a speed hump on the outskirts of La Haye-du-Puits.

We also lost part of the convoy when it took the wrong turning at Sousville and became temporarily marooned in the *marais*, but the treacherous quickmud pits claimed no victims today. Our steady progress also caused probably the longest traffic jam on the D2 that the area has seen since the Tour de France passed our way, but René Ribet's inspired idea of borrowing the uniform and motorcycle of a friendly traffic policeman and posing as our official escort ensured we completed the journey unmolested.

All our furniture and other belongings have been stowed away in the stable block at Le Marais, and we are now gathered at the bar in Sousville. To thank my friends for their help and to get to know the local people and regulars, I have put a large amount of euros behind the bar, and Madame tells me she is having her best night since the week-long celebrations following the Liberation. The offer of a free drink has had its predictable effect on the local people's normal reluctance to leave their homes on a weekday, and the party has spilled out on to the road.

The leading lights of the Sousville Hunting Club have turned out in full force and have thankfully left their weaponry at home. They are telling the usual tall tales and passing round photographs of past triumphs, and our Jolly Boys Club secretary, JayPay, has already made a list of possible dates for a combined onslaught on the wildlife of the *marais*. Henri Chartier has broken his usual rule of not venturing from his home in daylight hours, and his dramatic appearance has confirmed some of my friends' suspicions about this part of the peninsula. The Count of Nulléplace has said he intends accompanying me on a visit to Néhou and a JBC meeting in the near future, and Didier Bouvier has already taken orders for at least six plastic crucifixes from the more superstitious club members. An inter-village *boules* match is taking place on the gravel path leading to the church, and such is the conviviality of the occasion that there have been no serious accusations of cheating.

As it is a Wednesday, the Flaming Curtains at St Sauveur is closed for the evening, and a selection of the regulars have also made the long journey to drink to our health and happiness in the future. Jean-Claude Goulot is still wearing his suit of lights, but tells me he is considering closing down his escort agency. Business has not been good, so he is thinking of going back to his old *métier*. Now that we are leaving, he plans to call at La Puce when the new owners take over and ask if they would like him to continue the project of fitting a door or window into the hole at the ruined end of the mill cottage. Continuity is important, he says, and he will otherwise miss the calls he has been making for the past eight years to assess and prepare for the job.

Other old friends at our small celebration include my professional contacts, including the patron of the Café de Paris at Bricquebec and virtually every other bar owner in that town. Freddo says he organised the coach party when he heard the news of our departure from La Puce, and he and his colleagues have left their wives in charge for the night. As I will realise from the black armband that he is wearing, the occasion is more of a wake than a celebration for them as they will be losing their single most valuable customer when I bury myself in the marshlands.

It is after midnight, and still the party continues. My float behind the bar has long since expired, but everyone is having such a good time that there has been a whip-round to fund the festivities. The local people have lodged their desire to witness René Ribet's traditional Whirling Dervish routine, and it will take at least another dozen bottles of beer before he feels in peak condition.

~

We are returning to the mattress on the floor of the mill cottage, but have decided to stop off and see Le Marais in the moonlight. The big house is outlined against the otherwise unbroken arch of the sky above the silent plain, and without the polluting loom of light from any nearby town, the furthest stars appear as a milky sea. Apart from the occasional hoot of an owl, all is quiet. Then comes a rustle from the direction of the cornfield, and we see two shadows glide stealthily across the lane and through the hedge alongside what will soon be our gate.

I am glad to see that the fox and his mate have avoided the attentions of the local shooting club and the feral cat, and gladder still that the building where our chickens are now sleeping is made of such sturdy materials.

~

We have spent most of what will probably be our last night at La Puce looking for our balletic goose.

When we visited the big pond for another effort to persuade the two birds to leave the island, Ermintrude was nowhere to be seen and little Hen was swimming around the pond as if looking for her friend. After searching everywhere, we had to accept that Ermintrude has left us as suddenly and inexplicably as she arrived. Though it is a blow, I said to my wife that we should try not to be too sad. Ermintrude appeared when we returned to La Puce after a long absence, and now that we are leaving for the last time she has decided to move on. Perhaps she has returned to wherever she came from. Perhaps she may come back after we have gone. We both know in our hearts that little Hen will not be coming with us to our new home, and if Ermintrude returns, it will be good to think that the two friends will be together.

FRIDAY 13TH, 10.05 A.M.
We are saying goodbye to La Puce, and have reached the ancient, tree-ringed water basin we like to call the grotto.

I am thinking about all the times we have sat here watching our little stream tumble down on its endless journey to the sea. We move on past the hen-houses, now strangely silent. Through the archway of trees lies the water meadow, and I see that it will be a spectacular year for our flag irises. They are the ancient symbol for this part of France, and another money-making scheme I never saw through was the idea of culling and selling them to local garden centres each year.

We walk on past the rickety landing stage, and over the tombstone bridge that René Ribet claimed he bought cheaply from the undertaker at Bricquebec because the name etched on it had been misspelt.

Back along Hunters' Walk to the ford and stone chute that gave La Puce its name, and into the copse. Now we walk past the mill cottage and over the wooden bridge, and I think of all that has happened in this small dell across the years. It seems impossible that, like all those who have gone before us, we will leave no reminder of our guardianship of La Puce other than the physical signs of our occupation.

My thoughts are disturbed by the familiar buzz of a moped as our postman delivers his last package to the current owners of the Mill of the Flea. As he pulls up beside us, I see that Patrick has taken to wearing his official crash-helmet again. When I ask him why, he blows his cheeks out and says it would obviously be madness not to. When I ask if he is still taking his vitality potion, he gives a shrug and says that he discovered the so-called miracle medicine is nothing more than a cough linctus. As soon as he knew what it was, its effect somehow stopped working. To tell the truth, he is quite relieved that his time as a rampant stud is over. It was good while it lasted, but nice to be back to normal.

We shake hands and he says that he cannot say that he is sorry we are leaving as our absence will lighten his daily load considerably. But he wishes us well, and hopes to see us again when we come back to visit the area. I watch him ride carefully up the old mill track, then we begin to open our last delivery of mail. As I look at a circular advertising cut-price televisions, my wife gives a grunt of dry amusement and hands me the letter she has been reading. I see that it has the symbol of the European Union at the top, and that the letter is a further response to an enquiry I made some months ago. After all the unsuccessful grant applications I have sent on behalf of the Jolly Boys Club of Néhou, my request for information on possible subsidies for growing trees has borne fruit. The secretary to the relevant committee has written to say that there are several schemes to encourage the planting and nurturing of trees in certain parts of Normandy, and our fields at La Puce may well qualify for a significant grant. I smile at Donella and put the letter in the porch of the mill cottage for the attention of the new owners. They may be interested in the scheme, but for us it is too late. The page has turned and it is time for us to move on.

1.55 P.M.
Almost time to go. We have completed our walk through thirteen years of memories, and I am standing by the front door of the mill cottage. I have tied the mattress to the roof of the car and filled the back with the few remaining items that will travel with us to our meeting at Mr Remuen's office and then on to our new home. That is, of course, if all goes according to plan. As it is said, nothing is over until it is over, and unexpected things have a way of happening to us.

Donella is at the big pond saying goodbye to Hen, and before I call her I pick up a rusty nail from the gravel in the turning circle. On the day we arrived at La Puce, I was fascinated by a date and initials scratched by an unknown hand into the stone lintel over the door of the mill cottage. I have often looked at the lintel and wondered about the life and story of whoever made his or her small claim to immortality on that high summer's day in 1776. Now, I take the rusty nail and add our initials and the date. It is not much of a record, but we have left our mark on La Puce in so many other ways. Because of what we have done here, we know the mill cottage and farmhouse will live on, and perhaps even for centuries to come.

My wife arrives beside me and I put my arm across her shoulders. I can see that she has been crying, but she smiles when she sees what I have done before pointing out that I have used the wrong initial for her middle name. I say that it is just about par for the course that I should make one final cock-up before we leave, and we both hug each other and laugh before we cry. I hand my wife the key to the door, but she shakes her head and goes to wait in the car with Milly. I lock up for the last time. As I look around, I see that we are in for a bumper crop of chestnuts from the tree beside the wooden bridge. Then I remember that it will not be us who will harvest them.

Before getting into the car, I look at our old home and hope that it will treat the new owners as kindly as it has treated us across the years, and that they will be as happy here as we have been. I think it is true to say that home is where the heart is, and wherever our lives take us, a part of our hearts will always rest at La Puce and the Mill of the Flea.

Goodbye, old friend, and thanks for all the golden memories.

Glossary

~

There follows a list of what I think is meant by most of the French words, phrases and expressions in this book. On occasion, I have added further explanations, comments or historical notes. In practice, my interpretations and observations may not coincide with the official viewpoint, but that is all part of the fun of trying to understand and come to terms with a foreign culture.

Agent de nettoyage Posh name for a general cleaner.

A vendre For sale.

Bastide Usually very impressive and often quaint (nowadays) mediaeval fortified town.

Bocage The small fields hedged with trees that are a quintessential feature of the Norman countryside.

Chambre d'hôte Bed and breakfast establishment or service.

Chef de cuisine Literally 'boss of the kitchen'.

Choucroute A traditional regional dish of sauerkraut with pork and sausages. Not for the faint-hearted or those monitoring their cholesterol levels.

Cidre bouché Fizzy, rather than still, cider.

Curé Parish priest. At one time even more powerful than the mayor of a small community.

Département Like an English county, only smaller, and run by an elected civil servant, or *préfet*.

Entente cordiale A historic accord and pledge of friendship made between France and England in 1904. The 'friendly agreement' was actually signed on 8 April, but most informed observers agree the first day of that month would have been a much more appropriate date.

Epicerie anglaise English grocery shop.

Maison pleine My version of 'full house', but pretty meaningless in France. Care should be taken with the use of this adjective by English ladies at dinner, as a literal translation into French of the English 'I'm full' is a colloquialism for being pregnant.

Gendarmerie Collective noun for the national military police force, the local station or barracks. Administratively part of the armed forces, the *gendarmerie* is responsible for policing countryside areas and towns with a population of fewer than a thousand inhabitants.

Gîte Any self-catering and usually overpriced holiday cottage, which will inevitably be owned and run by optimistic Britons trying to make a living out of living in France.

Lingua franca Technically any language of convenience. The term originates from how Mediterranean traders communicated before the eighteenth century.

Manoir Any big farmhouse with embellishments and attitude.

Marais Huge swathe of mostly desolate marshlands bisecting the Cotentin peninsula.

Métier Specialist skill or job.

Notaire Public notary and, in rural France, a cross between a family solicitor, property conveyancer, local dispute-settler and tax collector.

Petite hutte Little shack.

Pissoir A very public urinal, either official or established by local tradition in any convenient spot.

Pompier As a noun, fireman. As a singular adjective, pompous or affected. In the case of some fire officers I have dealt with, both explanations may apply.

Potage paysan Countryman's soup. Always thick – the soup and not the countryman, that is.

PMU Very civilised combination of a betting shop and bar.

Poule au pot Chicken and vegetable casserole, which the traditional recipe demands should be boiled to a slurry. It was the ambition of Henry IV (1553–1610) that every labourer in his realm should be able to dine on this dish.

Prix de l'Arc de Triomphe A famous horse race on the flat, held at the Longchamp course in Paris on the first Sunday in October.

Rideau Cramoisi Flame red or crimson curtains. The official name of my local at St-Sauveur-le-Vicomte and the title of a work by the town's other celebrated author, Jules Barbey d'Aurevilly (1808–89).

Salle Literally 'room', but used in context to mean one of the tens of thousands of village halls (*salles des fêtes*) in rural France.

Salle des fêtes See *salle* above.

Sans culottes The political movement behind the French Revolution, and so called because the middle-class members chose to abandon their knee-breeches and dress like the working class.

Serge de Nîmes A cloth made of wool and silk produced in the French town, then adopted and adapted by the British to become 'denim'.

Syndicat d'initiative Tourist information bureau.

Sûreté Elite specialist and highly secretive government investigative body.

Tempête Serious storm.